The Embodied
Teaching

NEW PERSPECTIVES ON LANGUAGE AND EDUCATION
Founding Editor: Viv Edwards, *University of Reading, UK*

Series Editors: Phan Le Ha, *University of Hawaii at Manoa, USA* and
Joel Windle, *Monash University, Australia*

Two decades of research and development in language and literacy education have yielded a broad, multidisciplinary focus. Yet education systems face constant economic and technological change, with attendant issues of identity and power, community and culture. This series will feature critical and interpretive, disciplinary and multidisciplinary perspectives on teaching and learning, language and literacy in new times.

All books in this series are externally peer-reviewed.

Full details of all the books in this series and of all our other publications can be found on http://www.multilingual-matters.com, or by writing to Multilingual Matters, St Nicholas House, 31–34 High Street, Bristol BS1 2AW, UK.

NEW PERSPECTIVES ON LANGUAGE AND EDUCATION: 75

The Embodied Work of Teaching

Edited by
**Joan Kelly Hall and
Stephen Daniel Looney**

MULTILINGUAL MATTERS
Bristol • Blue Ridge Summit

Joan: For Bella and Josephine, my two best teachers
Stephen: For my parents, Sam and Terry Looney

DOI https://doi.org/10.21832/HALL5495
Library of Congress Cataloging in Publication Data
A catalog record for this book is available from the Library of Congress.
Names: Hall, Joan Kelly, editor.
Title: The Embodied Work of Teaching/Edited by Joan Hall and Stephen Looney.
Description: Bristol; Blue Ridge Summit: Multilingual Matters, [2019] |
Series: New Perspectives on Language and Education: 75 | Includes bibliographical references
    and index. | Summary: "The chapters in this volume build on a growing body of
    ethnomethodological conversation analytic research on teaching in order to enhance our
    empirical understandings of teaching as embodied, contingent and jointly achieved with
    students in the complex management of various courses of action and larger instructional
    projects"—Provided by publisher.
Identifiers: LCCN 2019018870 (print) | LCCN 2019980776 (ebook) | ISBN 9781788925488
    (paperback) | ISBN 9781788925495 (hardback) | ISBN 9781788925525 (kindle edition) |
    ISBN 9781788925518 (epub) | ISBN 9781788925501 (pdf)
Subjects: LCSH: Interaction analysis in education.
Classification: LCC LB1034 .E43 2019 (print) | LCC LB1034 (ebook) | DDC 371.102/2—dc23
LC record available at https://lccn.loc.gov/2019018870
LC ebook record available at https://lccn.loc.gov/2019980776

British Library Cataloguing in Publication Data
A catalogue entry for this book is available from the British Library.

ISBN-13: 978-1-78892-549-5 (hbk)
ISBN-13: 978-1-78892-548-8 (pbk)

Multilingual Matters
UK: St Nicholas House, 31–34 High Street, Bristol BS1 2AW, UK.
USA: NBN, Blue Ridge Summit, PA, USA.

Website: www.multilingual-matters.com
Twitter: Multi_Ling_Mat
Facebook: https://www.facebook.com/multilingualmatters
Blog: www.channelviewpublications.wordpress.com

The policy of Multilingual Matters/Channel View Publications is to use papers that are
natural, renewable and recyclable products, made from wood grown in sustainable forests.
In the manufacturing process of our books, and to further support our policy, preference is
given to printers that have FSC and PEFC Chain of Custody certification. The FSC and/or
PEFC logos will appear on those books where full certification has been granted to the
printer concerned.

Typeset by Nova Techset Private Limited, Bengaluru and Chennai, India.
Printed and bound in the UK by Short Run Press Ltd.
Printed and bound in the US by NBN.

Contents

Contributors   vii
Transcription Conventions   xi
Preface   xiii

1   Introduction: The Embodied Work of Teaching   1
Joan Kelly Hall and Stephen Daniel Looney

2   Attending to the Interpersonal and Institutional
Contingencies of Interaction in an Elementary Classroom   15
Nadja Tadic and Catherine DiFelice Box

3   What's Symmetrical? A Teacher's Cooperative Management
of Learner Turns in a Read-aloud Activity   37
Joan Kelly Hall, Taiane Malabarba and Daisuke Kimura

4   Managing Disaligning Responses: Sequence and
Embodiment in Third-turn Teases   57
Stephen Daniel Looney and Jamie Kim

5   A Tale of Two Tasks: Facilitating Storytelling in the
Adult English as a Second Language Classroom   81
Elizabeth Reddington, Di Yu and Nadja Tadic

6   Teacher Embodied Responsiveness to Student Displays
of Trouble within Small-group Activities   100
Drew S. Fagan

7   Gaze Shifts as a Resource for Managing Attention
and Recipiency   122
Hansun Zhang Waring and Lauren B. Carpenter

8   Mutual Gaze, Embodied Go-aheads and their Interactional
Consequences in Second Language Classrooms   142
Olcay Sert

9   The Use of Embodied Self-directed Talk in Teaching Writing   160
Innhwa Park

10   Embodied Actions and Gestures as Interactional Resources
     for Teaching in a Second Language Writing Classroom   181
     Yumi Matsumoto

11   Collective Translations: Translating Together in a
     Chinese Foreign Language Class   198
     Abby Mueller Dobs

12   The Embodied Accomplishment of Teaching: Challenges for
     Research and Practice   218
     Stephen Daniel Looney

     Index   227

Contributors

Catherine DiFelice Box is a lecturer in Educational Linguistics at the University of Pennsylvania, PA. Her research focuses on talk in educational settings, particularly in multilingual, cross-cultural contexts. A central tenet of her work entails using the conversation analytic framework to study naturally occurring unfolding interaction between teachers and students, and between teacher trainers and pre-service teachers. She is the co-editor of *Talk in Institutions: A LANSI Volume* (2014, Cambridge Scholars Press), and her work has been published in *Learning and Individual Differences, Journal of Applied Linguistics and Professional Practice, Applied Linguistics Review* and *Working Papers in Applied Linguistics & TESOL*.

Lauren B. Carpenter is a doctoral student in the Applied Linguistics Program at Teachers College, Columbia University, NY. As a former New York City Teaching Fellow and current student-teacher supervisor, her scholarly interest is in classroom discourse and embodied interaction in the K-12 English as a new language classroom (ENL). Her current longitudinal research project focuses on using conversation analysis to intervene with the development of a student-teacher in a middle school ENL classroom.

Abby Dobs is a TESOL instructor for Greensboro College, NC, and editorial assistant for the *Journal of Language Aggression and Conflict (JLAC)*. Her work appears in *JLAC*, as well as *Journal of Pragmatics* and *Language Learning*. Her research focuses on teaching and learning in and through classroom interaction. Under this purview, she also examines the identities teachers and students enact in the classroom and explores the roles of both conflict talk and playful talk.

Drew S. Fagan is Associate Clinical Professor of Applied Linguistics and Language Education, Coordinator of the TESOL Program and Associate Director of the Multilingual Research Center at the University of Maryland, College Park, MD. His research bridges the fields of classroom discourse, teacher cognition and second language acquisition. Currently, he is examining the influence of PreK-12 mainstream teacher–classroom interactions on English learners' academic and language learning opportunities. His work has appeared in such journals as *TESOL Quarterly,*

System and *Classroom Discourse*, as well as edited volumes across the fields of teacher education and discourse analysis.

Joan Kelly Hall is Professor of Applied Linguistics and Director of the Center for Research on English Language Learning and Teaching (CRELLT) at the Pennsylvania State University, PA. Her research centers on documenting the specialized interactional practices and actions of teaching-and-learning found in instructional settings. Her work appears in journals such as *Applied Linguistics, Journal of Pragmatics, The Modern Language Journal* and *Research on Language and Social Interaction.* Her most recent book is *Essentials of SLA for L2 Teachers: A Transdisciplinary Framework* (2019, Routledge).

Jamie Kim is a PhD candidate in the Department of Applied Linguistics at the Pennsylvania State University, PA. Her research interests include classroom discourse, second language (L2) teaching and learning and L2 teacher education. She is particularly interested in using the theoretical framework of conversation analysis to examine classroom discourse. Her dissertation research specifically focuses on how teachers mobilize and engender student participation in classroom interaction. She has published work in *Linguistics and Education* and *Mentoring & Tutoring.*

Daisuke Kimura is Project Assistant Professor at the University of Tokyo. Trained primarily in conversation analysis, he studies second language and lingua franca interactions in diverse contexts and configurations. His doctoral dissertation explored longitudinally the experiences of international and local students at Thai universities with respect to their language practices and social networks. His research interests include English as a lingua franca, multilingualism, multimodality, academic discourse socialization and study abroad. His work has appeared in *Journal of Pragmatics, Gesture, Journal of English as a Lingua Franca* and *The Routledge Handbook of English as a Lingua Franca.*

Stephen Daniel Looney is Associate Teaching Professor in Applied Linguistics and Director of the International Teaching Assistant (ITA) program in the Department of Applied Linguistics at the Pennsylvania State University, PA. His research takes a conversation analysis approach to analyzing teacher–student interaction in university STEM classrooms. Specifically, he is interested in the management of epistemics and affect in classroom interaction. He is an associate editor for the *International Journal of Teaching and Learning in Higher Education,* and his work has appeared in *Journal of Pragmatics* and *Linguistics and Education.*

Taiane Malabarba is Adjunct Professor of Applied Linguistics in the Department of English and American Studies at University of Potsdam, Germany. Her research interests center on applying ethnomethodological conversation analysis and interactional linguistics to studies on second language pedagogy, classroom interaction and teacher education. Her work has appeared in *Classroom Discourse* and *Calidoscópio* and she recently co-edited a book on EFL learning, teaching and testing.

Yumi Matsumoto is Assistant Professor in the Educational Linguistics division of the Graduate School of Education at the University of Pennsylvania, PA. Her research interests include English as a lingua franca, intercultural communication, gesture and second language learning/development, laughter and humor construction, and materials use in L2 classroom interactions. She has published in *The Modern Language Journal*, *Language Learning*, *TESOL Quarterly*, *Journal of English as a Lingua Franca*, *Journal of Multilingual and Multicultural Development*, *Teacher Development* and *Linguistics and Education*.

Innhwa Park is Associate Professor of TESOL in the Department of Languages and Cultures at West Chester University, PA. Her primary research interest is in conversation analysis, together with its applications in the fields of applied linguistics and education. Specific research topics have covered word search, conversational repair, advice delivery and Q-A sequences. Her current research projects include microteaching practices in the classroom as well as workplace meeting interactions. She has published her work in refereed journals such as *Applied Linguistics Review, Discourse Studies, Journal of Pragmatics* and *Linguistics and Education*.

Elizabeth Reddington is a doctoral candidate in Applied Linguistics at Teachers College, Columbia University, NY, where she is also an adjunct instructor. Having taught English in higher education settings in the USA and Poland, she is particularly interested in applying conversation analysis in the study of classroom interaction to gain insight into relationships between teacher talk, student participation and opportunities for language learning. Her work, often in collaboration with other members of The Language and Social Interaction Working Group (LANSI), has appeared in journals such as *Classroom Discourse, Discourse & Communication* and *Linguistics and Education*.

Olcay Sert is a Senior Lecturer in the School of Education, Culture and Communication at Mälardalen University, Sweden. He is the editor of *Classroom Discourse* (Routledge) and the author of *Social Interaction and L2 Classroom Discourse* (Edinburgh University Press), which was shortlisted for the BAAL Book Prize in 2016 and became a finalist for the AAAL first book award in 2017. His research deals with classroom discourse, second language talk and language teacher education.

Nadja Tadic is a doctoral candidate in Applied Linguistics at Teachers College, Columbia University, NY, and editor of *Teachers College, Columbia University Working Papers in Applied Linguistics & TESOL*.

Nadja's research interests include classroom interaction and critical pedagogy, with a focus on identifying interactional patterns that can help increase marginalized students' participation, learning and achievement. She has published in *Language and Education*, *Linguistics and Education* and *Working Papers in Applied Linguistics & TESOL*, and has presented research at national and international conferences such as AAAL, IIEMCA and IPrA.

Hansun Zhang Waring is Associate Professor of Linguistics and Education at Teachers College, Columbia University, NY, and founder of The Language and Social Interaction Working Group (LANSI). As an applied linguist and conversation analyst, Hansun has primarily been interested in understanding the discourse of teaching and learning. She is the author of *Theorizing Pedagogical Interaction: Insights from Conversation Analysis* (2016), *Conversation Analysis and Second Language Pedagogy* (with Jean Wong; 2010, 2nd edn forthcoming) and *Discourse Analysis: The Questions Discourse Analysts Ask and How they Answer Them* (2018). Her current book projects include: *Communicating with the Public: Conversation Analytic Studies* (with Elizabeth Reddington; Bloomsbury); *Storytelling in Multilingual Interaction: A Conversation Analytic Perspective* (with Jean Wong; Routledge); and *Micro-reflection on Classroom Communication: A FAB Framework* (with Sarah Creider; Equinox).

Di Yu is a doctoral student in Applied Linguistics at Teachers College, Columbia University, NY. Her research interests include media discourse, political discourse, humor and the use of multimodal resources in interaction. Di has presented her research at conferences such as AAAL, IPrA, IIEMCA and AILA. Di is currently serving as President of The Language and Social Interaction Working Group (LANSI), and her co-authored work has appeared in *Language Learning Journal*, *Research on Children and Social Interaction* and *Working Papers in Applied Linguistics & TESOL*.

Transcription Conventions

[ ]	overlapping utterances or nonverbal conduct
{ }	nonverbals and speech, pause or gap co-occurrences
=	contiguous utterances (latching)
(( ))	*nonverbal behaviors*
(.)	micro-pause; a number inside the parentheses represents the length of the pause
:	elongation (more colons demonstrate longer stretch)
.	fall in intonation at the end of an utterance
,	slight rise in intonation at the end of an utterance
?	rising in intonation at the end of an utterance
-	an abrupt stop in articulation
↑ in speech	marked upstep in pitch
↓ in speech	marked downstep in pitch
hhh	out-breath
.hhh	in-breath
@haha, @hhh	marks laughter
wo(h)rd	marks aspiration within a word
CAPS	loud speech
°word°	soft speech
<u>word</u>	stress/accentuation
<	hurried start of the turn
>word<	surrounds talk that is spoken faster
<word>	surrounds talk that is spoken more slowly
word	*description of nonverbal conduct*
(word)	uncertain utterances; surrounds the transcriber's best guess
(xxxx)	unintelligible syllables; the number of Xs represents the number of syllables
$word$	smiley, laughing voice
#word#	creaky voice

Preface

This volume arose from a two-day research symposium on teaching which was held at the Pennsylvania State University in May 2016 and sponsored by Penn State's Center for Research on English Language Learning and Teaching. The symposium brought together an international group of about 20 faculty and graduate students to share research interests and discuss the advantages and challenges of using ethnomethodological conversation analysis (EMCA) to study the practices and actions by which teaching is accomplished. The research studies reported in many of the volume's chapters were first presented at the symposium and have benefitted from extended collegial discussion over the two days. In addition to our fellow contributors to this volume, we extend our appreciation to Jean Wong, Carol Lo, Sarah Creider, Michael Amory, Karen Johnson and Mari Haneda, who also participated in the 2016 research symposium, for their contributions to our discussions on the specialized nature of teaching during the symposium. Finally, we extend our appreciation to Anna Roderick and the series editors for their help and support.

As each of the studies will show, teaching is indeed sophisticated work, comprising a wide range of actions and courses of action accomplished through the simultaneous and sequential use of a wide range of embodied practices. The chapters' analyses are not offered as exemplars of best practices; that is, they do not claim to showcase how teaching *should be* accomplished. Rather, they demonstrate how it *is* accomplished, by documenting its real-world, complex, embodied achievement in particular settings, by particular teachers with particular pedagogical goals and with particular students. Such detailed descriptions of the routine grounds of teaching offer to scholars of teaching, teacher educators, teachers and other stakeholders the opportunity to develop a reflective capacity for understanding the specialized nature of teaching and making sensible decisions in their own contexts of teaching.

1 Introduction: The Embodied Work of Teaching

Joan Kelly Hall and Stephen Daniel Looney

Building on a growing body of ethnomethodological conversation analytic research on teaching, the chapters in this volume further empirical understandings of teaching as embodied, contingent and jointly achieved with students in the complex management of various courses of action and larger instructional projects. Together, the chapters make three specific contributions to research on teaching. First, they further document the embodied accomplishment of teaching by identifying specific resources that teachers use to manage instructional projects. Secondly, the chapters demonstrate that teaching entails both alignment and affiliation work. Finally, each chapter shows the significance of using high-quality audio-visual data to document the sophisticated work of teaching. By providing analytic insight into routine grounds of the highly specialized work of teaching, the studies make a significant contribution to a practice-based understanding of teaching.

Introduction

The chapters in this volume take as their focus the organization of the specialized work of teaching. In addition to instructing or directing others, teaching involves devising and implementing pedagogical projects to facilitate the development of learners' subject-specific understandings and skills, maintaining their shared attention and promoting their participation, while displaying and engendering demonstrations of positive affect from the learners and attending to and managing individual learners' experiences and needs (Ball & Forzani, 2009, 2011; Cohen, 2011; Macbeth, 2011, 2014).

Although we know that *how* teachers teach 'is the proximal and most powerful factor in student engagement and learning' (National Research Council, 2004: 60), such work is typically represented in educational literature on teaching as propositional knowledge *about* teaching rather than as practices and actions for *doing* teaching. In addition, there remains a view of teaching as highly improvisational and rooted in personal preferences (Ball & Forzani, 2009, 2011). Consequently, the practices and actions by which teaching is accomplished remain at best understudied and poorly articulated.

The practical organization of the intricate and complex work of teaching has been a focus of ethnomethodological conversation analysis (EMCA) studies for over 40 years (Baker, 1992; Heap, 1990, 1992; Hester & Francis, 1995, 2000; Lee, 2007; Lerner, 1995; Macbeth, 1991, 2000, 2011, 2014; McHoul, 1978; Mehan, 1979; Payne & Hustler, 1980). EMCA is based on two interrelated sociological approaches to the study of social life, both of which are concerned with the local organization of concrete social activities: ethnomethodology (EM) and conversation analysis (CA). EM considers social order to be fundamentally empirical and locally accomplished (Garfinkel, 1964, 1967, 1996, 2002). It was founded by Garfinkel as a radical alternative to sociological theories which posit the existence of an objective social order and appeal to theoretical constructs to explain the lived experiences of members of society. According to Garfinkel, such theories explain the production of stability in everyday life as compliance by members of society to 'pre-established and legitimate alternatives of action that the common culture provides' (Garfinkel, 1964: 244). Members have no influence on these action options; they can only internalize them and act in response to them. Garfinkel argued that such formal analyses of social life treat individuals as 'cultural dopes' (Garfinkel, 1964: 244), that is, passive bearers of theorized constructs.

As a radically different approach to the study of social life, EM makes no distinction between a theorized social world and individuals' experiences of it. Rather, it considers the facts of social life to be practical constructions, produced in and through mutually recognizable common-sense reasoning methods used by members of society to achieve social order in their local contexts (Garfinkel, 1967, 2002; Heritage, 1984; Maynard, 2012; Maynard & Clayman, 2003). These methods are the observable, reflexively accountable ways in which members of society jointly construct their social worlds. People take for granted that what is done at any local moment is understood on the basis of these shared methods. These methods do not stand for something else; that is, they are not texts that represent or signify an abstract concept. They are exhibits of social order, and thus 'constitutive of their own reality' (Garfinkel, 2002: 97). These observable, common-sense methods through which individuals produce and recognize courses of action in actual, not hypothesized, settings are the topics of EM study.

CA emerged from EM's interests in the empirical study of the methods by which members of society achieve social order and from Goffman's commitment to the study of interaction as a coherent domain of inquiry (Goffman, 1981; Heritage, 2008; Schegloff, 1988). Founded by Sacks in association with Schegloff and Jefferson and asserting a fundamental role for interaction as 'the primordial site of human sociality' (Schegloff, 2006: 70), CA posited social order to be a fundamentally cooperative, sequential achievement informed by stable, observable interactional structures to which individuals normatively orient (Enfield & Sidnell, 2014; Heritage, 1984; Sacks, 1984, 1992, 1995). These structures comprise a common-sense knowledge, that is, an interactional competence, which is possessed by all ordinary members of society and exhibited in the methods they use in their interactions with others to achieve social order (Maynard, 2012).

Specification of the interactional methods comprising the interactional infrastructure used to achieve social order has formed the research program of CA. Methods documented thus far include the systems of turn taking, sequence organization and repair (Dingemanse *et al.*, 2015; Stivers *et al.*, 2009). Turn taking concerns the construction and distribution of turns among individuals in an interaction. Sequence organization is the 'vehicle for getting some activity accomplished' (Schegloff, 2007: 2), and concerns the relative positioning of actions or turns. CA considers the positioning of an action to be 'fundamental to the understanding of its meaning and to the analysis of its significance as an action' (Stivers, 2012: 191). The basic unit of sequence organization is the adjacency pair, which consists of two turns that are normatively fitted to each other such that the first utterance projects a next action. As explained by Schegloff (1968: 1083), 'given the first, the second is expectable; upon its occurrence it can be seen to be a second item to the first; upon its nonoccurrence it can be seen to be officially absent – all this provided by the occurrence of the first item'. Repair is the 'self-righting' mechanism (Schegloff *et al.*, 1977: 381) by which troubles in maintaining shared understandings are dealt with such that the action, the action sequence and the larger interactional project can move to possible completion (Levinson, 2012). Repair practices do not address '*all* divergences or difficulties of understanding' (Schegloff, 1992: 1341, italics added). Instead, they deal with 'only the narrower domain of understanding what someone has just said' (Schegloff, 2000: 207), that is, with difficulties presented by 'the production and uptake of the talk itself' (Schegloff, 1992: 1341).

Key to understanding the structural relationships between turns in a sequence or course of action is preference (Pomerantz, 1984). Many action types involve at least two relevant options that differ in terms of how they forward the interaction. An action that complies with the expectation of the prior turn is the preferred action. For example, greetings anticipate return greetings; questions project answers. Preferred actions are typically offered straight away, without delay or any kind of qualification. Dispreferred actions do not comply with the expectations of prior actions and are designed with delays, mitigating particles, e.g. *well*, *uh*, accounts, and other features that mark deviation from the expected action. Individuals orient to the relevance of preference to manage and display to each other their ongoing understanding of what they are doing together.

Closely tied to preference are the concepts of alignment and affiliation, which have to do with how cooperation is achieved in interaction (Lindström & Sorjonen, 2012; Steensig, 2012; Stivers, 2008; Stivers *et al.*, 2011). Aligning actions are preferred actions; they match the formal design preference of the preceding turn, accept the proposed presuppositions and interactional roles made relevant in the prior turn, and thereby facilitate the progression of the activity or sequence. For example, a student response to a teacher question that is formally matched to the design of the question and accepts its presuppositions supports the structural preference of the activity turn and thus is an aligning action. A student response that is structurally or otherwise unrelated to the question is a dispreferred, disaligning action.

While alignment has to do with structural cooperation, affiliation has to do with the affective level of cooperation. Turns that match a speaker's conveyed stance or perspective toward some action or occasion are affiliative actions (Stivers, 2008; Stivers *et al.*, 2011). Indices of affiliation include lexical intensifiers such as *really*, prosodic cues such as high pitch, vowel elongation and loudness, and other embodied cues such as head nods, smiling and laughter (Haakana, 2010; Lehtimaja, 2011; Ochs, 1996; Piirainen-Marsh, 2011; Stivers, 2008). Use of such cues can display a range of emotions such as happiness, anger, intimacy, sadness, excitement and so on. In storytelling, for example, nodding following the telling of story elements that make visible the teller's stance toward those elements display affiliation (Stivers, 2008). Aligning and affiliative actions support sociability and solidarity while disaligning and disaffiliative responses do not (Heritage, 1984). Moreover, while alignment is relevant at every turn at talk, affiliative actions are potentially relevant only when a speaker's evaluative stance toward the unfolding action or some state of affairs is displayed (Steensig, 2012; Stivers *et al.*, 2011).

EMCA program of research on teaching

An EMCA program of research on teaching has the following four interconnected characteristics. First, it is descriptive. As EMCA's central concern is with the practical methods that participants routinely use in making sense of their social worlds, the purpose of EMCA research on teaching is to describe the natural features of classroom life as they are produced 'in their situated and lived detail' (Francis & Hester, 2004: 187). Secondly, it is indifferent. To do indifferent research on teaching does not mean that anything goes or that methodological and analytic care is not exercised by the researcher. Rather, an EMCA approach assumes that, because interaction always entails the construction of social order, researchers of teaching can analyze any teaching interaction and find interesting processes of the formation of action and courses of action. As Koschmann *et al.* (2004: 4) note, for the purposes of studying teaching, 'any circumstance, situation or activity that participants treat as one in which instruction and learning is occurring can be investigated for how instruction and learning are being produced by and among participants'. This stance of indifference also suggests not only that the examination of any activity of teaching will demonstrate some occurrence of import, but also that 'such a demonstration can be based on a single case' (Koschmann *et al.*, 2004: 4).

Thirdly, EMCA research on teaching does not yield causative variables nor it is concerned with using abstract concepts about teaching to interpret findings or demonstrating whether some occasion of teaching is successfully implemented based on exogenous criteria (Erickson, 2012; Francis & Hester, 2004; Koschmann *et al.*, 2004). Rather, EMCA research is concerned with how the life of the classroom, as lived by its members, is accomplished. What is treated as relevant on any occasion is up to the members of that occasion to work through in their interaction; it is the researcher's task 'to discover what these relevancies might be' (Koschmann *et al.*, 2004: 8).

The final characteristic has to do with the production of video-recorded data. What distinguishes an EMCA research program is its 'careful and precise attention to temporally and sequentially organized details of actions that account for how co-participants orient to each other's multimodal conduct, and assemble it in meaningful ways, moment by moment' (Mondada, 2016: 240). According to Kimura *et al.* (2018), two distinctive institutional characteristics of second language (L2) teaching contexts afford special consideration in the production of video-recordings: the multiplicity of participation frameworks and physical arrangements and the interplay of interactional routines and pedagogical projects. Regarding the first, they note that L2 teaching contexts typically comprise multiple pedagogical activities within one time period or lesson, which engender different participation frameworks and different arrangements of, for example, desks and chairs, the placement of instructional artifacts and devices and so on. This requires the researchers to be nimble, that is, able to respond quickly to adjustments of recording devices as needed. In terms of the second consideration, L2 teaching actions are organized by larger institutional projects. This means that not only is any one action contingent on the prior turn, but it is also oriented to a larger pedagogical project, which at the same time amplifies and constrains the meaning of any one action (Levinson, 2012). To describe the assemblage of an activity as the participants who are responsible for its production understand it, then, requires that video-recordings capture extended stretches of interaction not only within a lesson but also across multiple lessons.

Research on Classroom Settings

Early EMCA studies in classroom settings focused on describing two interactional systems: the specialized nature of sequence organization and the turn allocation system (Gardner, 2012; Kapellidi, 2013; Macbeth, 1990, 1991, 2000; McHoul, 1978; Mehan, 1979). Early studies on the organization of instructional sequences found a ubiquitous teacher-fronted three-action sequence known as the IRF, where I refers to a teacher directive or question, R to a student response, and F to the teacher turn that follows up on the student response (Hall & Walsh, 2002; McHoul, 1978; Mehan, 1979; Nassaji & Wells, 2000).

Receiving a great deal of the attention on the IRF instructional sequence, the third turn has been shown to play an important role in providing feedback to student responses and promoting or hindering student participation (Fagan, 2015; Hall, 1997; Margutti & Drew, 2014; Waring, 2008, 2009). Lee (2007) offers perhaps the most detailed examination of teacher management of learner turns, showing the practical and procedural details of a range of complex pedagogical actions that the third turn accomplishes in responding to and acting on student responses. These actions include breaking problematic questions into component parts, steering the direction of the interaction toward the teacher's objective, providing clues for more desired answers, and managing the attention of the cohort and at the same time moving the instructional project forward. Additional work on this instructional sequence includes Sert's (2013) study of teacher management of student displays and claims of insufficient knowledge in the second turn, Waring's (2008, 2009) studies of explicit positive assessments and learner post-expansion turns, Park's (2014) study of teacher repetitions of student responses in the third turn, and Jacknick's (2009) study of teacher management of student-initiated sequences.

Studies on the turn-taking system in classroom contexts have revealed that, unlike in informal interaction where any participant has the right to self-select as next speaker (Sacks et al., 1974), the responsibility for coordinating turns lies largely with the teacher (Käänta, 2012; Lerner, 1995; McHoul, 1978; Mehan, 1979; Mortensen, 2009; Sahlström, 2002; Waring et al., 2013). It is the teacher who determines whether students are to wait to be called on before speaking, whether and how they can bid for the opportunity to speak, when they can speak at will and whether the turn is to be taken by a single student, two or more students or as a collective turn by the cohort, as well as student behaviors for bidding for and securing turns.

Embodied resources

Early EMCA studies of teaching primarily used audio-recordings of interactions for their analyses; consequently, they focused on descriptions of participants' vocal behaviors, i.e. prosodic cues and word choice, in the design of actions and sequences of actions. Impelled by technological advancements in video-recording resources over the last two decades, EMCA research on teaching has expanded its analytic scope to consider the use of *embodied*[1] resources including gesture, gaze, head movements, facial expressions, body posture and body movements in addition to verbal ones in designing turns and sequences of actions (Nevile, 2015; Streeck *et al.*, 2011).

One strand of research has documented the embodied practices and actions by which instructional turn-allocation routines are accomplished (e.g. Kääntä, 2012; Mortensen, 2008, 2009; Mortensen & Hazel, 2011; Sahlström, 2002). Findings show that students and teachers both use shared gaze and aligned body positions to indicate willingness to take next turns and to allocate turns. Another strand has demonstrated the integral role of gesture to teaching. Gestures are used by teachers to enrich their explanations (Gullberg, 2006; Lazaraton, 2004; Matsumoto & Dobs, 2017; Smotrova, 2017), teach vocabulary (Waring *et al.*, 2013; Watanabe, 2017) and achieve and maintain intersubjectivity (aus der Wieschen & Sert, 2018).

Another group has investigated the shared embodied resources that teachers and students use to manage sensitive moments such as when glitches with the use of instructional materials or devices arise or when students have difficulty in responding to teacher questions (e.g. Fagan, 2015; Hall & Smotrova, 2013; Kääntä, 2014; Looney & Kim, 2018; Sert & Jacknick, 2015). These studies show how talk, gaze, facial expression and gesture work simultaneously and sequentially to mitigate correction, hold the floor, display cognitive states and invite participation and/or empathy from students. Additional studies that have looked mainly or solely at gestures and objects have found them to be pedagogical resources used for various purposes, including to orient learners' attention during correction, explanation and elicitation sequences and to transition between activities (Looney *et al.*, 2017; Matsumoto & Dobs, 2017; Sert, 2015).

Summaries of Chapters

Building on this growing body of research, the chapters in this volume further empirical understandings of teaching as embodied, contingent and jointly achieved with students in the complex management of various courses of action and larger instructional projects. The setting for the study by Tadic and Box (Chapter 2) is an elementary classroom in a US public school. Drawing on Goffman's (1974, 1981) concept of *framing*, they show how the teacher attends simultaneously to institutional expectations and students' interpersonal needs through his use of prosody, gaze, body posture and instructional materials. Similar to Tadic and Box, the context for Chapter 3 by Hall, Malabarba and Kimura is an elementary classroom in a US public school. In their investigation of the teacher's cooperative management of learner turns in a read-aloud activity, they show the significant work the teacher's embodied actions do in the simultaneous management of potentially disaligning student turns and displays of affiliation as the activity unfolds.

Looney and Kim's chapter draws on data from a US university undergraduate Geosciences lab (Chapter 4). They analyze the embodied practices the teacher uses for doing third-turn teases in negative follow-up turns to disaligning student responses in IRFs. They find that exaggerated prosody, gaze, facial expression and laughter are used by the teacher to manage student affect while delivering negative assessments of student responses. The context for Chapter 5 by Reddington, Yu and Tadic is a community adult English as a second language (ESL) classroom in the United States. Their examination of two storytelling activities shows how the teacher utilizes a variety of linguistic and embodied resources to engage with learners, and how shifts in the teacher's embodied actions shape opportunities for student participation. Also located in a community adult ESL class in the United States, Chapter 6 by Fagan examines the complexities of doing teaching when students are engaged in small group work. He finds two embodied actions – marking the path and mobilizing elaboration – are used by the teacher to respond to students' embodied displays of trouble. These actions not only address the trouble, but they also ensure that the small-group work remains student led.

Chapter 7 by Waring and Carpenter reports on the role of gaze in the management of attention in an adult ESL classroom. Specifically, the authors show that teacher gaze shifts from individual students to the cohort of students in order to call attention to information that is relevant to the entire class and, thus, to facilitate the achievement of larger pedagogical projects, such as the presentation, practice and review of pronunciation, vocabulary and grammar for which the attention and participation of the class as a collective is crucial. Sert's study in Chapter 8 is also concerned with gaze. The setting is an 11th grade English as a foreign language (EFL) class in a European country. His analysis shows the significant role that mutual gaze between the teacher and individual students plays in creating a space for student participation. Sert concludes that his findings provide further evidence that gaze is an important resource in the management of epistemic stance and institutional roles and responsibilities in the classroom.

Chapter 9 by Park uses data from a US university-level writing tutorial and shows the role that a tutor's self-directed talk – marked by averted gaze and other embodied practices such as lower volume, thinking gestures and rhetorical questions – plays in suggesting revisions, giving reasons why a revision should be made and managing time. The content area of Matsumoto's study (Chapter 10) is also writing, but the context is a university-level ESL writing class in a US university. She looks at how, during moments when students display trouble in understanding via embodied actions, the teacher directs and incorporates students' embodied actions into her own teaching in ways that capture the students' attention and facilitate their understanding. The final study, Chapter 11 by Dobs, examines how collective translations, a frequently occurring instructional activity in a Chinese foreign language classroom in a US university, unfold. She finds that the teacher's use of prosodic and embodied resources such as elongated vowels, rising intonation, lip positioning and head nodding cue students as to when to commence collective translations.

In addition to illuminating the complexities of teaching in various classroom settings, the chapters make three specific contributions to research on teaching. First, they further document the embodied accomplishment of teaching by identifying specific resources that teachers use to manage instructional projects. Gaze is revealed to be a particularly significant resource for displaying affiliation (Hall *et al.*; Looney & Kim), managing participation and attention (Sert; Tadic & Box; Waring & Carpenter), initiating choral repetitions (Dobs), and responding to student displays of trouble (Fagan). Gesture is shown to be a resource for managing participation (Hall *et al.*) and explaining course content (Matsumoto). In addition, many studies demonstrate how lexis, prosody, facial expression, gaze, gesture and body position come together in embodied actions to accomplish activities such as negotiations of turn taking during storytellings and read-alouds (Hall *et al.*; Reddington *et al.*), collective translations (Dobs), self-directed talk (Park) and third-turn teases (Looney & Kim).

Secondly, the chapters demonstrate that teaching entails both alignment and affiliation work. This is significant in that, while a great deal of literature has suggested that affective relationships between teachers and students are linked to academic performance (National Research Council, 2004; Pianta *et al.*, 2012), there has been little systematic attention to how affiliation is accomplished as instruction unfolds. The studies here show its embodied achievement and how it is interwoven into instructional projects like storytelling (Tadic & Box; Reddington *et al.*), read-alouds (Hall *et al.*) and the IRF (Looney & Kim).

Finally, each chapter shows the significance of using high-quality audio-visual data to document the sophisticated work of teaching. Dobs' study on collective translations in particular draws our attention to the need for high-quality data to capture fully the complex interactional details involved in accomplishing such sophisticated work. As noted by Garfinkel (2002: 220), without 'analyzable audio and video documents', classroom practice 'cannot seriously be identified, formulated, or solved'. The collection of studies in this volume make a significant contribution toward documenting the complexities entailed in teaching.

Conclusion

Teaching is indeed sophisticated professional work. By providing analytic insight into the embodied, endogenous, witnessable 'routine grounds'

(Garfinkel, 1967) of the highly specialized work of teaching, the studies shift the focus from what teachers know and believe to a focus on what teachers do and, in so doing, make a significant contribute to a practice-based understanding of teaching (Ball & Forzani, 2009, 2011). More specifically, they contribute to the development of a specialized language for describing its many constituent parts at a level of articulation that motivates alternate readings, as instructed actions or pedagogies (Garfinkel, 2002). Such descriptions are 'at once a *curriculum* in that practice, and a pedagogy for those who would learn how to do it' (Macbeth, 2011: 99).

Making visible the practices and actions of how teaching is accomplished can help teachers and other stakeholders in the profession of teaching build professional vision, that is, 'socially organized ways of seeing and understanding that are answerable to the distinctive interests of a particular social group' (Goodwin, 2018: 408). Such close scrutiny of the details of teaching can reveal, to teachers, researchers, policy makers and other stakeholders, instructive distinctions between their idealized understandings of the work of teaching and 'its interactional reality' (Freebody, 2013: 73). This, in turn, can facilitate the development of a reflective capacity for understanding such work and informing 'prudent judgments' (Erickson, 2012: 688) and sound decision making in their own teaching contexts. As Heap (1990: 43) noted, 'if some activity is important in our lives, then knowing how it is organized may make a difference to how we act'.

Note

(1) An alternative term is multimodal, which includes the mobilization of objects in organizing action (Mondada, 2014).

References

aus der Wieschen, M. and Sert, O. (2018) Divergent language choices and maintenance of intersubjectivity: The case of Danish EFL young learners. *International Journal of Bilingual Education and Bilingualism.* doi:10.1080/13670050.2018.1447544

Baker, C. (1992) Description and analysis in classroom talk and interaction. *Journal of Classroom Interaction* 27, 9–14.

Ball, D.L. and Forzani, F.M. (2009) The work of teaching and the challenge for teacher education. *Journal of Teacher Education* 60 (5), 497–511.

Ball, D.L. and Forzani, F.M. (2011) Building a common core for learning to teach. *American Educator* 35 (2), 17–21, 38–39.

Cohen, D. (2011) *Teaching and its Predicaments.* Cambridge, MA: Harvard University Press.

Dingemanse, M., Roberts, S.G., Baranova, J., Blythe, J., Drew, P., Floyd, S. and Rossi, G. (2015) Universal principles in the repair of communication problems. *PloS One* 10 (9), e0136100.

Enfield, N. and Sidnell, J. (2014) Language presupposes an enchronic infrastructure for social interaction. In D. Dor, C. Knight and J. Lewis (eds) *The Social Origins of Language* (pp. 92–104). Oxford: Oxford University Press.

Erickson, F. (2012) Comments on causality in qualitative inquiry. *Qualitative Inquiry* 18, 686–688.

Fagan, D. (2015) Managing language errors in real-time: A microanalysis of teacher practices. *System* 55, 74–85.

Francis, D. and Hester, S. (2004) *An Invitation to Ethnomethodology*. London: Sage Publications.

Freebody, P. (2013) School knowledge in talk and writing: Taking 'when learners know' seriously. *Linguistics and Education* 24, 64–74.

Gardner, R. (2012) Conversation analysis in the classroom. In J. Sidnell and T. Stivers (eds) *The Handbook of Conversation Analysis* (pp. 593–612). New York: Wiley-Blackwell.

Garfinkel, H. (1964) Studies of the routine grounds of everyday activities. *Social Problems* 11, 225–250.

Garfinkel, H. (1967) *Studies in Ethnomethodology*. Englewood Cliffs, NJ: Prentice-Hall.

Garfinkel, H. (1996) Ethnomethodology's program. *Social Psychology Quarterly* 59, 5–21.

Garfinkel, H. (2002) *Ethnomethodology's Program: Working Out Durkheim's Aphorism*. Lanham, MD: Rowman & Littlefield.

Goffman, E. (1974) *Frame Analysis: An Essay on the Organization of Experience*. Cambridge, MA: Harvard University Press.

Goffman, E. (1981) *Forms of Talk*. Philadelphia, PA: University of Pennsylvania Press.

Goodwin, C. (2018) *Co-operative Action*. Cambridge: Cambridge University Press.

Gullberg, M. (2006) Handling discourse: Gestures, reference tracking, and communication strategies in early L2. *Language Learning* 56, 155–196.

Haakana, M. (2010) Laughter and smiling: Notes on co-occurrences. *Journal of Pragmatics* 42 (6), 1499–1512.

Hall, J.K. (1997) Differential teacher attention to student utterances: The construction of different opportunities for learning in the IRF. *Linguistics and Education* 9, 287–311.

Hall, J.K. and Smotrova, T. (2013) Teacher self-talk: Interactional resource for managing instruction and eliciting sympathy. *Journal of Pragmatics* 47, 75–92.

Hall, J.K. and Walsh, M. (2002) The links between teacher–student interaction and language learning. *Annual Review of Applied Linguistics* 22, 186–203.

Heap, J.L. (1990) Applied ethnomethodology: Looking for the local rationality of reading activities. *Human Studies* 13, 39–72.

Heap, J. (1992) Seeing snubs: An introduction to sequential analyses of classroom interaction. *Journal of Classroom Interaction* 27, 23–28.

Heritage, J. (1984) *Garfinkel and Ethnomethodology*. Malden, MA: Polity Press.

Heritage, J. (2008) Conversation analysis as social theory. In B.S. Turner (ed.) *The New Blackwell Companion to Social Theory* (pp. 300–320). Oxford: Blackwell.

Hester, S. and Francis, D. (1995) Words and pictures: Collaborative storytelling in a primary classroom. *Research in Education* 53, 65–88.

Hester, S. and Francis, D. (2000) Ethnomethodology and local educational order. In S. Hester and D. Francis (eds) *Local Educational Order: Ethnomethodological Studies of Knowledge in Action* (pp. 1–17). Amsterdam: John Benjamins.

Jacknick, C.M. (2009) A conversation-analytic account of student-initiated participation in an ESL classroom. Unpublished doctoral dissertation, Teachers College, Columbia University, New York.

Kääntä, L. (2012) Teachers' embodied allocations in instructional interaction. *Classroom Discourse* 3 (2), 166–186. doi:10.1080/19463014.2012.716624

Kääntä, L. (2014) From noticing to initiating correction: Students' epistemic displays in instructional interaction. *Journal of Pragmatics* 66, 86–105.

Kapellidi, C. (2013) The organization of talk in school interaction. *Discourse Studies* 15, 185–204.

Kimura, D., Malabarba, T. and Hall, J.K. (2018) Data collection considerations for classroom interaction research: A conversation analytic perspective. *Classroom Discourse* 9 (3), 185–204. doi:10.1080/19463014.2018.1485589

Koschmann, T., Stahl, G. and Zemel, A. (2004) The video analyst's manifesto. *Proceedings of the 6th International Conference on Learning Sciences (ICLS '04)* (pp. 278–285). Santa Monica, CA: International Society of the Learning Sciences.

Lazaraton, A. (2004) Gesture and speech in the vocabulary explanations of one ESL teacher: A microanalytic inquiry. *Language Learning* 54 (1), 79–117.

Lee, Y.A. (2007) Third turn position in teacher talk: Contingency and the work of teaching. *Journal of Pragmatics* 39, 1204–1230.

Lehtimaja, I. (2011) Teacher-oriented address terms in students' reproach turns. *Linguistics and Education* 22 (4), 348–363.

Lerner, G. (1995) Turn design and the organization of participation in instructional activities. *Discourse Processes* 19, 111–131.

Levinson, S.C. (2012) Action formation and ascription. In T. Stivers and J. Sidnell (eds) *The Handbook of Conversation Analysis* (pp. 103–130). Malden, MA: Wiley-Blackwell.

Lindström, A. and Sorjonen, M. (2012) Affiliation in conversation. In J. Sidnell and T. Stivers (eds) *The Handbook of Conversation Analysis* (pp. 350–369). New York: Wiley-Blackwell.

Looney, S.D. and Kim, J. (2018) Humor, uncertainty, and affiliation: Cooperative and co-operative action in the university science lab. *Linguistics and Education* 46, 56–69.

Looney, S.D., Jia, D. and Kimura, D. (2017) Self-directed okay in mathematics lectures. *Journal of Pragmatics* 107, 46–59.

Macbeth, D. (1990) Classroom order as practical action: The making and un-making of a quiet reproach. *British Journal of Sociology of Education* 11, 189–214.

Macbeth, D. (1991) Teacher authority as practical action. *Linguistics and Education* 3, 281–313.

Macbeth, D. (2000) Classrooms as installations: Direct instruction in the early grades. In S. Hester and D. Francis (eds) *Local Education Order: Ethnomethodological Studies of Knowledge in Action* (pp. 21–72). Philadelphia, PA: John Benjamins.

Macbeth, D. (2011) A commentary on incommensurate programs. In T. Koschmann (ed.) *Theories of Learning and Studies of Instructional Practice* (pp. 73–104). New York: Springer.

Macbeth, D. (2014) Studies of work, instructed action, and the promise of granularity: A commentary. *Discourse Studies* 16, 295–308.

Margutti, P. and Drew, P. (2014) Positive evaluation of student answers in classroom instruction. *Language and Education* 28 (5), 436–458.

Matsumoto, Y. and Dobs, A. (2017) Pedagogical gestures as interactional resources for teaching and learning tense and aspect in the ESL grammar classroom. *Language Learning* 67, 7–42.

Maynard, D. (2012) Everyone and no one to turn to: Intellectual roots and contexts for conversation analysis. In J. Sidnell and T. Stivers (eds) *The Handbook of Conversation Analysis* (pp. 11–31). Oxford: Wiley-Blackwell.

Maynard, D. and Clayman, S. (2003) Ethnomethodology and conversation analysis. In L. Reynolds and N. Herman-Kinney (eds) *Handbook of Symbolic Interactionism* (pp. 173–202). Walnut Creek, CA: Altamira Press.

McHoul, A. (1978) The organization of turns at formal talk in the classroom. *Language in Society* 7, 183–213.

Mehan, J. (1979) *Learning Lessons: Social Organization in the Classroom.* Cambridge, MA: Harvard University Press.

Mondada, L. (2014) The local constitution of multimodal resources for social interaction. *Journal of Pragmatics* 65, 137–156.

Mondada, L. (2016) Challenges of multimodality: Language and the body in social inter-action. *Journal of Sociolinguistics* 20, 336–366.

Mortensen, K. (2008) Selecting next speaker in the second language classroom: How to find a willing next speaker in planned activities. *Journal of Applied Linguistics* 5 (1), 55–79.

Mortensen, K. (2009) Establishing recipiency in pre-beginning position in the second language classroom. *Discourse Processes* 46, 491–515.

Mortensen, K. and Hazel, S. (2011) Initiating round robins in the L2 classroom – preliminary observations. *Novitas-ROYAL (Research on Youth and Language)* 5 (1), 55–70.

Nassaji, H. and Wells, G. (2000) What's the use of 'triadic dialogue': An investigation of teacher–student interaction. *Applied Linguistics* 21, 376–406.

National Research Council (2004) *Engaging Schools: Fostering High School Students' Motivation to Learn*. Washington, DC: National Academies Press.

Nevile, M. (2015) The embodied turn in research on language and social interaction. *Research on Language and Social Interaction* 48 (2), 121–151.

Ochs, E. (1996) Linguistic resources for socializing humanity. In J. Gumperz and S. Levinson (eds) *Rethinking Linguistic Relativity* (pp. 407–435). Cambridge: Cambridge University Press.

Park, Y. (2014) The roles of third-turn repeats in two L2 classroom interactional contexts. *Applied Linguistics* 35, 145–167.

Payne, G. and Hustler, D. (1980) Teaching the class: The practical management of a cohort. *British Journal of Sociology of Education* 1, 49–66.

Pianta, R., Hamre, B. and Allen, J. (2012) Teacher–student relationships and engagement: Conceptualizing, measuring, and improving the capacity of classroom interactions. In S.L. Christenson, A.L. Reschly and C. Wylie (eds) *Handbook of Research on Student Engagement* (pp. 365–386). New York: Springer Science + Business Media.

Piirainen-Marsh, A. (2011) Irony and the moral order of secondary school classrooms. *Linguistics and Education* 22 (4), 364–382.

Pomerantz, A. (1984) Agreeing and disagreeing with assessments: Some features of pre-ferred/dispreferred turn shapes. In J. Maxwell Atkinson and J. Heritage (eds) *Structures of Social Action: Studies in Conversation Analysis* (pp. 57–101). Cambridge: Cambridge University Press.

Sacks, H. (1984) On doing 'being ordinary'. In J. Maxwell Atkinson and J. Heritage (eds) *Structures of Social Action: Studies in Conversation Analysis* (pp. 413–429). Cambridge: Cambridge University Press.

Sacks, H. (1992) *Lectures on Conversation, Vol. 1*. Oxford: Basil Blackwell.

Sacks, H. (1995) *Lectures on Conversation, Vol. 2*. Oxford: Blackwell.

Sacks, H., Schegloff, E.A. and Jefferson, G. (1974) A simplest systematics for the organiza-tion of turn-taking for conversation. *Language* 50 (4), 696–735.

Sahlström, J.F. (2002) The interactional organization of hand raising in classroom inter-action. *Journal of Classroom Interaction* 37 (2), 47–57.

Schegloff, E. (1968) Sequencing in conversational openings. *American Anthropologist* 70, 1075–1095.

Schegloff, E. (1988) Goffman and the analysis of conversation. In P. Drew and T. Wootton (eds) *Erving Goffman: Exploring the Interaction Order* (pp. 89–135). Cambridge: Polity Press.

Schegloff, E. (1992) Repair after next turn: The last structurally provided defense of inter-subjectivity in conversation. *American Journal of Sociology* 97, 1295–1345.

Schegloff, E. (2000) When 'others' initiate repair. *Applied Linguistics* 21, 205–243.

Schegloff, E. (2006) Interaction: The infrastructure for social institutions, the natural ecological niche for language, and the arena in which culture is enacted. In N.J. Enfield and S. Levinson (eds) *The Roots of Human Sociality: Culture, Cognition and Interaction* (pp. 70–96). London: Berg.

Schegloff, E. (2007) *Sequence Organization in Interaction*. Cambridge: Cambridge University Press.

Schegloff, E., Jefferson, G. and Sacks, H. (1977) The preference for self-correction in the organization of repair in conversation. *Language* 53, 361–382.

Sert, O. (2013) 'Epistemic status check' as an interactional phenomenon in instructed learning settings. *Journal of Pragmatics* 45, 13–28.

Sert, O. (2015) *Social Interaction and L2 Classroom Discourse*. Edinburgh: Edinburgh University Press.

Sert, O. and Jacknick, C. (2015) Student smiles and the negotiation of epistemics in L2 classrooms. *Journal of Pragmatics* 77, 97–112.

Smotrova, T. (2017) Making pronunciation visible: Gesture in teaching pronunciation. *TESOL Quarterly* 51 (1), 59–89.

Steensig, J. (2012) Conversation analysis and affiliation and alignment. In K. Mortensen and J. Wagner (eds) *The Encyclopedia of Applied Linguistics: Conversation Analysis*. Cambridge: Wiley-Blackwell.

Stivers, T. (2008) Stance, alignment, and affiliation during storytelling: When nodding is a token of affiliation. *Research on Language and Social Interaction* 41 (1), 31–57.

Stivers, T. (2012) Sequence organization. In J. Sidnell and T. Stivers (eds) *The Handbook of Conversation Analysis* (pp. 191–209). Malden, MA: Wiley-Blackwell.

Stivers, T., Enfield, N.J., Brown, P., *et al.* (2009) Universals and cultural variation in turn-taking in conversation. *Proceedings of the National Academy of Sciences* 106 (26), 10587–10592.

Stivers, T., Mondada, L. and Steensig, J. (2011) Knowledge, morality and affiliation in social interaction. In T. Stivers, L. Mondada and J. Steensig (eds) *The Morality of Knowledge in Conversation* (pp. 3–26) Cambridge: Cambridge University Press.

Streeck, J., Goodwin, C. and LeBaron, C. (2011) Embodied interaction: Language and body in the material world. In J. Streeck, C. Goodwin and C. LeBaron (eds) *Embodied Interaction: Language and Body in the Material World* (pp. 1–28). Cambridge: Cambridge University Press.

Waring, H.Z. (2008) Using explicit positive assessment in the language classroom: IRF, feedback, and learning opportunities. *The Modern Language Journal* 92, 577–594.

Waring, H. (2009) Moving out of IRF: A single case analysis. *Language Learning* 59 (4), 796–824.

Waring, H., Creider, S. and Box, C. (2013) Explaining vocabulary in the second language classroom: A conversation analytic account. *Learning, Culture and Social Interaction* 2 (4), 249–264.

Watanabe, A. (2017) Developing L2 interactional competence: Increasing participation through self-selection in post-expansion sequences. *Classroom Discourse* 8 (3), 271–293.

2 Attending to the Interpersonal and Institutional Contingencies of Interaction in an Elementary Classroom

Nadja Tadic and Catherine DiFelice Box

Although at times treated as a violation of institutional participation norms (Lemke, 1990), conversational talk in the classroom can offer learners valuable opportunities to build social roles, nurture interpersonal relationships and develop understandings (Edwards & Mercer, 1987; Lemke, 1990; Mehan, 1979). In the second language (L2) classroom, such talk also allows learners to engage in authentic and spontaneous target language use not often available during more traditional classroom-sanctioned turn-taking patterns (Park, 2016; Waring, 2014). Therefore, skillfully attending to both the institutional and interpersonal concerns of the classroom is crucial to the interactional achievement of teaching.

In this chapter we analyze the ways in which one third-grade teacher attends to the interpersonal and instructional contingencies of the L2 classroom through a range of verbal and embodied resources. Drawing on Goffman's (1974, 1981) concept of *framing*, we show that the teacher uses prosody, gaze, body posture and instructional materials either to mark transitions from 'doing conversation' to 'doing instruction' or to embed instruction into conversation, thus interweaving the institutional and the interpersonal. We argue that such practices expand the notion of what constitutes teaching in the language classroom, and we consider possible implications for teachers who strive to incorporate students' funds of knowledge into the classroom to create a rich learning environment.

Introduction

While ordinary conversation varies greatly in terms of topic, length of utterance and turn allocation (Sacks *et al*., 1974), classroom interaction, as a form of institutional talk (Heritage, 2004; Seedhouse, 1996; van Lier, 1996; Walsh, 2006) tends, at least traditionally, to be structured more rigidly, with the teacher predominantly taking charge of topic initiation, topic development and speaking rights (McHoul, 1978; Mehan, 1979; Sinclair & Coulthard, 1975; van Lier, 1996). This is not to say, however, that teachers and students do not veer from these official participation norms and engage in talk more akin to ordinary conversation. In fact, engaging students in interactions that relax institutional norms and allow more spontaneous talk on topics of personal relevance to the participants is considered integral and crucial to instruction, as it helps participants build interpersonal relationships and create an environment conducive to learning (Bannink, 2002; Kramsch, 1985). In the L2 classroom, such departures from typical teacher–student roles and interactional patterns can additionally facilitate learners' language development, providing them with a space to engage in spontaneous L2 use as they would outside the classroom (Ädel, 2011; Coupland, 2000, 2003; Nguyen, 2007; Ohta, 2008; Park, 2016; Tsui, 1996; Waring, 2014) and to employ interactional practices to which they do not commonly have access in the traditional classroom, such as topic initiation, topic development and self-selection (Cazden, 1988; Lemke, 1990; Mehan, 1979).

With its potential to uncover fine-grained details about social interaction, conversation analysis (CA) has greatly helped illuminate the nature of conversational talk, particularly in the adult L2 classroom (e.g. Markee, 2005; Nguyen, 2007; Park, 2016; Waring, 2012, 2014). However, there is still a paucity of CA research examining how teachers discursively manage contingencies in interaction when working with young language learners, particularly those in public school classrooms in which mandated state and federal standards may drive both the pedagogical agenda and the teacher's pedagogical style. We aim to address this gap by examining how one English as a second language (ESL) teacher manages to attend to both the institutional and the interpersonal concerns of an elementary school classroom as a writing lesson unfolds.

Background

Unlike in ordinary conversation, interactants in institutional talk are primarily concerned with institution-specific goals, restricted in the nature of their interactional contributions and guided by institution- and activity-specific inferential frameworks (Drew & Heritage, 1992). In the classroom, these features of institutional talk emerge in the form of teacher-directed discourse, in which teachers control turn-taking and the topic of talk (see, for example, McHoul, 1978; Mehan, 1979; Seedhouse, 1996). Ordinary conversation, however, still can occur in the classroom, with students and teachers interacting as fellow-conversationalists with equal speaking rights and topic development rights (Richards, 2006). And even though student interactions resembling ordinary conversation are often treated as 'illegitimate' (Waring, 2012) or as violations of classroom participation norms, they offer learners valuable opportunities to build social roles, nurture relationships and develop understandings (Edwards & Mercer, 1987; Lemke, 1990; Mehan, 1979). A growing number of CA studies, focusing primarily on adult L2 instruction, have recently explored ordinary conversation in the classroom with an aim of uncovering its intricate nature and the learning opportunities it might engender for L2 students *in situ*. Markee (2005), for instance, examined a personal conversation or 'off-task' talk between two students during small group work, finding that such talk allowed the students to express their nuanced identities and address their actual interactional needs more than 'on-task' talk. Richards (2006) showed that teachers managed more conversational talk by enacting their non-institutional identities. Similarly, exploring 'playful' talk in an adult ESL classroom, Waring (2012: 205) found that teachers and students 're-key[ed] classroom talk as more conversational' by invoking different situational, personal and relational identities.

The CA framework allows for a detailed exploration into the ways in which teachers can incorporate ordinary conversation into the language classroom to build rapport and promote learning. Nguyen (2007) analyzed rapport in ESL college-prep classes and identified an array of verbal and nonverbal cues (e.g. word choice, prosody, facial expressions, gestures) that teachers employed in face-threatening situations (for example, correcting) to simultaneously attend to the instructional and interpersonal aspects of instruction. Similarly exploring how one ESL teacher navigated the tension between the interpersonal and institutional, Waring (2014) utilized Goffman's (1974) concept of frame. Examining the opening sequences of classroom interaction, she argued that the teacher strikes a balance between control and connection in one of two ways: (1) by embedding a conversational frame within an institutional one; or (2) by redirecting personal conversations to the institutional frame. Park (2016: 125) similarly found that teachers often built rapport with their Korean language students by engaging them in informal conversations on personal matters or by 'embedd[ing] a conversational frame into the instructional frame'. Both Waring (2014) and Park (2016) showed teacher–student interactions in the conversational frame to be more akin to peer interactions, while interactions in the institutional frame tended to reflect asymmetries tied to participants' institutional roles. When embedding a conversational into an institutional frame, teachers modified typical, instructional initiation-response-feedback (IRF) sequences by asking personally relevant instead of known-answer questions and by expressing appreciation as opposed to assessment of student responses. The teachers also cued their shifts from an institutional to a conversational frame by invoking co-membership with students in non-institutional roles (e.g. vacationers or writers) and by taking on a more intimate speech style or tone.

We aim to add to this line of research by exploring the granular details of how one teacher attends to the interpersonal and institutional contingencies of interaction in a third-grade ESL classroom. Building on the recent CA work that incorporates Goffman's (1974, 1981) concept of frame (Park, 2016; Waring, 2014), we identify a range of verbal and embodied interactional resources, including gestures, manipulation of instructional materials, and shifts in posture, prosody and gaze, on which the teacher and students draw to attend to both the institutional and interpersonal concerns of the classroom. Our findings contribute to the growing body of research on managing and promoting learner participation and teacher–student interaction in the L2 classroom, with possible benefits for teacher training. More broadly, we embrace the notion that the act of *teaching* can both be planned and unfold naturally as part of the sequence in either a conversational or an institutional frame.

Data and Method

The data for this study come from an hour-long video-recording of a third-grade English Language Arts class at a public school in the United States. The class was designed for ESL students and entailed content-based ESL instruction. The participants in this study are the teacher, Fred, and his four students – Anthony, Melissa, Alonso and Brendon (all names are pseudonyms). During the session, the class was working on a writing task requiring every student to write three imagined dialogues on the topic of his/her chosen future profession. As they worked on this instructional task, the participants often veered from canonical patterns of classroom interaction (McHoul, 1978; Mehan, 1979; Sinclair & Coulthard, 1975; van Lier, 1996) and discussed personal topics.

We transcribed the video-recording according to the notation system developed by Gail Jefferson (2004), slightly adapted to fit the nature of the data. We then examined the transcripts using CA principles and Goffman's concept of *frame*, which denotes the metamessages (e.g. prosodic, verbal and embodied cues) that define what is going on at any moment of an interaction (Goffman, 1974, 1981; Tannen, 1993). According to Goffman (see also Bateson, 1972), any social interaction consists of multilayered frames. In the context of classroom interaction, this includes the frames of 'doing conversation' and of 'doing instruction' (Park, 2016; Waring, 2014). Participants signal their shifts from one frame to another through subtle changes in the design of their utterances and through changes in the footing or alignment they take up to those utterances, to themselves and to others around them (Goffman, 1981). For instance, the whole class might shift from a conversational to an institutional frame at the beginning of a lesson; the teacher might walk to the front of the class and increase voice volume while addressing all of the students, and the students might interrupt conversations with their peers, turn to face the teacher and open their books. During a lesson, a subset of students might also embed a conversational frame within the larger institutional frame by turning to face one another instead of the teacher, lowering their voices and initiating a conversation on matters unrelated to official classroom business.

Here, we examine the ways in which an ESL teacher and his students draw on multiple verbal and embodied resources to establish conversational and institutional frames in the classroom. We show that the teacher uses his prosody, gaze, body posture and instructional materials either to mark transitions from the conversational to the institutional frame or to embed the latter within the former. We argue that such practices expand the notion of what constitutes teaching in the ESL classroom, as participation in both frames contributes to learner engagement with the language, albeit in different ways.

Analysis

In this section we delineate the interactional practices used to establish the conversational and institutional frames in the classroom, focusing primarily on the teacher's orientation to the interactional contingencies of the two frames displayed through verbal and embodied action. First, we examine how the teacher aligns with the students' initiations of personally relevant conversational talk and shows appreciation for their contributions before initiating a shift back to the institutional frame. We then turn our attention to instances when the teacher embeds the institutional frame as subordinate (Goffman, 1981) to the conversational frame, attending again to the students' personal interests and identities before re-establishing the institutional frame and orienting the whole class to the planned pedagogical agenda.

Shifting frames through embodied action

Our first excerpt demonstrates ways in which the teacher draws on verbal and embodied resources to indicate shifts between the conversational and the institutional frames. Prior to the first excerpt (which occurs near the outset of the class), the participants reviewed what they learned the previous week, before moving on to the pedagogic agenda or teaching point of the day. We can see the configuration of the classroom space, materials and participants in Figure 2.1. The teacher, Fred, and the

Figure 2.1 Classroom layout

students are sitting in a circle – Anthony and Brendon to Fred's right and left, respectively, Alonso across from Fred, and Melissa between Alonso and Anthony. The board is positioned between Fred and Brendon, slightly in the back, and a back desk with extra instructional materials is located behind Fred, to his slight right. Outside the camera frame, behind Brendon, two school staff members are doing administrative work. They share the space with Fred's class, but they do not participate in their class sessions.

Just before we join the class, one student, Brendon, reads what Fred terms the 'teaching point' for the day's lesson from the board. Fred subsequently starts repeating the teaching point to the class, but he soon interrupts this action to turn off the air conditioning unit in the classroom (outside the camera frame), since it is, as Fred states, 'a little loud'. Fred's management of the air conditioning unit leads to a brief crossplay (Goffman, 1981) between himself and the two school staff members sharing the classroom space (ST1 and ST2). We join the class at the end of this interaction between Fred and the staff members, as ST1 and ST2 share their assessments of the classroom temperature (Lines 1–5). For ease of reference, teacher moves that index the institutional frame will be marked with a bold arrow (➜) and moves that index a conversational frame with a regular arrow (→). Embodied actions will be marked with an arrow when they are not accompanied by speech or are not aligned with the frame of the teacher's speech (e.g. when the teacher's verbal conduct indexes a conversational frame but his embodied conduct indexes the institutional frame).

Excerpt 1: really hot

```
1    ST1:      >it's (.) r::e::ally cold or re:ally warm.
2    ST2:      ye[ah.
3    FRE:        [[yeah.
4                {((smiles and looks at BRE))
5    ST2:      (XXXXX)=
6    FRE:      ={>one or the other. exactly.
7         ➜      {((looks and points at board))
```

Figure 2.2 Lines 6–7: Addresses ST2, looks at board

```
 8    FRE:          {((looks at BRE))
 9          →        {[BRENDON. CAN YOU READ tha-
10    MEL:           [yesterday was=
11    FRE:          ((looks at MEL))
```

Figure 2.3 Lines 8–9: Looks at and addresses BRE

Figure 2.4 Line 11: Turns to MEL

```
12    MEL:          =really hot.
13                  (.)
14    FRE:          what's that?
15    MEL:          yesterday was [really hot.
16    FRE:   →                     {[>yesterday got
17                               {((nods))
18                  pretty hot.< >today's supposed to get< even hotter.=
19    MEL:          =<eighty six degrees.>
20    ALO:          ((looks at FRE, points at his own arm))
21    FRE:   →      why- {do you watch the news?
22                      {((squints))
23    ALO:                {((shakes his hand))
24    MEL:          {↑no::, i just (check) on my compu:ter.
25    ALO:          {((repeatedly points at arm))
26    FRE:          {((raises eyebrows, shifts gaze toward ALO))
27           →      {oh, you checked on your computer?
28    ALO:          {((continues to point at his arm))
29    FRE:   →      ↑and what did {you do outside in e:ighty six degree
30                                {((points to ALO))
31                  ↑weather.
```

Figure 2.5 Lines 29–31: Looks at and addresses ALO

```
32                    (0.2)
33    ALO:            {(((gestures to full mouth))
34    FRE:   →        {playing football?
35    ALO:            ((nods once))
36    FRE:   →        {oh, okay. ((smiles))
37    ALO:            {mm,
38                    {(((shakes head))
39    FRE:   →→       no. (.) {(((turns to BRE)) [okay. we'll COM-
40    ANT:                    {(((looks at FRE)) [I was playing fo-
41    FRE:            ((turns to ANT))
```

Figure 2.6 Lines 39: Looks at and addresses BRE

Figure 2.7 Line 41: Turns to ANT

```
42    ANT:           I was playing football.
43    FRE:   →       you were playing football? [°alright.°
44    ALO:                                       [i was playing <soccer.>
45    FRE:   →       ((looks at ALO)) {°soccer?° (.) {°okay.°
46           →→                       {((nods))       {((turns to BRE))
```

Figure 2.8 Lines 45–46 ('soccer'): Looks at and addresses ALO

Figure 2.9 Lines 45–46 ('okay'): Looks at and addresses BRE

```
47    FRE:   →      {BRENDON, ONE MORE TIME UP here please,
48                  {((turns and points to board))
49                  ((looks at BRE))
50    BRE:          {students will a:dd (.)
51                  {((reads off board))
```

Triggered by the air conditioner drowning out the students' voices, the crossplay between Fred and the two staff members, while still concerned with institutional, classroom issues, ends up halting the progressivity of the ongoing *instructional* activity on the main classroom floor – the introduction of the teaching point. We can see Fred's orientation to a return to this instructional activity in his summative response to ST1 and ST2 (Line 6), which is verbally aligned with the staff members' room temperature telling, but nonverbally disaligned from it, with Fred shifting his body away from the tellers and to the board (Figure 2.2) and then to Brendon (Figure 2.3). Fred's orientation to the lesson is further seen in his subsequent initiation of an instructional sequence. Immediately after expressing agreement with the staff members' assessment of the room temperature, Fred asks Brendon to read the teaching point to the class with a marked increase in volume (Line 9), signaling a transition to a new activity (Dorr-Bremme, 1990).

However, in overlap with Fred's reading request, Melissa self-selects and pursues the crossplay topic on the main classroom floor by shifting the focus from institutional issues of classroom temperature to her own experience with the recent hot weather outside the institutional, classroom space (Lines 10–12). Melissa's self-selection and topic expansion based on personal experience index a symmetry in student–teacher interaction (Lemke, 1990; Mehan, 1979; van Lier, 1996) more in line with a conversational than with a typical institutional frame. In response, Fred abandons his instructional sequence with a cut-off (Line 9), aligns with Melissa's course of action by turning to her (Figure 2.4) and initiating repair of her turn (Line 14), and affiliates with Melissa through an agreement in recognitional overlap (Jefferson, 1984) (Line 16). The conversational frame implicit in Melissa's self-selection and topic pursuit in Lines 10 and 12 is then further taken up by Fred, as he elaborates on Melissa's topic (Line 16), asks her a follow-up question (Line 21), and engages another student, Alonso, in the conversation (Figure 2.5, Lines 29–31) (possibly having understood Alonso's gestures in Lines 20, 23, 25 and 28 as bids for the floor). As Alonso is temporarily unable to speak due to his mouth being full, Fred seems to initiate a closing of the hot weather topic and a resumption of the ongoing instructional activity (Line 39): he delivers a transition-implicative 'okay' and noticeably increases his volume (Dorr-Bremme, 1990) as he turns to Brendon once again (Figure 2.6), just as he did when attempting to resume the ongoing activity previously (Figure 2.3).

Fred's attempt at shifting back to the institutional frame is once again interrupted, now by Anthony, who self-selects in overlap to offer his own contribution to the topic (Line 40). Fred aligns with Anthony's turn by shifting his gaze toward him (Figure 2.7) and then responding with a full-repeat of Anthony's utterance in rising intonation, along with an acknowledgement delivered in *sotto voce* and in transitional overlap with Alonso's contribution to the topic (Line 43). Fred similarly responds to Alonso's contribution by first turning toward him (Figure 2.8) and then providing a nod, a partial repeat in rising intonation and a softly spoken acknowledgement (Line 45) – an acknowledgement now accompanied by Fred's simultaneous shift in gaze toward Brendon (Figure 2.9). Fred's verbal alignment (an acknowledgement) coupled with his nonverbal disalignment (shift in gaze) from the current sequence is reminiscent of his initial attempt to transition to the instructional activity while responding to the staff members' room temperature assessments (Line 6, Figure 2.2). He now successfully initiates the target instructional sequence by pointing to the whiteboard and asking Brendon, at a noticeably higher volume, to once again read the teaching point (Lines 47–48). This time, Fred's directive (Line 47, 'one more time up here') lacks any explicitly stated action to guide Brendon's response (compare to Line 8, 'can you *read*'). Nevertheless, Brendon responds appropriately, starting to read the teaching point from the board without any delay.

Throughout this excerpt, Fred's speech and body signal several vacillations between two frames; the institutional frame ostensibly appears to be more closely oriented to pre-planned, focused language learning (i.e. 'the teaching point'), while the conversational frame seems more organically tied to immediate and recent personal experiences. We see that, as Fred attempts to reinitiate the instructional activity in the institutional frame through his embodied actions, the students orient to the conversational frame as (still) open for contributions, an orientation with which Fred aligns. Melissa comments on the weekend weather and Anthony proffers his weekend activity, both of which occur after Fred has cued a return to the pedagogical task at hand. Yet, Fred aligns with both contributions, thereby validating (and in the case of Melissa, expounding upon) the talk, exhibiting his willingness to postpone the instructional frame in order to attend to the budding conversational talk, at least for a certain amount of time. During these moments, the students demonstrate their ability to both adhere to the stated pedagogical agenda and participate in unfolding conversational sequences through self-selection, topic pursuit and topic expansion. By promoting a space in which both frames exist *in tandem*, Fred, therefore, creates opportunities for various types of student participation.

Embedding frames through embodied action

While the previous excerpt shows the ways in which Fred draws on verbal and embodied resources to temporarily align with the conversational before shifting back to the institutional frame, here we demonstrate how he manages to attend to both frames simultaneously by *embedding* the institutional within the conversational frame. The interactional sequence we examine in the next two excerpts occurs later in the lesson. Anthony has just shared one of his dialogues with the class, which Fred positively evaluates before announcing a new class task. At the start of Excerpt 2, Fred is setting up the next task by finding additional sheets of paper for the students (Lines 1–3). Melissa and Anthony take advantage of this indeterminate space between class activities (Dorr-Bremme, 1990; Markee, 2005) to initiate resistance to the teacher's plan of, as he says, 'getting back to work'.

Excerpt 2: *soccer*

```
1    FRE:   →     so right now we're getting back to work.
2                 {((turns to back desk))
3                 {I have more [blank sheets here.
4    MEL:                      [what?
5                 (0.2)
6    MEL:         no[:::::::.=
7    FRE:           [well [cuz-
8    ANT:                 [so-
9    MEL:         =o:[::::
10   ANT:            [mr. johnson? ((looks at FRE, smiles))
11   FRE:         {((looks at MEL)) {((looks at back desk))
12        →       {ms. melissa?      {thank you?}
13   MEL:         [ma::n.
14   ANT:         [mr. johnson?
15   FRE:         {((looks at ANT))
16                {yes.
17   ANT:         {((looks straight, smiles))
18                {.h my brother can beat a 18-year-old in
19                so:c{cer.
20                    {((looks at FRE))
21   FRE:   →     {wow.              {how o:ld is your brother.
22        →→      {((looks at ANT's work)) {((looks at ANT, hands him
23                back his work))
```

Figure 2.10 Lines 21–22 ('wow'): Looks at materials and addresses ANT

Figure 2.11 Lines 21–22 ('how old...'): Addresses and looks at ANT and hands him the materials

```
24   ANT:         thirteen.
25   FRE:   →     {(.)that's pretty good.
26        →→      {((moves head from ANT to blank papers in wide nod))
```

Figure 2.12 Lines 25–26: Moves head from ANT to materials in wide nod

```
27    FRE:  ➔      ((stacks papers))
```

Figure 2.13 Line 27: Looks at and stacks papers

```
28    MEL:        when my {dad=
29    FRE:  ➔→             {((taps papers loudly on desk, looks at MEL))
```

Figure 2.14 Line 29: Taps papers on desk and looks at MEL

```
30    MEL:        =was playing so:ccer: and now he do:esn't? he: he:
31                was the last °one to {(be on the ↑team.°)
32                                     {((looks down to the side))
33                [(°he was the-°)
34    FRE:  →     {[↑he was the last one to do ↑what.
35                {((slouches, speaks in loud whisper))
36                ((gestures toward himself))
37                (.)
```

```
38    MEL:        ((looks at FRE)) °↑i <forgot,>° (.)
39    FRE:        [(he-) {((looks down and points to ground))
40    MEL:        [so    {i >saw a< {<picture> of it.
41    FRE:                         {(((looks at MEL, raises eyebrows,
42         →      nods)) was he a good soccer player?
43    ALO:        [mm::::.
44    MEL:        [yeah. he u- he had a [ma::wha::wk,
45    FRE:  ➔          ((looks at ALO)) [°alonso.° ((points to front of
46          ➔→      room, slides hand left to right, looks back at MEL))
```

Figure 2.15 Line 45: Looks at and addresses ALO

Figure 2.16 Line 46: Turns to MEL

```
47    ALO:        ((starts cleaning crumbs off his desk))
48    MEL:        ((looks at FRE)) whe:n he was young:er:,
49    FRE:   →    okay,
((MEL continues her telling))
```

As the participants are transitioning to the new class task, we notice a slight misalignment in their orientations to the frame. Fred explicitly refers to the institutional nature of the current activity ('getting back to work', Line 1) and manipulates instructional materials, seemingly indicating his orientation to the institutional frame (Lines 2–3). On the other hand, Melissa explicitly resists Fred's course of action with a *wh*-question (Line 4) which, delivered in rising intonation and with added stress, functions as an other-initiated repair. She then more explicitly disaligns from Fred's transition to a new task with a significantly elongated 'no' (Lines 6, 9), indexing a relationship with Fred which is much more symmetrical and equal than a traditional relationship between a teacher and a student. This disalignment is quickly (and temporarily) resolved as Fred invokes a disciplinary action by implicitly reprimanding Melissa for her behavior through a summons (Line 12) and thus reinforcing the institutional frame. Nevertheless, Anthony establishes the conversational frame by securing the teacher's attention through a generic pre-sequence (Lines 10, 14) and by making an announcement (Lines 18–19) on a topic of personal relevance to him – his brother's athletic acumen.

Just as he did when responding to Melissa's topic pursuit in Excerpt 1, Fred now aligns with Anthony's telling: he verbally marks it as newsworthy ('wow', Line 21), asks a follow-up question (Line 21), and provides a positive assessment of Anthony's news (Line 25). However, while verbally aligning with Anthony's personal telling, Fred nonverbally orients to the transition from one instructional task to the next, gazing at and returning Anthony's already-written work (Figures 2.10 and 2.11) and organizing the blank sheets of paper for the students' next writing assignment (Figure 2.13). Moreover, as Fred's assessment in Line 25 works to show heightened involvement in Anthony's telling and simultaneously indexes a potential transition to the next sequence (Goodwin & Goodwin, 1992), Fred's gaze to the stack of blank papers in this moment (Figure 2.12) and his subsequent loud tap of the paper stack against the desk (Figure 2.14) might underscore the *instructional* nature of the upcoming sequence. However, in partial overlap with Fred's tap of the blank-paper stack, Melissa launches a 'my side' telling (Pomerantz, 1980) on Anthony's soccer topic (Line 28), further preserving the conversational and deferring the institutional frame.

Fred immediately shifts his gaze to Melissa (Figure 2.14) and aligns with her telling as a listener, encouraging her to speak louder (Lines 34–36), nodding (Line 42) and asking a follow-up question (Line 42). Interestingly, in the midst of Melissa's telling, Fred does temporarily orient to another student, Alonso, shifting his gaze toward him (Figure 2.15), summoning him in *sotto voce* (Line 45), and issuing a nonverbal directive in the form of a clearing gesture (Line 46), to which Alonso responds by cleaning the food crumbs off his desk (Line 47). This brief byplay (Goffman, 1981) between Fred and Alonso appears to be set within the institutional frame, with Fred issuing a disciplinary directive and Alonso abiding by it. Noticeably, however, this disciplinary action is constructed as clearly subordinate to Melissa's telling (Goffman, 1981). It is designed to minimally interfere with Melissa's action on the classroom floor, consisting of two quiet or entirely embodied turns. As soon as Fred completes his directive, he shifts his gaze back to Melissa (Figure 2.16), again aligning with her telling by providing a response token (Line 49).

As we can see, through employing hand gesturing, gaze and prosodic packaging, Fred managed to complete institutional tasks while engaging the students in interactions that unfolded organically and provided them with opportunities to produce extended output. This output both (1) linked to the students' personal worlds, and (2) gave them a space to develop and demonstrate their interactional competence (see Hall *et al.*, 2011) as storytellers – to meaningfully and appropriately initiate, develop and build on each other's personal tellings at moments when the institutional frame had not yet been firmly established.

Throughout the rest of Melissa's telling, the conversational frame is uninterrupted, with Fred continuing to align as a recipient of Melissa's personally relevant story. At the beginning of our final excerpt, Melissa's story reaches its climax (Line 55) and a transition back to the institutional frame again becomes potentially relevant. It is at this point that we once again see Fred's embodied orientation to the institutional frame.

Excerpt 3: *then he grew fat*

```
((MEL continues her telling))
55    MEL:          and then he grew fat. ((smiles))
56    FRE:    →     then h(h)e g(h)re(h)w {f(h)a(h)
57            →                           {((looks at blank paper))
```

Figure 2.17 Lines 56–57 ('fat'): Looks at materials and addresses MEL

```
58    MEL:          @hh
59    FRE:    →     $↑and then he grew fa:t. i won't tell him you said
60                  that. [we'll keep that {a secret.$
61                                         {((looks at MEL))
62    ANT:          [why did he grow fat.
63    FRE:    →     {.hh          {↓i don't know.
64            →→    {((looks at ANT)){((looks at stack of blank paper,
65                  shakes head slightly, raises eyebrows))
```

Figure 2.18 Lines 63–64 ('.hh'): Turns to ANT

Figure 2.19 Lines 63–65 ('I don't know'): Looks at materials and responds to ANT

```
66    FRE:    →     ((taps stack of blank paper on desk))
```

Figure 2.20 Line 66: Taps materials on desk

```
67    FRE:    →    {sometimes that tends to happen with {adults.
68                 {((looks down))                        {((looks at MEL))
```

Figure 2.21 Lines 67–68: Looks down as he responds to ANT's question

Figure 2.22 Lines 67–68 ('adults'): Looks at MEL as he responds to ANT's question

```
69    FRE:    →    {they get- they're re:ally athletic
70                 {((opens eyes wide))
71                 when they're young and then what happens.=they get
72                 la:zy when they get older.
73    MEL:           yeah, [they drink=
74    FRE:                 {[or they-
75                         {((extends arm toward MEL))
76    MEL:           =[wa:ter.
77    ANT:            [I-
78    FRE:           ((looks at MEL, raises eyebrows, nods))
79    ANT:           I'm not fat.
80    FRE:    →    {som- sometimes    {they have melissa as a daughter,
81                 {((looks at ANT)) {((extends arm toward MEL))
82                 ((looks at MEL))
```

Figure 2.23 Lines 80–81: Looks at ANT as he expands response to ANT's question

Figure 2.24 Line 82: Looks at MEL as he expands response to ANT's question

```
83    FRE:    →    {and               {then they have to (deal)
84                 {((looks at ALO)){((extends arm toward MEL))
85                 with (.) with {melissa,
86                               {((looks at MEL, opens eyes wide))
```

Figure 2.25 Lines 83–84: Looks at ALO as he expands response to ANT's question

Figure 2.26 Lines 85–86: Looks at MEL as he expands response to ANT's question

```
87                    (.)
88    MEL:            he::y,=
89    FRE:     →      =who's a little ((looks at ALO)) $crazy and
90                    {((opens up arms, opens eyes wide))
91                    {[then they DON'T HAVE TIME$=
92    MEL:            [i'm NO:T FA:T.=
93    FRE:     →      =$to EXERCISE {ANYMORE          {nah$, i'm just
94             →→                   {((looks at MEL)) {((looks down))
95             →      kidding. ((taps stack of blank paper on desk))
```

Figure 2.27 Lines 93–95 ('nah...'): Looks down as he responds to MEL

Figure 2.28 Line 95: Taps materials on desk

```
96    FRE:     →      oKAY. ↑how many do we have over there Alonso?
97                    how many did you write so far?
98    ALO:            two.
99    FRE:     →      ↑you wrote two? >okay. i'm gonna come over
100                   there and take a look melissa< how many did you
101                   write?
102   MEL:            TWO::.
```

As Melissa brings her story to an end (Line 55), Fred affiliates with her through laughter and a repetition of the climax, showing appreciation for her personally relevant telling. Notably, while Fred's gaze was directed at Melissa throughout most of her telling (except during the brief byplay with Alonso described above), as soon as Melissa's story reaches its climax, Fred's gaze shifts to the blank sheets of paper he has prepared for the upcoming task (Figure 2.17), even as he verbally responds to the climax of Melissa's story (Line 56). Fred's orientation to the institutional frame at this point is still only fleeting, however, and he continues to affiliate with Melissa on a personal level: he invokes a close relationship with her by referring to the two of them together as a team sharing a secret (note the first person plural pronoun in 'we'll keep that a secret', Line 60). In this way, Fred simultaneously shows appreciation for Melissa's telling and implicates its closing. Before the closing is initiated, however, Anthony asks a follow-up question, expanding the telling sequence.

In response to Anthony's follow-up question, Fred temporarily shifts his gaze to Anthony (Figure 2.18) before looking down at the stack of blank-paper sheets (Figure 2.19) and claiming lack of knowledge (Line 63). He then again taps the stack of papers against his desk (Figure 2.20), possibly indicating his orientation to the next instructional activity (as in Excerpt 2); however, this very light tap of the paper stack is followed not by an instructional task but by two candidate responses to Anthony's question. As Fred delivers his first candidate response (Lines 67–72), he initially looks down at the stack of papers (Figure 2.21) but then settles his gaze on Melissa (Figure 2.22), who joins him in answering (Lines 73, 76). During his second candidate response, delivered in the form of a teasing (Lines 80–93), Fred repeatedly shifts his gaze from one student to the other (Figures 2.23–2.26), seemingly trying to engage each student in his teasing response turn. Fred's light-hearted teasing of Melissa at this point indicates a friendly personal relationship and, just as the reference to their shared secret at the previous sequence-closing juncture (Line 60), it helps highlight Fred's involvement in the current conversational frame while simultaneously implicating a closing of it. This time, however, Fred manages to successfully close the telling sequence by shifting his gaze from the students down to the stack of papers (Figure 2.27) and by lowering his voice as he marks his teasing as humorous (Lines 93, 95). He then cues the transition to the institutional frame with a comparably loud tapping of the blank-paper stack against the desk (Figure 2.28) (just as in his initial transition attempt after Anthony's telling in Excerpt 2) and a loud discourse marker ('okay', Line 96). The transition is finally followed by a question on the students' task progress thus far (Line 96) and, even though this question lacks an explicit reference to the target instructional task ('how many did you write' as opposed to, for example, 'how many dialogues did you write'), the students indicate no problems in responding. The institutional frame is firmly established, and the logistics of the writing task can now be properly addressed.

While Fred tended to, and indeed cultivated, his conversation with Melissa and Anthony in this excerpt, his gaze and gestures toward task materials reveal that the instructional work is, literally and figuratively, close at hand. From their immediate responses to Fred's anaphoric referent for 'how many' in Line 96, we can also see that the students orientated to the fleeting nature of the conversational frame and to the instructional nature of Fred's embodied actions. It therefore appears that embodied practices allowed Fred to operate in both frames simultaneously, pushing forward the pedagogical agenda while creating a space for sharing and appreciating a personally relevant telling, thus nurturing a classroom climate in which personal stories and pedagogical tasks alike abound.

Discussion and Conclusion

In this chapter we have explored the ways in which a teacher can draw on embodied resources to attend to both the institutional and interpersonal contingencies of interaction in an elementary language classroom. The teacher in our data used prosody, gaze, gesture, body orientation and class materials to align with his students in 'doing conversation' and subsequently or simultaneously orient to 'doing instruction'. As we could see, he regularly aligned and affiliated with the learners' personally relevant topic initiations and tellings, asking clarifying and follow-up questions, providing acknowledgements and assessments and showing interest in and appreciation of their contributions, before or while orienting to instructional tasks as well. When simultaneously orientating to conversation and instruction, the teacher tended to treat the institutional frame as subordinate to the conversational, participating in the latter verbally and in the former mostly nonverbally. This suggests that a 'division of labor' (Kääntä, 2012: 181) can be employed not only within frames (e.g. when verbally responding to one student and nonverbally allocating a turn to another student), but also across frames (when verbally responding to one student's personal story and nonverbally disciplining another student's actions). In the case of sequential orientation to conversation and instruction, it was only after showing heightened involvement with the learners' conversational contributions (through appreciation, positive assessment and laughter) that the teacher would cue a transition to instruction with an increase in volume, shift in gaze and/or manipulation of instructional materials.

The teacher's multilayered orientations to both the institutional and conversational frames underscore the complex nature of instruction, in which the interpersonal and institutional are finely intertwined (Kramsch, 1985). By drawing on an array of verbal and embodied resources to attend to the two frames, the teacher in our data managed to strike a balance between 'control and connection' (Waring, 2014: 52), completing instructional tasks while promoting and validating his students' personally relevant stories and experiences. And even though he did not appear to orient to conversational talk as occasioning 'teachable moments' (cf. Waring, 2014), by aligning with the students' personal tellings and by prioritizing the conversational over the institutional frame, even briefly, the teacher allowed the students to employ (and potentially develop) interactional practices that are not as readily available to them in more traditional structures of classroom talk – practices such as self-selection, topic initiation and pursuit, and storytelling.

It should also be noted that the students in our study seemed to pursue conversational talk only at moments recognizable as transitions between class activities (Dorr-Bremme, 1990; Markee, 2005). It might be the case that the learners engaged in conversational talk at these moments precisely because they oriented to them as, in fact, breaks in the ongoing instructional activity – spaces where other, loosely related topics and actions could be pursued. Overall, the students oriented to and aligned with the teacher's verbal and embodied shifts to the institutional frame, even when these shifts were more implicit. And when they were not immediately oriented to by the learners, the teacher's cues were disregarded only at transition relevance places (when the floor was up for the taking) and in instances of overlap. Therefore, the students' orientation to frame shifts and their pursuit of conversational talk in indeterminate spaces and at transition relevance places could in fact indicate these learners' interactional competence – their ability to engage in interpersonal conversations and express their personal concerns and experiences at, what they came to recognize as, appropriate moments during a lesson.

The findings of this study contribute to the growing body of research on simultaneously managing and promoting learner participation in the language classroom. As our analysis has shown, while conversational talk might appear to be a departure from official class business, when encouraged and managed skillfully by the teacher, these breaks in the institutional frame can promote learners' use of a variety of interactional practices, allow them to express their identities and even help them build relationships with their teacher, which could in turn help motivate their engagement in class tasks (Lee *et al.*, 2009). Moreover, given the need for teachers to appropriate their students' personal interests, experiences and funds of knowledge into the classroom for the purpose of making formal education more relevant and effective (e.g. Barton & Tan, 2009; Canagarajah, 1997; Heath, 1983; Moll *et al.*, 1992), conversational frames, where learners freely bring up their interests and experiences, could be a rich source for teachers to draw on in determining which topics students are concerned with or which funds of knowledge they possess. The role of conversational talk in the classroom also complicates the notion of what constitutes *teaching*. Although public school teachers often must adhere to predetermined objectives and rigid standards, the work that ostensibly occurs outside of the pedagogical agenda may, in fact, co-exist with it and carry learning opportunities of equal importance to the sanctioned ones. Preparing ESL teachers to maximize these opportunities by deploying multimodal resources may prove particularly fruitful.

Finally, it should be noted that this study did not attend to participants who were less verbally active or who remained quiet throughout the focal segments. Future research would need to take into account students' lack of verbal contributions in conversational frames as well, exploring precisely when and how these seeming absences of participation are enacted. A detailed examination of both more and less active participants' conduct could help uncover the potential interactional and social factors that might shape learners' participation (or lack thereof) in the conversational frame and even suggest some pedagogical practices for eliciting contributions from various students. Research exploring ways of appropriating conversational talk for instructional purposes could help educators and curriculum developers better gauge and draw on their learners' interests, experiences and funds of knowledge.

References

Ädel, A. (2011) Rapport building in student group work. *Journal of Pragmatics* 43 (12), 2932–2947.

Bannink, A. (2002) Negotiating the paradoxes of spontaneous talk in advanced L2 classes. In C.J. Kramsch (ed.) *Language Acquisition and Language Socialization: Ecological Perspectives* (pp. 266–289). New York: Continuum.

Barton, A.C. and Tan, E. (2009) Funds of knowledge and discourses and hybrid space. *Journal of Research in Science Teaching* 46 (1), 50–73.

Bateson, G. (1972) *Steps to an Ecology of Mind*. New York: Ballantine Books.

Canagarajah, A.S. (1997) Safe houses in the contact zone: Coping strategies of African-American students in the academy. *College Composition and Communication* 48 (2), 173–196.

Cazden, C.B. (1988) *Classroom Discourse: The Language of Teaching and Learning*. Portsmouth, NH: Heinemann.

Coupland, J. (2000) *Small Talk*. Harlow: Longman.

Coupland, J. (2003) Small talk: Social functions. *Research on Language and Social Interaction* 36 (1), 1–6.

Dorr-Bremme, D.W. (1990) Contextualization cues in the classroom: Discourse regulation and social control functions. *Language in Society* 19 (3), 379–402.

Drew, P. and Heritage, J. (1992) Analyzing talk at work: An introduction. In P. Drew and J. Heritage (eds) *Talk at Work* (pp. 3–65). Cambridge: Cambridge University Press.

Edwards, D. and Mercer, N. (1987) *Common Knowledge: The Development of Understanding in the Classroom*. London and New York: Methuen.

Goffman, E. (1974) *Frame Analysis*. New York: Harper & Row.

Goffman, E. (1981) *Forms of Talk*. Philadelphia, PA: University of Pennsylvania Press.

Goodwin, C. and Goodwin, M.H. (1992) Assessments and the construction of context. In A. Duranti and C. Goodwin (eds) *Rethinking Context: Language as an Interactive Phenomenon* (pp. 147–190). Cambridge: Cambridge University Press.

Hall, J.K., Hellermann, J. and Pekarek Doehler, S. (eds) (2011) *L2 Interactional Competence and Development*. Bristol: Multilingual Matters.

Heath, S.B. (1983) *Ways with Words*. Cambridge: Cambridge University Press.

Heritage, J. (2004) Conversation analysis and institutional talk. In R. Sanders and K. Fitch (eds) *Handbook of Language and Social Interaction* (pp. 103–146). Mahwah, NJ: Lawrence Erlbaum.

Jefferson, G. (1984) Notes on some orderlinesses of overlap onset. *Discourse Analysis and Natural Rhetoric* 500, 11–38.

Jefferson, G. (2004) Glossary of transcript symbols with an introduction. In G. Lerner (ed.) *Conversation Analysis: Studies from the First Generation* (pp. 13–31). Amsterdam: John Benjamins.

Käänta, L. (2012) Teachers' embodied allocations in instructional interaction. *Classroom Discourse* 3 (2), 166–186.

Kramsch, C.J. (1985) Classroom interaction and discourse options. *Studies in Second Language Acquisition* 7 (2), 169–183.

Lee, N., Mikesell, L., Joaquin, A.D.L., Mates, A.W. and Schumann, J.H. (2009) *The Interactional Instinct: The Evolution and Acquisition of Language*. Oxford: Oxford University Press.

Lemke, J.L. (1990) *Talking Science: Language, Learning, and Values*. Norwood, NJ: Ablex.

Markee, N. (2005) The organization of off-task classroom talk in second language classrooms. In K. Richards and P. Seedhouse (eds) *Applying Conversation Analysis* (pp. 197–213). Basingstoke: Palgrave Macmillan.

McHoul, A. (1978) The organization of turns at formal talk in the classroom. *Language in Society* 7 (2), 183–213.

Mehan, H. (1979) *Learning Lessons*. Cambridge, MA: Harvard University Press.

Moll, L.C., Amanti, C., Neff, D. and González, N. (1992) Funds of knowledge for teaching: Using a qualitative approach to connect homes and classrooms. *Theory into Practice* 31 (2), 132–141.

Nguyen, H.T. (2007) Rapport building in language instruction: A microanalysis of the multiple resources in teacher talk. *Language and Education* 21 (4), 284–303.

Ohta, A.S. (2008) Laughter and second language acquisition: A study of Japanese foreign language classes. In J. Mori and A.S. Ohta (eds) *Japanese Applied Linguistics: Discourse and Social Perspectives* (pp. 213–242). New York: Continuum.

Park, M.Y. (2016) Integrating rapport-building into language instruction: A study of Korean foreign language classes. *Classroom Discourse* 7 (2), 109–130.

Pomerantz, A. (1980) Telling my side: 'Limited access' as a 'fishing' device. *Sociological Inquiry* 50 (3–4), 186–198.

Richards, K. (2006) Being the teacher: Identity and classroom conversation. *Applied Linguistics* 27 (1), 51–77.

Sacks, H., Schegloff, E.A. and Jefferson, G. (1974) A simplest systematics for the organization of turn-taking for conversation. *Language* 50 (4), 696–735.

Seedhouse, P. (1996) Classroom interaction: Possibilities and impossibilities. *ELT Journal* 50 (1), 16–24.

Sinclair, J.M. and Coulthard, M. (1975) *Towards an Analysis of Discourse: The English Used by Teachers and Pupils*. London: Oxford University Press.

Tannen, D. (ed.) (1993) *Framing in Discourse*. New York: Oxford University Press.

Tsui, A. (1996) Reticence and anxiety in second language learning. In D. Bailey and M. Swan (eds) *Voices from the Language Classroom: Qualitative Research in Second Language Education* (pp. 145–167). Cambridge: Cambridge University Press.

van Lier, L. (1996) *Interaction in the Language Curriculum: Awareness, Autonomy and Authenticity*. New York: Longman.

Walsh, S. (2006) *Investigating Classroom Discourse*. New York: Routledge.

Waring, H.Z. (2012) Doing being playful in the second language classroom. *Applied Linguistics* 34 (2), 191–210.

Waring, H.Z. (2014) Managing control and connection in an adult ESL classroom. *Research in the Teaching of English* 49 (1), 52.

3 What's Symmetrical? A Teacher's Cooperative Management of Learner Turns in a Read-aloud Activity

Joan Kelly Hall, Taiane Malabarba and Daisuke Kimura

This chapter investigates teacher management of learner turns in an American second-grade classroom during a read-aloud activity. A read-aloud is a whole-group instructional activity which involves a teacher reading aloud a book to a cohort of students as they listen (Tainio & Slotte, 2017). Using ethnomethodological conversation analysis (EMCA) and drawing on the concepts of alignment and affiliation (Steensig, 2012; Stivers, 2008; Stivers *et al.*, 2011), we investigate how embodied practices such as gaze, facial expressions, body positioning and gestures in addition to verbal practices are used by the teacher separately and together to respond to learner turns in ways that keep the learners affectively engaged and, at the same time, ensure the orderly progression of the lesson. Our analysis shows that teacher cooperative management of learners' turns involves: (1) orienting to them as affiliative tokens in order to neutralize their disaligning force while still treating learners as cooperative participants in the activity; and (2) managing turns not only according to their sequential positions and the actions they project but, just as importantly, to the larger instructional project being accomplished. The study contributes to the re-specification of the everyday grounds of teaching in order to broaden understandings of the specialized nature of such work (Macbeth, 2014).

Introduction

Teaching is deliberate and sophisticated professional work (Ball & Forzani, 2007, 2009, 2011; Cohen, 2011; Macbeth, 2011; Waring, 2016).

In addition to instructing or directing others, teaching involves maintaining the attention of a cohort of students as lessons unfold while, at the same time, attending to and managing individual learner turns. Teacher management of learner turns in the whole-group instructional activity known as the IRF has been the subject of much EMCA research (e.g. Heap, 1992; Hellermann, 2005; Hester & Francis, 2000; Lee, 2007; Macbeth, 2000, 2011; Margutti, 2006; Mehan, 1979; Nassaji & Wells, 2000; Park, 2014; Waring, 2008). The IRF, which consists of a sequence of three actions – a teacher initiation, a student response and a teacher follow-up – is typically used to check or review learners' understandings of the material being taught.

Lee (2007) offers perhaps the most detailed examination of teacher management of learner turns in the IRF by showing the procedural particulars of a range of actions that the third turn, i.e. the follow-up, accomplishes in responding to student turns and at the same time moving the instructional project forward. Additional work has examined teachers' enactment of explicit positive assessments in the third turn to mark student responses as adequate (e.g. Waring, 2008), their management of student responses that display or claim insufficient knowledge (e.g. Sert, 2013), and the role that teacher repetitions of student responses play in managing learner turns (Park, 2014). This chapter is similarly concerned with teacher management of learner turns but in a different type of whole-group instruction: a read-aloud activity.

Read-alouds

The read-aloud is a common type of whole-group instructional activity in elementary and middle grades. It usually involves a teacher reading aloud a book to a cohort of students as they listen (Tainio & Slotte, 2017). Research on read-alouds suggests that they increase student motivation for reading, build background knowledge of a topic, improve learner listening comprehension skills, expand learner vocabulary and raise their language awareness (Albright & Ariail, 2005; Damber, 2015; Hurst & Griffity, 2015; Kraemer et al., 2012; Tainio & Slotte, 2017).

Despite their pedagogical importance, we were able to locate only two studies that have examined naturally occurring read-alouds in the classroom context from an EMCA perspective. Hester and Francis (1995) offer an ethnomethodological examination of storytelling in a primary school classroom. In their analysis, they describe how the telling of the story constitutes an interactional partnership involving both the teacher and the students. It also involves coordination of the verbal with the visual; as the story is read, the storybook pictures are displayed to the students. They conclude that, rather than being unique to the classroom they studied, both features – the collaborative storytelling and the integration of the pictures with narration – are likely routine features of literacy activities in many primary classrooms.

A more recent study is Tainio and Slotte's (2017) conversation analytic examination of read-aloud activities found in the sixth grade of Finnish comprehensive schools.[1] It differs from Hester and Francis (1995) in that, rather than describing a single occasion, it describes commonalities in actions and action sequences across different types of read-aloud events. A key finding is the highly influential role that embodied resources such as gaze, gestures and facial expressions play in the organization of the events. They observed, for instance, that when learners have visual access to what is being read by the teacher or a peer, they typically follow the reading from the text available to them as it is being read aloud. Learners who are gazing elsewhere during the read-aloud are commonly instructed to redirect their gaze to the text being read.

Our study of a read-aloud in a second-grade classroom adds to this small body of research in the following ways. First, like Hester and Francis (1995), our focus is on the details of actions comprising one activity rather than on commonalities found across activities, as reported in Tainio and Slotte (2017). Like Tainio and Slotte, and unlike Hester and Francis who account only for verbal practices, we consider embodied practices such as gaze, facial expressions, body positioning and gestures in addition to the verbal practices used by the teacher. Unique to this study is the focus on the varied ways in which the teacher uses multiple embodied and verbal practices, separately and together, to respond cooperatively to learner turns such that the learners continue to be affectively engaged and, at the same time, the orderly progression of the lesson is ensured. To show the varied details of teacher management of learner turns, we draw on the concepts of alignment and affiliation.

Alignment and Affiliation

Basic to EMCA is the premise that interaction is fundamentally cooperative (Levinson, 2006). Alignment and affiliation are two dimensions of interactional cooperation (Lindström & Sorjonen, 2012; Steensig, 2012; Stivers, 2008; Stivers et al., 2011). Alignment involves the structural level of cooperation. Aligning actions match the formal design preference of the preceding turn and thereby facilitate the progression of the sequence or activity. For example, storytelling involves several consecutive turns by the teller of the story. The use of mid-telling vocal continuers such as *mm* and *uh huh* by the recipient at transition relevance places (TRPs) treats the storytelling activity as still in progress and thereby aligns with or supports the structural preference of the activity, i.e. that the teller has the floor until the completion of the story (Stivers, 2008). A participant's contribution during storytelling that offers a mid-telling response that impedes progress of the activity is a dispreferred turn and thus is considered to disalign with the activity.

Affiliation has to do with cooperation at the level of action and affective stance (Stivers *et al.*, 2011). Affiliative responses are 'maximally prosocial' (Stivers *et al.*, 2011: 21), matching the action preference of the prior turn, regardless of the format. Likewise, responses that endorse or match the speaker's conveyed evaluative stance toward some action or occasion display affiliation. Whereas alignment is relevant at every turn at talk, affiliative actions are not always relevant.

As noted by Stivers and colleagues (Steensig, 2012; Stivers, 2008; Stivers *et al.*, 2011), alignment and affiliation are not categorical. Rather, the degrees of cooperation displayed in actions fall along two continua: they can be more or less aligning to non-aligning and more or less affiliative to non-affiliative (Steensig, 2012; Stivers, 2008; Stivers *et al.*, 2011). Moreover, utterances that align with prior turns may or may not affiliate with the speaker, and vice versa. In the case of storytelling, for example, in contrast to a minimal vocal continuer such as *mmhm* uttered by a recipient in a mid-telling position, which aligns with the storytelling but does not affiliate with the speaker, an extended comment, such as *Oh my goodness, I can't believe that happened, how could he do such a thing*, affiliates with the speaker's evaluative stance toward the events being narrated. However, at the same time, it disaligns with the ongoing activity by projecting a reply by the teller that has the potential to undermine the continuation of the storytelling.

The few studies concerned with affiliative actions in classroom interactions have examined the ways in which students display affiliation to teachers and to each other (Jacknick, 2013; Petitjean & González-Martínez, 2015; Sert & Jacknick, 2015). Their findings show how students' use of laughter and smiles facilitate the pursuit of affiliation in moments of interactional difficulties. Our study contributes to this research by focusing on how both alignment and affiliation figure into a teacher's management of learner turns in a read-aloud activity.

The Study: Data and Methods

The context of this study is a second-grade classroom[2] in a public school[3] located in the United States. The class was participating in a two-week unit on geometry in design (Lehrer & Curtis, 2000). The data comprise a 12-minute video-recording of a read-aloud activity involving the teacher and a cohort of students that occurred during the two-week period. In our analysis, we draw on the theoretical framework and methodological tools of EMCA. EMCA considers the nature and source of human sociality to be fundamentally cooperative, locally accomplished and grounded in real-world activity (Schegloff, 2006, 2007). Its central concern is with uncovering the practical reasoning and meaning-making methods used by individuals to achieve social order in their local contexts. Their methods are exhibits of social order, and thus 'constitutive of their own reality' (Garfinkel, 2002: 97). Its theoretical strength lies in its grounding of mutual understanding in the sequential organization of interaction. Its methodological strengths are that it is data driven and analytically inductive, substantiating claims about 'just how' (Garfinkel, 2002: 106) actions are built and interpreted in public observables.

After viewing the video several times, we completed a basic transcription of the entire activity and from the transcript identified a total of six episodes in which learners do more than display their embodied alignment with the activity by, for example, maintaining their gaze toward the teacher and the book as the story is being read. We further transcribed these episodes using CA conventions with modifications to capture eye gaze, facial expressions, gestures and other modes of action in addition to the verbal. In the process of transcribing, we relied on the visible orientation of the participants' bodies and actions to specific features of the context as the lesson unfolded as a guide for determining what to include (Goodwin, 2000).

Findings

Before the activity begins, the teacher sits on a chair and the students sit on the floor in a semicircle around the chair, facing the teacher. We can see this configuration in Figure 3.1. The goal of the activity is to introduce the students to the concept of symmetry. The title of the book being read to the students is *The Bedspread* by Sylvia Fair. The story is about two old sisters who each live at the end of a long bed and who decide to embroider the ends of their bedspread with their recollections of the house they grew up in. The designs should be symmetrical, but they end up very differently because the women remember different things about their house.

Figure 3.1 The read-aloud activity

Once she begins to read, the teacher holds the book in her hands and moves her gaze back and forth between the page she is reading and the students, simultaneously monitoring the students' engagement as she advances the story. The book is held in such a way that the depictions on the pages are visible to the students as the teacher reads. In its seating arrangement, and the mutually visual accessibility to a common object, i.e. the book being read, the contextual configuration of the activity creates what Goffman (1963: 95) refers to as an 'ecological huddle', that is, a publicly shared organization of visual and cognitive attention to multiple fields simultaneously.

Unlike the IRF, in which turns alternate between the teacher and students, in the read-aloud the teacher and the learners work together to allow for the teacher's production of extended turns at talk. In this way, it is more similar to the activity of storytelling, which entails the production of multiple turn constructional units by the teller in the recounting of events (Jefferson, 1972; Mandelbaum, 2012; Sacks, 1974; Stivers, 2008). This distinctive feature of turn taking is identifiable by the contextual configuration of the activity; its specialized configuration also works to secure learners' alignment to the reading of the story. The teacher also displays to the learners her 'affective treatment of the events' (Stivers, 2008: 27), i.e. her affiliative stance toward the events being recounted. This is done through her use of prosodic cues such as varied intonation, stress and vowel elongation as she reads (Ochs, 1996).

The learners are active recipients of the teacher's actions. As they listen to the story, they lean forward, orienting their bodies toward the teacher, and alternate the direction of their eye gazes between the teacher and the pages of the book being read, and in so doing display their alignment to the unfolding activity. On five occasions, the learners do more than display their embodied alignment as the activity unfolds. They also initiate vocal turns, which display varying degrees of alignment to the activity and affiliation with the teacher. Our analysis reveals that the teacher's cooperative management of these learner turns involves a range of multimodal actions. Furthermore, our analysis reveals that the variation in teacher management is linked to the interactional work being accomplished by the learner turn, its sequential placement and its relationship to the larger instructional project. In the following five excerpts we show how the specifics of teacher responsiveness are linked to the details of learner initiations.

The cooperative management of minimal vocal continuers

Excerpt 1 illustrates how the teacher cooperatively manages a minimal vocal turn by one of the learners. The excerpt begins with the teacher reading from the book and reaching a point in the story where the illustrations on the page become relevant to the unfolding plot (Lines 1–6). Upon finishing the end of the sentence she is reading, she looks at the students and projects the book forward, moving it slowly to the right (Lines 7–8). Immediately after this, one student produces a vocal assessment, a declarative statement *w-oh*, uttered with falling intonation (Line 9). In its design and placement, the assessment indicates that the learner is attending to and aligning with the story. At the same time, it displays affiliation with the stance conveyed by the teacher in her varied use of stress and elongation in the reading of the story. The teacher responds to the learner's affiliative assessment with a reciprocal, embodied token of affiliation, a smile (Line 10), and resumes the reading.

***Excerpt 1:** w-oh⁴*

```
1      TEA:   amelia's windows were crooked. a:nd frayed.
2             and they were framed in string that wouldn't
3             lie flat. but flowers bloo:med in window boxes
4             on every floor and on the balcony she stitched
5             herself, with maud, and their father and mother
6             and a::ll their brothers and sisters.
7             ((looks at students, projects the book forward,
8             moves the book slowly to the right))
9      STU:   w-oh.
10     TEA:   ((smiles))
11             on wednesday maud said ↑today we shall make the walls
12             ((continues reading))
```

On four occasions, the learners do more than offer affiliative continuers as the activity unfolds. They offer mid-telling comments which have the potential to stall the progression of the story. In two cases the comments are upshot formulations (Heritage & Watson, 1979), i.e. inferences based on the previously recounted events of the story, and in two cases the comments display unexpected or troubled understandings. Teacher management of these turns is complicated work involving simultaneously and sequentially enacted actions that exhibit varying degrees of cooperation. In the next section we show how these learner turns are managed by the teacher.

The cooperative management of mid-telling formulations

Excerpts 2 and 3 illustrate how the teacher manages two potentially disaligning learner turns. In Excerpt 2 the teacher is reading from the book, and as she reads, her body is oriented toward the group while her head is turned toward the book she is holding in her hand. The stress and pitch variations in her utterances as she reads (Lines 1, 3, 5, 8) display heightened affect toward the events she is recounting. As she approaches the end of the sentence, the teacher turns her gaze to the class (Line 10) and then completes the sentence (Line 11).

Excerpt 2: *i think i know what they*

```
1       TEA:   {↑LOOK exclaimed maud ↑my ↑thimble still fits.
2              {((looking at book))
3       TEA:   {and so do my ↑scissors ↓said amelia
4              {((looking at book))
5              {snipping excitedly at the air,
6              {((looking at book; raises her LA/LH and gestures))
7              ((rests her LA/LH on her lap))
8       TEA:   {eagerly they threaded their needles,
9              {((looking at book))
10             ((turns face to left side of classroom))
11             {and then stopped.=
12      SAM:   {((leans forward))
13 ──►         =>i think i know what they {°(    )°<
14 ──► TEA:                                {((turns face to book))
15             they didn't know what to ↑sew.
16             (1.0)
17             they stared <↑empty faced> at one another.
18             (0.6)
19             until {amelia (.)
20                   {((looks at class))
21             had {an idea.
22                 {((looks at book))
```

At this TRP, one of the students, Sam, leans forward, latches onto the teacher's turn, and offers an upshot formulation, anticipating the next actions of the story, stating, *i think i know what they* (Line 13). His self-selected turn is delivered quickly and includes the clauses 'i think' and 'i know', which claim a degree of epistemic primacy (Stivers *et al.*, 2011) toward the unfolding event and suggest that he has more to say. His displayed excitement is affiliative but its position as a mid-telling comment makes it a disaligning action. If taken up by the teacher, Sam's action has the potential to interrupt the progression of the story.

As we see, rather than responding to Sam's comment, which would serve to disalign with the ongoing activity, the teacher treats it as an aligning move. As Sam finishes speaking, the teacher turns her gaze back to the book (Line 14) and resumes reading (Lines 15–22). In orienting to Sam's turn as a cooperative rather than a disaligning action, the teacher's actions both neutralize the potential of Sam's comment to interrupt the continuation of the story and forward the progression of the activity. At the same time, they convey to Sam and the other learners what the teacher considers to be appropriate displays of their roles as recipients of the story being read to them.

Excerpt 3 shows a similar sequence. It begins as the teacher finishes reading from a page in the book (Lines 1–3) and points to a picture of a portion of the quilt being made that she had just described (Lines 4–5). In Line 7, in overlap with the teacher's in-breath as she restarts the reading of the book, a student offers a mid-telling formulation of what she anticipates the next actions of the story will be, stating *i bet hers is gonna be.* Similar to the previous excerpt, if taken up by the teacher the action has the potential to at least stall the progression of the reading activity. However, here again, the teacher orients to it as an aligning move rather than as a potentially disaligning comment, by latching onto the student's turn and continuing to read. She does not ignore the comment, however. As she begins to read again (Line 8), she displays affiliation to the comment with a nod of her head (Line 9).

Excerpt 3: *i bet hers is gonna be*

```
1       TEA:   she chose pearl thread for the balcony and
2              wove it into lozenges of knots(.)with intercrossed
3              ba::rs.
4              {°°xxx here°°
5              {((looks and points at book.
6       TEA:   [.h
7 ──▶   ALI:   [i bet hers is gonna be=
8       TEA:   ={amelia's windows were crooked. a:nd frayed.
9                {((nods))
10             and they were framed in string that wouldn't
11             lie flat.
```

To recap, in these two excerpts we observed two upshot formulations of the unfolding plot offered by learners at mid-telling positions. Both turns exhibit affiliation with the teacher's reading of the story, but at the same time they disalign with the activity by making relevant a response from the teacher which, howsoever temporarily, would stall the ongoing activity. In both cases, the teacher does not provide verbal uptake and instead continues with the read-aloud. In so doing, she neutralizes their disaligning force by treating the learner comments as cooperative affiliative tokens and, by extension, the learners as cooperative participants in the activity.

The cooperative management of unexpected or troubled understandings

The next two excerpts illustrate the teacher's cooperative management of a different type of learner action. Unlike the turns in Excerpts 2 and 3, here the learner comments reveal potential confusion about a particular occurrence in the story. As we show, teacher management of these turns involves more interactional work.

Excerpt 4: *one is upside down*

```
1       TEA:   and then when they were about
2              a ↑hundred and three years old, (0.4)
3              the sisters died,
4              and their bedspread
5              was put in a museum, (.) for a:ll to see.
6              (0.7)
```

```
7     ST1:   uh well
8            (1.9)
9     ST2:   ↑one's upside do:wn.
10    ST3:   (          ).=
11    TEA:   =↑mmhm and that was the problem.=
12           ={listen what they did (.) about that problem.
13            {((turns page))
14           (0.4)
15    TEA:   [ON MONdays, wednesdays, and fridays,
16           it hangs so that maud's house is right side up.
17           (0.5)
```

Excerpt 4 begins as the teacher finishes reading the last sentence of the page (Lines 1–5). She marks the final information item as notable through the use of a brief pause, elongation and falling intonation *(.) for a:ll to see.* (Line 5). After a gap, Sam self-selects and offers a noticing *one's upside do:wn* (Line 9), which shows his orientation to the picture of the bedspread displayed on the page that the teacher has just finished reading. The prosodic cues of high pitch and vowel elongation used in its delivery mark the information that is displayed in the illustration as unexpected by the learner. Unlike the mid-telling formulations, and perhaps because it displays some apparent confusion about a key component of a particular moment in the story, this contribution receives a more elaborate response from the teacher. After a high-pitched acknowledgement token ↑*mmhm*, which affiliates with the learner's turn, the teacher aligns with it by endorsing the noticing as a relevant concern, with the comment *and that was the problem* (Line 11). However, the teacher does not directly take up the problem raised by the student's comment. Instead, she issues an invitation to the class to *listen what they did about the problem* (Line 12), and resumes reading the story (Lines 15–16). This action serves to keep the instructional project moving forward.

Toward the end of the instructional activity, a similar type of learner turn is offered. This is illustrated in Excerpt 5. Before she completes the reading of the story, the teacher directs a question to the students about the illustration of the bedspread depicted on the last page of the book (Line 1). This question reconfigures the pedagogical interaction to an IRF sequence of action, making it relevant for the students to respond to the teacher's initiation, which several do (Line 2). At this point, the teacher turns the book upside down (Line 4). As noted earlier, each sister embroiders her end of the bedspread with her recollections of the house in which they grew up. Their different memories result in different depictions. Turning the book upside down is an apparent attempt to draw the students' attention to a key component of the story, i.e. that the museum displaying the bedspread rotates it on a regular basis so that each end can be in full view.

Excerpt 5: *now those people are upside down*

```
1     TEA:   whose house is right side up now?
2     STS:   amelia's.
3     TEA:   amelia's.but then {on the other days of the week
4                             {((turns book upside down))
5            they turn it around,
6            [the people-
7     SAM:   [$but now {those people are upside down.$
8     TEA:            {((turns to SAM, holds book forward))(see Fig.3.2)
9            {yeah. well, they wouldn't turn the people.
10           {((tilts head to the left)) (see Fig.3.3)
11           >they'd just turn the bedspread.<
12           >>and i can do that by turning the book.<<
13           and then maud's house would be right [side up.
14    SAM:                                        [°you can't
15           quite- you can't turn [the people°
16    TEA:                         [{°°(okay)°°
17                                 {((closes the book))
```

Figure 3.2 Excerpt 5, Line 8

Figure 3.3 Excerpt 5, Line 10

This turn is cut off by Sam, who delivers a noticing *but now those people are upside down*. (Line 7). Although it is delivered with declarative syntax, it comes out of turn and is uttered with a smiley voice, which displays the learner's affiliation toward the event depicted in the illustration and at the same time indicates an uncertain or unexpected understanding of it.

Similar to the turn in Excerpt 4, Sam's turn engenders actions from the teacher that both align and affiliate with it. She first turns to Sam (Figure 3.2), holds the book forward and then acknowledges his comment with two simultaneously enacted actions – a verbal *yeah*, and an embodied head tilt (Lines 9–10, Figure 3.3). She then produces an explanation that serves to clarify the student's apparent confusion but does not project further learner participation (Lines 11–13). In taking up the learner turn and in its manner of delivery, i.e. its change in tempo, the teacher's response in Lines 8–13 treats the learner comment as 'in some sense relevant' (Jefferson, 1972: 294) to the ongoing activity. The teacher then moves to return to the instructional project to complete the reading of the book, which is marked by a shift to her story voice, uttered with slower tempo (Line 13). Sam formulates another statement that displays his clarified understanding of the depiction, thus aligning with the teacher's explanation. In overlap with the end of Sam's turn, the teacher utters a sequence-closing 'okay' and closes the book, signaling an end to the read-aloud activity (Line 16).

Delaying alignment with a disaligning learner initiation

Not every learner turn that disaligns with the ongoing activity is so easily dealt with. In the next excerpt we examine a learner initiation that resembles the one examined in the two previous excerpts in that it also displays a student's troubled understanding of a component of the unfolding story. At the time it is offered, it appears to disalign with the unfolding instructional moment by making relevant a side sequence. However, as we will show, the teacher responds to it differently from how she deals with the other disaligning turns.

Excerpt 6: *What's symmetrical?*

```
1    TEA:   today, (.) we will <turn> the bedspread around,
2           >so that< i can see your house, and you can see mine.
3           {(0.6)
4           {((looking at book))
5    TEA:   so they <turned> the bedspread carefully around, and saw
6           at once {(.) that it was not symmetrical at <a:ll.>
7                   {((turns face to class))
8           {((turns face to book))
9           {(0.7)
10   ALI:   {what's symmetrical=
11          {((leans backward))
12   TEA:   =$i↑:::{m$ afraid my stitching isn't quite as tidy as yours
13                 {((raises LH index finger to belly, looks at ALI, nods
14                    twice)) (see Fig. 3.4)
15          {↓stammered amelia
16   ALI:   {((smiles)) (see Fig. 3.5)
```

Figure 3.4 Excerpt 6, Line 14

Figure 3.5 Excerpt 6, Line 16

The teacher is continuing to read the story to the students as Excerpt 6 begins. She indicates that she has reached the end of the sentence by her use of slowed speech and falling intonation and a reorientation of her gaze and head position from the book to the class (Lines 5–7). Together, the prosodic cues and embodied actions mark a TRP. After a short gap during which the teacher looks back to the page she is reading (Lines 8–9), Alicia self-selects and asks *what's symmetrical* (Line 10), referring to a lexical item used in the teacher's previous utterance (Line 6).

This learner turn constitutes an initiation of repair (Schegloff *et al.*, 1977) since it concerns Alicia's understanding of the concept of symmetry, apparently unknown to her (and perhaps to the whole class) at this point. The repair is other-initiated (OIR), which typically comprises 'a short sequence – ostensibly devoted to sorting out a trouble in speaking, hearing or understanding – which suspends the otherwise ongoing action in which the participants are engaged' (Kitzinger, 2012: 249).

The expectation is that the teacher will align with the OIR and respond to the question to sort out the apparent trouble in understanding, as she did in Excerpt 5. Instead, she continues to read the story (Line 12). She does not, however, ignore the question. We see that as she resumes reading, she uses multiple means to display heightened affiliation to Alicia. As she continues reading, she produces an elongated, high-pitched *i::* in a smiley voice at the same time as she raises her left index finger and moves it toward Alicia while nodding (Lines 13, 14, Figure 3.4). The simultaneous use of a smiley voice and a gesture oriented to Alicia allows the teacher to both acknowledge the question and display affiliation to Alicia and, at the same time, to stay on task (Lavin & Maynard, 2001). Alicia reciprocates the affiliative display by smiling (Line 16, Figure 3.5).

While the teacher immediately displays affiliation, her lack of response to Alicia's question displays disalignment with it. It is only by looking ahead, when the teacher is finished reading the story, that it becomes apparent that the teacher's response is not missing, but rather delayed. As we show in Excerpt 7, the lack of immediate alignment is directly connected to the subsequent components of the lesson and is explained by the outcomes that are being pursued by the teacher. Excerpt 7 is comprised of two parts. In Excerpt 7.1 the teacher brings up the question posed by Alicia earlier to which she had not responded. The second part reveals the reason for the delay.

Excerpt 7.1: *Excellent question*

```
1       TEA:    alicia asked an excellent question
2               ↓while i was reading the book.
3               (0.2)
```

```
4      TEA:   and i didn't ignore her question, (.hhh) u:m (0.8)
5             i've been ↑thinking about it,
6             >and now i'm gonna ask< you to think about it.
7             u:m there's >two places in the book< that
8             {i want to reread to you quickly
9             {((browses through the pages))
10            (.) and the:n, (1.0)
11            {uh (.) then i want us to talk
12            {((turns face to class, leans slightly forward))
13     TEA:   about the {question alicia asked during the story.=
14                      {((points at ALI with L index finger))
15            =y- probably didn't hear her
16            >if you were sitting in the back<
17            >because she said it< pretty quietly
18            (.)
19     TEA:   but it was a good question.=
20            =and you might have been thinking this question
21            while i was reading too.
22            ((TEA rereads the part of the story where Alicia asked her
              question))
```

Upon completing the reading of the story, the teacher revisits the previously held-off question, stating *alicia asked an excellent question* (Line 1). Her positive assessment of the question shows continued affiliation and, in taking up the question now, the teacher aligns with Alicia's earlier turn. As a further display of affiliation, she offers an account for not addressing the question when Alicia first asked it (Lines 4–5). However, rather than answering the question at this moment, she brings the question to the attention of the group, asking them to think about it as she rereads two sections of the story that are apparently relevant to the question (Lines 6–8). Her use of the inclusive pronoun *us* and her changed body positioning and eye gaze direction (Lines 11–12) make clear that the question is meant to be of relevance to everyone in the class, and not just to Alicia, who initiated the repair. Why the teacher continues to hold off answering Alicia's question can only be answered by looking at what happens next.

Excerpt 7.2: Don't say anything yet though

```
23     TEA:   alicia >while she was listening to the story said<
24            {<what's symmetrical.>
25            {((leans forward)) (see Fig. 3.6)
26     SEV:   ((raise hands))
27     TEA:   w- don't {say anything yet ↓though.
28                     {((covers mouth with RH)) (see Fig. 3.7)
29            (0.3)
30     TEA:   what we're gonna to do::, (0.5)
31            >is we're gonna go back,<=
32            =be↑fore we talk about that word, (0.5)
33            >we're gonna put our<
34            beginning ideas >on what we think<
35            it ↑might mean or have to do with, (0.2)
36            in our <quilting journal.>
37            (0.3)
38     TEA:   >then we're gonna< come back together
39            and talk about that ↓word,
40            a::nd uh: (1.1)
41            and f- learn >more and more<
42            ↑about that word.
```

Figure 3.6 Excerpt 7.1, Line 25   **Figure 3.7** Excerpt 7.2, Line 28

Excerpt 7.2 begins with the teacher reanimating Alicia's question after having reread the relevant parts of the story. The teacher restates the question slowly (Lines 23–25) and as she does, she leans forward, toward the cohort (Figure 3.6). These simultaneously enacted verbal and embodied actions display the teacher's heightened affective stance toward the question. Now that the reading activity appears to be coming to a close, the learners display an orientation to the restatement of the question as a reconfiguring of the instructional project to an IRF and to the question as the first action of the sequence by raising their hands to bid for the opportunity to respond (Line 26, Figure 3.7).

However, the teacher rejects the students' projected contributions with two simultaneously enacted actions. She states, *don't say anything yet though* as she covers her mouth (Lines 27, 28, Figure 3.7). She then uses the question as a transition to the next activity by explaining what is going to happen next, i.e. an exploration of the concept of symmetry (Lines 30–42). In her reframing of the question and redirection of the students' attention, the teacher's instructional goal for the read-aloud activity becomes fully observable, and the goal of the activity – to introduce the concept of symmetry to the learners – and the reason for the teacher's delayed alignment to Alicia's question are now made clear. That the teacher's displays of affiliation were heightened at the same time as she delayed alignment demonstrates in real time the multimodal complexity involved in attending to and affiliating with an individual student's action while keeping the cohort of learners focused on the ongoing instructional project.

Summary and Implications

As our findings have shown, the cooperative management of learner turns in a read-aloud activity is multifaceted, complex work requiring a 'fine sensitivity' to the 'rich nuances' (Waring, 2016: 141) of learner turns. Drawing on the notions of alignment and affiliation to capture the empirical details of such sensitivity, we have shown the varied vocal and embodied ways in which the teacher manages learner turns in ways that keep students affectively engaged, while at the same time ensuring the orderly progression of the lesson. We showed that even a mid-telling minimal continuer offered by a learner is responded to in ways that both acknowledge and affiliate with it and at the same time advance the instructional activity. We also showed the multifaceted, embodied, affiliative work the teacher undertakes to respond to disaligning learner turns while maintaining the progression of the lesson. Finally, we have provided evidence of how the management of learner turns is linked not only to the sequential position of the turn and the action it projects but, just as importantly, to the larger instructional project being accomplished. We saw this most clearly in the teacher's different responses to similar types of learner turns in Excerpts 5 and 6. Recall, learner turns in both excerpts concerned a troubled understanding of a moment in the story being recounted by the teacher. In Excerpt 5 the teacher explicitly addressed the misunderstanding in the next turn, both affiliating and aligning with it, to quickly resolve the trouble. However, in Excerpt 6, while she displayed heightened affiliation through prosodic and embodied cues to the learner question, she delayed alignment to it until after she had completed reading the story.

Given that the learner turns in Excerpts 5 and 6 are largely comparable in their sequential position and content, to uncover the reason for the variation cannot be fully understood by looking only at the immediate sequential context. As shown in Excerpt 7, to understand fully the work the teacher undertakes to manage learner turns we needed to look across moments, over the larger instructional project being accomplished. In this case, the learner question about the term 'symmetry' was apparently the instructional goal of the read-aloud activity, i.e. to bring learners' awareness to the term for use in subsequent exploratory activities. Responding to the turn when it was first posed by the learner would have treated it as an individual concern; by delaying alignment to the question and through use of varied embodied behaviors, the teacher made it relevant to the entire cohort.

In sum, these findings contribute to understandings of the verbal and embodied achievement of teaching as it is accomplished in one type of instructional project, the read-aloud, by showing the varied means by which a teacher attends to individual learner turns in ways that align with the unfolding lesson and at the same time support, i.e. affiliate, with learners' contributions. Our intent behind unpacking the details of teacher management of learner turns in a read-aloud activity is not to impose a view of how management of learner turns in such activities *should* be done. Rather, it is to illuminate the taken-for-granted complexities of teaching in read-alouds and, in so doing, to reveal instructive distinctions between idealized understandings of the work of teaching and its 'interactional reality' (Freebody, 2013: 73; Macbeth, 2014). More generally, the study contributes to CA's project of re-specifying the everyday grounds of teaching by broadening understandings of the specialized nature of such work (Macbeth, 2014).

On a practical level, studies like this can be of immense benefit to teachers and teacher educators. Classroom teaching is highly demanding work. As we know, teaching practices are not improvisational or resistant to specification. Nor are they rooted in personal preferences or intuition. Rather, like medical practices, they are highly professionalized and specifiable and thus, ultimately, teachable and learnable (Ball & Forzani, 2007, 2009, 2011; Cohen, 2011). Nonetheless, the routine manner in which an experienced teacher handles and controls his/her class is likely to be such a taken-for-granted aspect that s/he cannot easily tell others how it is done (Grossman, 2011). When novice teachers are told to observe another teacher, they usually do not know what to look for or what is worth noticing. What they are to attend to often remains obscure. The empirical details provided in studies like this one can develop in students of teaching a professional vision (Goodwin, 1994), i.e. ways of seeing and understanding the specialized nature of teaching. Examining the careful ways in which the teacher redirects potentially disaligning learner turns while displaying reciprocal affiliation with the students can reveal to students of teaching the subtle yet complex actions by which teaching is accomplished. It also reveals the crucial role that embodied actions play in this work. Such enhanced understandings can ultimately inform 'prudent judgments' (Erickson, 2012: 688) and sound decision making by teachers in their own teaching contexts.

Acknowledgements

Earlier versions of this paper were presented at the 2015 AAAL and LANSI conferences. We acknowledge with gratitude the many helpful comments we received from the conference participants.

Notes

(1) Finnish comprehensive schools are nine-year compulsory schools, taking students from age seven to 16.
(2) Second grade is the second year of primary school; it corresponds to Year 3 in the UK.
(3) Public schools in the United States are funded by state and federal taxation and provided free of charge to all students who live within the geographical areas that they serve.
(4) All names are pseudonyms. Abbreviations for participants' pseudonyms are as follows:

TEA	Teacher
ALI	Alicia
SAM	Samuel
SEV	Several students

References

Albright, L. and Ariail, M. (2005) Tapping the potential of teacher read-alouds in middle schools. *Journal of Adolescent & Adult Literacy* 48 (7), 582–591.

Ball, D.L. and Forzani, F.M. (2007) What makes education research 'educational'? *Educational Researcher* 36 (9), 529–540.

Ball, D.L. and Forzani, F.M. (2009) The work of teaching and the challenge for teacher education. *Journal of Teacher Education* 60 (5), 497–511.

Ball, D.L. and Forzani, F.M. (2011) Building a common core for learning to teach. *American Educator* 35 (2), 17–21, 38–39.

Cohen, D. (2011) *Teaching and its Predicaments.* Cambridge, MA: Harvard University Press.

Damber, U. (2015) Read-alouds in pre-school – a matter of discipline? *Journal of Early Childhood Literacy* 15 (2), 256–280.

Erickson, F. (2012) Comments on causality in qualitative inquiry. *Qualitative Inquiry* 18, 686–688.

Freebody, P. (2013) School knowledge in talk and writing: Taking 'when learners know' seriously. *Linguistics and Education* 24, 64–74.

Garfinkel, H. (2002) *Ethnomethodology's Program: Working out Durkheim's Aphorism.* Lanham, MD: Rowman & Littlefield.

Goffman, E. (1963) *Behavior in Public Places.* New York: Free Press.

Goodwin, C. (1994) Professional vision. *American Anthropologist* 96 (3), 606–633.

Goodwin, C. (2000) Action and embodiment within situated human interaction. *Journal of Pragmatics* 32 (10), 1489–1522.

Grossman, P. (2011) Framework for teaching practice: A brief history of an idea. *Teachers College Record* 113 (12), 2836–2843.

Heap, J. (1992) Seeing snubs: An introduction to sequential analysis of classroom interaction. *Journal of Classroom Interaction* 27, 23–28.

Hellermann, J. (2005) Syntactic and prosodic practices for cohesion in series of three-part sequences in classroom talk. *Research on Language and Social Interaction* 38, 105–130.

Heritage, J. and Watson, R. (1979) Formulations as conversational objects. In G. Psathas (ed.) *Everyday Language: Studies in Ethnomethodology* (pp. 123–162). New York: Irvington.

Hester, S. and Francis, D. (1995) Words and pictures: Collaborative storytelling in a primary classroom. *Research in Education* 53, 65–88.

Hester, S. and Francis, D. (2000) Ethnomethodology and local educational order. In S. Hester and D. Francis (eds) *Local Educational Order: Ethnomethodological Studies of Knowledge in Action* (pp. 1–17). Amsterdam: John Benjamins.

Hurst, S. and Griffity, P. (2015) Examining the effect of teacher read-aloud on adolescent attitudes and learning. *Middle Grades Research Journal* 10 (1), 31–47.

Jacknick, C. (2013) 'Cause the textbook says ...': Laughter and student challenges in the ESL classroom. In P. Glenn and E. Holt (eds) *Studies of Laughter in Interaction* (pp. 185–200). London: Bloomsbury Academic.

Jefferson, G. (1972) Side sequences. In D.N. Sudnow (ed.) *Studies in Social Interaction* (pp. 294–333). New York: Free Press.

Kitzinger, C. (2012) Repair. In J. Sidnell and T. Stivers (eds) *The Handbook of Conversation Analysis.* New York: Wiley-Blackwell.

Kraemer, L., McCabe, P. and Sinatra, R. (2012) The effects of read-alouds of expository text on first graders' listening comprehension and book choice. *Literacy Research and Instruction* 51, 165–178.

Lavin, D. and Maynard, D.W. (2001) Standardization vs. rapport: Respondent laughter and interviewer reaction during telephone surveys. *American Sociology Review* 66 (3), 452–479.

Lee, Y.-A. (2007) Third turn position in teacher talk: Contingency and the work of teaching. *Journal of Pragmatics* 39, 1204–1230.

Lehrer, R. and Curtis, C.L. (2000) Why are some solids perfect? *Teaching Children Mathematics* 6 (5), 324.

Levinson, S. (2006) 'On the human 'interaction engine''. In N.J. Enfield and S. Levinson (eds) *Roots of Human Sociality* 3 (pp. 9–69). Oxford: Berg.

Lindström, A. and Sorjonen, M. (2012) Affiliation in conversation. In J. Sidnell and T. Stivers (eds) *The Handbook of Conversation Analysis* (pp. 350–369). New York: Wiley-Blackwell.

Macbeth, D. (2000) Classrooms as installations: Direct instruction in the early grades. In S. Hester and D. Francis (eds) *Local Education Order: Ethnomethodological Studies of Knowledge in Action* (pp. 21–72). Philadelphia, PA: John Benjamins.

Macbeth, D. (2011) Understanding understanding as in instructional matter. *Journal of Pragmatics* 43, 438–451.

Macbeth, D. (2014) Studies of work, instructed action, and the promise of granularity: A commentary. *Discourse Studies* 16 (2), 295–308.

Mandelbaum, J. (2012) Storytelling in conversation. In J. Sidnell and T. Stivers (eds) *The Handbook of Conversation Analysis* (pp. 492–508). Cambridge: Cambridge University Press.

Margutti P. (2006) 'Are you human beings?' Order and knowledge construction through questioning in primary classroom interaction. *Linguistics and Education* 17, 313–346.

Mehan, H. (1979) *Learning Lessons*. Cambridge, MA: Harvard University Press.

Nassaji, H. and Wells, G. (2000) What's the use of 'triadic dialogue'? An investigation of teacher–student interaction. *Applied Linguistics* 21, 376–406.

Ochs, E. (1996) Resources for socializing humanity. In J. Gumperz and S. Levinson (eds) *Rethinking Linguistic Relativity* (pp. 407–438). Cambridge: Cambridge University Press.

Park, Y. (2014) The roles of third-turn repeats in two L2 classroom interactional contexts. *Applied Linguistics* 35, 145–167.

Petitjean, C. and González-Martínez, E. (2015) Laughing and smiling to manage trouble in French-language classroom interaction. *Classroom Discourse* 6 (2), 89–106.

Sacks, H. (1974) An analysis of the course of a joke's telling in conversation. In R. Bauman and J.F. Sherzer (eds) *Explorations in the Ethnography of Speaking* (pp. 337–353). Cambridge: Cambridge University Press.

Schegloff, E. (2006) Interaction: The infrastructure for social institutions, the natural ecological niche for language, and the arena in which culture is enacted. In N.J. Enfield and S. Levinson (eds) *The Roots of Human Sociality: Culture, Cognition and Interaction* (pp. 70–96). London: Berg.

Schegloff, E. (2007) *Sequence Organization in Interaction*. Cambridge: Cambridge University Press.

Schegloff, E.A., Jefferson, G. and Sacks, H. (1977) The preference for self-correction in the organization of repair in conversation. *Language* 53, 361–382.

Sert, O. (2013) 'Epistemic status check' as an interactional phenomenon in instructed learning settings. *Journal of Pragmatics* 45, 13–28.

Sert, O. and Jacknick, C.M. (2015) Student smiles and the negotiation of epistemics in L2 classrooms. *Journal of Pragmatics* 77, 97–112.

Steensig, J. (2012) Conversation analysis and affiliation and alignment. In K. Mortensen and J. Wagner (eds) *The Encyclopedia of Applied Linguistics: Conversation Analysis* (pp. 944–948). Cambridge: Wiley-Blackwell.

Stivers, T. (2008) Stance, alignment, and affiliation during storytelling: When nodding is a token of affiliation. *Research on Language and Social Interaction* 41, 31–57.

Stivers, T., Mondada, L. and Steensig, J. (2011) Knowledge, morality and affiliation in social interaction. In T. Stivers, L. Mondada and J. Steensig (eds) *The Morality of Knowledge in Conversation* (pp. 3–26). Cambridge: Cambridge University Press.

Tainio, L. and Slotte, A. (2017) Interactional organization and pedagogic aims of reading aloud practices in L1 education. *Nordic Journal of Literacy Research* 3, 61–82.

Waring, H.Z. (2008) Using explicit positive assessment in the language classroom: IRF, feedback, and learning opportunities. *The Modern Language Journal* 92, 577–594.

Waring, H. (2016) *Theorizing Pedagogical Interaction: Insights from Conversation Analysis*. New York: Routledge.

4 Managing Disaligning Responses: Sequence and Embodiment in Third-turn Teases

Stephen Daniel Looney and Jamie Kim

This chapter investigates two practices that a university science lab teacher uses to tease students following disaligning response turns in initiation-response-follow-up (IRF) sequences (Mehan, 1979; Sinclair & Coulthard, 1975). The two practices for teasing are reusing student responses with transformation (Goodwin, 2013, 2018) and noting the inadequacy of response design. We investigate how a teacher draws on various embodied resources including lexis, prosody and facial expression to design teases that affiliate with humorous stances displayed by students in and around disaligning responses while also delivering negative assessment. The analysis reveals that third-turn teases are contingent embodied actions which are tightly interwoven into the instructional project of the classroom. This is made apparent in fourth turns in which either the teacher self-selects to initiate a new IRF or provide an explanation, or students self-select and provide further candidate responses. We argue that third-turn teases are dualistic actions that a teacher uses to manage disaligning turns in an affiliative manner.

Introduction

While third turns in IRF sequences (Mehan, 1979; Sinclair & Coulthard, 1975) overwhelmingly involve delivering positive assessment (Margutti & Drew, 2014; Seedhouse, 2004), teachers inevitably encounter moments when they must provide negative assessment, perhaps to turns that disalign (Stivers, 2008; Stivers *et al.*, 2011) with the action projected by the prior initiation. The interactional work teachers do in the IRF is complex and follow-up turns take various shapes and accomplish and mobilize a variety of actions (Hall, 1997; Hellermann, 2003; Lee, 2007;

Nassaji & Wells, 2000; Park, 2014; Waring, 2008, 2016). While much has been said about the impact positive evaluation has on the unfolding of classroom sequences, we know little about how teachers manage disaligning responses. In this paper, we look at how a university science teacher uses third-turn teases in IRFs to manage response turns that do not align with the projected action of the prior initiation turn (Stivers, 2008; Stivers *et al.*, 2011). We argue that teasing is an action for affiliating with humorous stances while delivering negative assessment and resetting the interaction on a serious trajectory. The analysis of teasing in IRF sequences has significant implications for classroom conversation analysis (CA) research and teacher preparation.

Managing Dispreferred and Disaligning Actions

In Asian, European and North American contexts including K-12, university, STEM and second language/foreign language (L2/FL) classrooms, extensive work has been conducted to unpack the complexity of the individual components of the IRF sequence, i.e. the I, the R and the F. Follow-ups, or third turns, have garnered the lion's share of attention and can be broadly placed in two categories: those that provide positive assessment and those that provide negative assessment (Hellermann, 2003; Margutti & Drew, 2014; Seedhouse, 2004; Waring, 2008). Positive assessment is typically delivered without hesitation in the form of a verbatim repetition with falling intonation and/or explicit positive assessment, e.g. yes or correct (Hellermann, 2003; Margutti & Drew, 2014; Waring, 2008). Follow-up turns that provide positive assessment are preferred actions (Pomerantz, 1984; Waring, 2016), are more frequent (Margutti & Drew, 2014; Seedhouse, 2004), and have been more widely discussed in the literature than those that provide negative assessment. Nonetheless, when providing negative assessment, teachers do nuanced interactional work.

Because positive assessment is preferred, it only makes sense that negative assessment is dispreferred. One indication of this dispreference is the fact that negative assessment is often in a delayed position and perhaps prefaced with the discourse marker *well* (Jucker, 1993; Macbeth, 2004). In fact, students orient to the withholding of follow-up as negative assessment. When verbally designing negative assessment, teachers may reuse lexis from responses while altering the prosodic pattern to contrast with the prior turn (Hellermann, 2003; Seedhouse, 2004). Negative assessment can also be delivered nonverbally, for instance by using gesture and gaze to mobilize further candidate responses (Waring, 2016). Seedhouse (2004) reports that in his data explicit negative assessment, e.g. no, is rare. While some have proposed that positive assessment may limit opportunities for student participation (Hall, 1997; Waring, 2008), negative assessment in follow-up has been shown to engender extended participation. Following negative feedback or the withholding of follow-up turns, students may self-select and account for the prior response or provide another candidate response (Hellermann, 2003, 2005; Margutti & Drew, 2014; Park, 2014; Zemel & Koschmann, 2011).

In short, the actions of teacher third turns in IRFs are complex. They manage epistemic positioning, interactional trajectories and affective stances. The work they do is more nuanced than just positive or negative evaluation of student turns. For example, follow-up turns might contain assessment as well as seeking clarification or justification (Nassaji & Wells, 2000; Park, 2014). Lee (2007) elegantly demonstrates that terms like follow-up, feedback and evaluation cannot precisely describe the complex interactional work of third turns and actually obfuscate and downplay the interactional complexities of teaching. A 'teacher's third turns display multiple layers of meaning making as she punctuates the discourse in this pedagogical way for both the content of the lesson [and] steering the discourse interactionally and purposefully' (Lee, 2007: 195).

In addition to assessing student responses, teachers may have to manage responses that do not align (Stivers, 2008; Stivers et al., 2011) with the projected action of the initiation turn. A handful of studies look specifically at follow-up turns in which teachers manage disaligning student turns. In disaligning second turns, students provide absurd, inappropriate or sarcastic responses (Berge, 2017; Lin, 1999; Piirainen-Marsh, 2011; Roth et al., 2011). Piirainen-Marsh (2011: 380) calls such turns '(designedly) inappropriate or cheeky answers'. During cheeky responses, students display humorous stances in part by providing responses that disalign with prior turns and alter the trajectory of interaction (Reddington & Waring, 2015). In addition to disaligning turn design, displays of humorous stances in response turns rely on a collection of embodied resources such as, but not limited to, lexis, smile, gesture and gaze.

Following cheeky responses, teachers affiliate with students' humorous stances (Hutchby, 1992: 346; Stivers, 2008), if only momentarily, before redirecting the course of action seriously. Teachers' humorous follow-up 'turns can serve as a resource for invoking the normative order of instructional talk while still addressing the playful or subversive elements of prior talk' (Piirainen-Marsh, 2011: 369). Thus, teacher humorous turns are dualistic, affiliating with humorous stances while also projecting a serious trajectory for the interaction. Piirainen-Marsh (2011: 373) notes that ironic teacher turns, the focus of her study, are rare and seem 'to be used only on occasions where the student's answer is itself hearable as ironic or displays a critical attitude'. This suggests that humor allows teachers to affiliate with students' stances while simultaneously asserting their institutional authority and realigning the interactional project of the class (Lehtimaja, 2011; Piirainen-Marsh, 2011; Roth *et al.*, 2011).

A shared history in the classroom makes recurrent sequences like the IRF opportune locations for displaying humorous stances (Poveda, 2005). Students and teachers become socialized into routines, and certain classes may establish rapport such that students and teachers playfully improvise during routine moments. Humorous turns and laughter also index some level of intimacy (Drew, 1987; Roth *et al.*, 2011; Thonus, 2008). For example, students in a seventh-grade science class playfully use the name of the teacher's husband in response turns (Roth *et al.*, 2011). While the students may not personally know the husband, knowing the husband's name indexes more than a passing familiarity with the teacher. Berge (2017) shows that humorous responses are recurrent when students are struggling with content and provide answers hesitantly. Thus, we see that in second and third turns in IRFs, students and teachers negotiate personal and institutional identities and manage epistemic positioning while doing the instructional project. While acknowledging the resistant nature of humor, our paper builds on past classroom research by showing how teasing (Drew, 1987; Glenn, 2003) is an embodied affiliative action for managing disaligning turns during a specific, recurrent and well-documented sequence of classroom interaction.

Teasing as Sequential Action

Teases are turns within definable sequences that utilize comic devices such as exaggeration, irony and mockery to deliver criticism or negative assessment (Glenn & Holt, 2017). While the body of literature on teases is small, two findings are relevant for this chapter: teases are sequential and dualistic in design and action. Teases do not emerge freely but are contingent upon prior turns and mobilize specific forms of receipts. Drew (1987: 250, emphasis in original) writes, 'teasing is not freely occurring in conversation but occurs in a certain *sequential* context, post utterance by the tease recipient, in which they have been doing one of a limited class of activities', e.g. complaining or bragging. Teasing sequences have three parts: a teasable, the tease and the receipt (Drew, 1987; Glenn, 2003). Thus, teases, as turns, are subsumed in teasing sequences and contingent upon the teasable actions of prior speakers that create the opportunity for a tease. In addition, teases mobilize responses that fall on a spectrum from more to less affiliative. Excerpt 1 is an example of a tease in classroom interaction. The teasing sequence involves three participants: Nora (the teacher), Tim (a student) and Sadie (a student). We have used arrows to mark the teasable, the tease and shared laughter.

Excerpt 1: *so much worlds more*

```
1    TIM:        >section x has greater deposition< (0.2)
2    TIM:        u:h than section y.
3    NOR:        how much (0.5) greater.
4    TIM:    →   so much more.
5    NOR:    →   @haha
6    SAD:    →   @haha
7    NOR:    →   ↑so ↑much {↑worlds more. no.
8    NOR:                  {((widens eyes))
9                (0.5)
10   NOR:        find the rate,
```

In Excerpt 1 Nora and the students are in the midst of a series of IRFs. In Line 3 Nora initiates an IRF with an open-ended *wh*-interrogative. In the second turn, Tim provides a disaligning response (Stivers, 2008; Stivers *et al.*, 2011) (Line 4). This disaligning response is the teasable. Following the disaligning turn, Sadie and Nora laugh (Lines 5–6) before Nora teases Tim by reusing his response and altering the intonation and lexis in an extreme fashion (Line 7). This structure demonstrates that teases do not occur in isolation but are contingent actions that arise in response to prior turns and project turns that fall on a spectrum from affiliative to disaffiliative.

Teases are dualistic (Drew, 1987; Glenn, 2003) in that they deliver a negative message, e.g. casting the teased as a gossip or sexual deviant, but package the turn so as to display a humorous stance. In Excerpt 1 Nora does not explicitly cast Tim in a negative light, but her turn is dualistic. She playfully provides negative evaluation, a matter that is usually dealt with seriously. In terms of turn design, teases are characterized by their exaggerated and contrastive design. When teasing, 'speakers [...] signal – to leave recipients in no doubt – that they are not to be taken seriously' (Drew, 1987: 232). This signaling can be accomplished using exaggerated intonation, laughter and/or relaying information that speakers know is to the contrary. In Excerpt 1 Nora ups the ante on Tim's vague response by modifying 'more' with 'worlds'. The prosody of her turn is also exaggerated and contrastive. The exaggerated turn design, which relies on both verbal and nonverbal features, makes it clear that Nora is treating Tim's response as non-serious and that she too should not be taken seriously at this exact moment.

While both Drew (1987) and Glenn (2003) note that embodied resources play a role in teasing, neither provides detailed analysis of non-verbal resources, focusing solely on lexicogrammatical turn design and laughter. As numerous studies have shown, the analysis of embodied actions is crucial for understanding the interactional and pedagogical work of the classroom (Matsumoto & Dobs, 2017; Mortensen, 2008, 2009; Mortensen & Hazel, 2011; Sahlström, 2002; Sert, 2015; Sert & Jacknick, 2015). The analysis below contributes to this growing body of classroom CA as well as to CA research on teasing by looking at third-turn teases in a university science lab, and by providing detailed analysis of the verbal and nonverbal resources that make up teasing sequences as embodied actions for accomplishing classroom interaction.

Methods

The third-turn teases presented in this chapter come from an upper-level undergraduate geosciences lab at a large US research university. The data consist of six hours of video-recordings from five class sessions (1–1.5 hours per class session) which are part of a collection of 120 hours of video-recorded STEM classroom interaction (Corpus of English for Academic and Professional Purposes, 2014). The analysis focuses on five students (Daniel, Isaac, Larry, Sadie and Tim) and one graduate teaching assistant (Nora). All names used in this chapter are pseudonyms. The recordings were made by the first author and transcribed by the second author according to the adapted Jeffersonian conventions used in this volume.

Conversation analysis is the lens for examining the data. CA's primary concern is with participants' sequential practices for accomplishing social order in their everyday lifeworlds. To illuminate the actions and practices, i.e. members' methods (Sacks, 1992), through which interlocutors get the work of the here and now done, CA takes an emic approach to analysis. In other words, conversation analysts look at how participants themselves orient to the action of unfolding sequences. CA is particularly apt for analyzing classroom teases and IRFs due to its precise attention to sequence and embodied action (Drew, 1987; Glenn, 2003; Goodwin, 2000, 2013, 2018; Jefferson, 1979; Sacks, 1974).

During the unmotivated looking (Psathas, 1995; Schegloff, 1996) phase of the analysis, a preponderance of IRFs and laughter was noticed. Through repeated viewings, we located 282 IRF sequences and 28 teasing sequences in the data. As discussed in the previous section, teases are three-turn sequences which are comprised of a teasable, the tease and the receipt. Cases upon which we could not confidently agree were excluded. After the data were transcribed, they were submitted to an iterative line-by-line analysis, precisely accounting for nonverbal resources such as gaze, gesture and facial expression in addition to lexical and grammatical turn design to the greatest extent possible. The co-authors collaborated on refinement of the transcription and analysis. A recurrent sequential location for teasing sequences was in overlap with IRFs, with the teasable being the response turn and the tease being the follow-up. The five examples of third-turn teases presented in this chapter were chosen because they clearly demonstrate two practices for doing third-turn teases: reusing resources with transformation and noting the inadequacy of response turns. In addition, they demonstrate the embodied nature of teasing and the complexity of managing response turns. Third-turn teases do dualistic work, both providing negative assessment and affiliating with humorous stances displayed by students.

Analysis

The analysis is presented in four sections. The first section analyzes two IRFs in which Nora provides negative assessment in the third turn but neither Nora nor the students display humorous stances. The second section analyzes teasing sequences in which the teacher, Nora, teases the students by repeating their responses with transformation in the third turn. The third section analyzes third-turn teases in which Nora teases the students by noting the inadequacy of response turn design. Thus, the teasables in all the examples in the second and third sections are response turns and the teases are follow-up turns. When doing both forms of teasing, Nora draws on various embodied resources including lexis, prosody, smiling, laughing, voice quality and gesture to affiliate with humorous stances taken by the students while also providing negative assessment. The fourth section analyzes a tease that mobilizes a disaffiliative receipt and suggests that both sequence and embodied resources are integral to teases that mobilize more affiliative receipts.

Negative assessment

In our data, positive assessment is more common than negative assessment and, in turn, negative assessment that is delivered seriously is more common than assessment delivered as a tease (Margutti & Drew, 2014; Piirainen-Marsh, 2011; Seedhouse, 2004). The following two excerpts are instances of IRFs in which Nora delivers negative assessment that does not involve any teasing. In Excerpt 2 we note the delayed and hesitant nature of the follow-up, while in Excerpt 3 we highlight the nonverbal design of the follow-up.

Excerpt 2: well not exactly

```
1    NOR:       so in order to not (.) move (.) a:
2               (1.2)
3               what has to happen to this boundary.
4               (2.8)
5    MIN:       move to here,
6               (0.5)
7    NOR:  →    .hh yeah we::ll not exactly cause (.)
8               >remember<, so {if- (0.5) if b is moving
9                              {((smiles))
10              at a hundred kilometers (.) per million year
11              relative to a: (.) the:n (1.0) >what do you
12              have to do< at midoceanic ridge.
```

In the first turn of the IRF, Nora asks Mingyu an open-ended *wh*-display question about two plate boundaries (Lines 1–3). A fairly long gap ensues (Line 4), indicating interactional difficulty (Pomerantz, 1984). Nonetheless, his response in Line 5 aligns with the initiation turn. In other words, Mingyu's response 'cooperate[s] by facilitating the proposed activity or sequence; accepting the presuppositions and terms of the proposed action or activity; and matching the formal turn design preference of the turn' of the initiation turn (Stivers *et al.*, 2011: 21). Nora's negative assessment 'not exactly' is delayed and preceded by an in-breath, 'yeah', and an elongated discourse marker (Lines 6–7). These perturbations are recognizable signs of interactional trouble and upcoming negative assessment (Hellermann, 2003; Jucker, 1993; Macbeth, 2004). In the fourth turn (Park, 2014), Nora initiates another IRF (Lines 8–12). Nora does smile while negatively assessing Mingyu's turn, but the turn is in no other way marked as humorous and Mingyu does not display a humorous stance.

Excerpt 3: *shaking head*

```
1    NOR:        what's c.
2                (1.0)
3    ETH:        like (.) the:: >environment<?
4                ((turns head and gazes at NOR))
5                (1.0)
6    NOR:    →   ((shakes head))
7    ETH:        ((turns head and looks back at his lab sheet))
8                (1.8)
9    ETH:        ((turns head and gazes at NOR))
10               what's the question you asked me?
11               (0.4)
12   NOR:        what is c. what does c stand for.
```

Excerpt 3 is another instance of Nora negatively assessing a student response, this time by simply shaking her head. In Line 1 Nora produces an initiation turn in which she poses a *wh*-interrogative asking Ethan about plate boundary c on his lab sheet. After a gap, Ethan gives an answer that contains a micropause, an elongated vowel and a rising intonation, all of which display uncertainty about his answer (Lines 2–3). Despite the hesitation and uncertainty displayed in Ethan's turn, it still aligns with the action of the instructional project (Stivers *et al.*, 2011). After another gap (Line 5), Nora shakes her head from side to side. Although she does not produce any verbal feedback, shaking her head delivers explicit negative assessment. In the ensuing turns, Ethan self-selects to make a clarification request (Lines 9–10) and Nora produces a reformulation of her initial question (Line 12).

There are three aspects of these IRF sequences that bear similarity to those in the next two sections. In both examples, the response turns and follow-up turns are preceded by a gap, and in the case of Excerpt 2 false starts and discourse markers, which are all indications of uncertainty on the part of the students and impending negative assessment (Hellermann, 2003; Macbeth, 2004). Secondly, nonverbal resources are integral to the follow-up turn in Excerpt 3. Specifically, Nora shakes her head from side to side, delivering negative evaluation in the follow-up position. And thirdly, in fourth turns, either Nora self-selects to initiate a new IRF (Excerpt 2) or a student self-selects (Excerpt 3). In contrast to the next five excerpts, neither Nora nor the students display humorous stances. Also, in the remaining excerpts, student response turns disalign with the initiation turns whereas in the first two excerpts the response turns align with the action of the instructional sequence. Disaligning response turns disrupt the ongoing instructional project, reject the presuppositions and terms of the proposed action or activity and/or do not match the formal turn design preference the initiation turn projects (Stivers *et al.*, 2011). The five excerpts presented in the following two sections demonstrate starkly different practices for producing negative evaluation as well. Upon receiving disaligning responses to initiation turns, Nora teases the students.

Third-turn repeats with transformation

The three excerpts presented in this section are IRFs in which Nora repeats student responses with transformation in the third turns. Prior to Excerpt 4, a group of students asks Nora about an angle, and Nora responds by asking them what the angle means. As the students struggle to answer, Nora launches a series of IRFs. Lines 1–2 of Excerpt 4 are Tim's response to a prior initiation.

Excerpt 4: *so much worlds more*

```
1    TIM:    >section x has greater deposition<  (0.2)
2    TIM:    u:h than section y.
3    NOR:    how much (0.5) greater.
4    TIM:    so much more.
5    NOR:    @haha
6    SAD:    @haha
```

Frame 4.1

```
7    NOR:    →  ↑so ↑much {↑worlds more. no.
8    NOR:                 {((widens eyes))
```

Frame 4.2

```
9             (0.5)
10   NOR:     find the rate,
11            (0.5)
12   NOR:     >how're you gonna find the rate<,
```

Following Tim's response in Lines 1–2, Nora initiates an IRF (Line 3). The initiation is an open-ended *wh*-display question (Lee, 2006). In Line 4 Tim says, 'so much more' with falling intonation. By reusing 'much' and replacing 'how' with 'so' and 'greater' with 'more', Tim decomposes and reuses resources (Goodwin, 2013, 2018) from Nora's initiation turn to create a vague response that disaligns with the action of the IRF by rejecting the terms and presuppositions of Nora's initiation turn, i.e. to provide a quantitative value. Tim's response mobilizes coordinated laughter from Nora and Sadie who turn to each other, laugh and smile (Lines 5–6, Frame 4.1). Tim's cheeky response (Berge, 2017; Piirainen-Marsh, 2011) sets the stage for the tease. Nora repeats the prior turn, adding 'worlds' and using exaggerated intonation and facial expression, i.e. eyes opened wide (Lines 7–8, Frame 4.2). She then immediately produces a sharply contrasting deadpan 'no' with falling intonation. The intonation of the explicit negative assessment contrasts starkly with the first part of the tease. In overlap with Nora's tease, Sadie smiles at Nora and laughs. Thus, the tease is acknowledged but not taken up (Drew, 1987; Glenn, 2003). In the fourth turn (Park, 2014) of the IRF, Nora gives explicit instructions.

In Excerpt 4 Nora's third-turn tease playfully provides negative assessment to a disaligning response that participants oriented to as humorous. Like serious negative feedback turns, this one repeats the past turn with a non-matching intonational contour (Hellermann, 2003; Seedhouse, 2004). In addition, the tease lexically modifies the response and contains explicit negative assessment. It is also important to note that the tease, much like Piirainen-Marsh's (2011) ironic teacher turns, is preceded by a humorous student turn and student smiling, perhaps cueing Nora into a tease-relevant position. The decomposition and reuse of materials with transformation (Goodwin, 2013, 2018) are central to the unfolding of the IRF and the teasing sequence in Excerpt 4. Nora's tease (Line 7) decomposes and reuses Tim's response, highlighting its vagueness and providing negative assessment. The transformation of the third-turn tease also involves pitch and facial expression. Such playful mockery serves to uphold the moral order of the classroom in the face of a cheeky response turn (Piirainen-Marsh, 2011; Roth *et al.*, 2011).

Excerpt 5 is a similar example of third-turn teasing that arises during a teacher-fronted moment in class. Just before these overlapping IRF and teasing sequences unfold, Nora has stopped group work to address a challenge about which multiple groups have asked.

Excerpt 5: *rararow*

```
1    NOR:        what's walther's law?
2    STS:        °xxx°
3    NOR:    →   rararow[row:: @hhhh] what is ↑it?
4    STS:               [xxx        ]
```

Frame 5.1

```
5               (2.5)
6    NOR:       you guys are not all gonna say the same thing but
7               you should just yell out whatever version of walther's
8               law you keep in your head.
```

Excerpt 5 begins with Nora's initiation, an open-ended *wh*-display question (Lee, 2006) (Line 1). The students produce an unintelligible response (Line 2) that disaligns with the prior turn by not advancing the instructional project or matching the projected preferred turn design. The unintelligible response becomes the teasable when Nora produces a non-sense response which is followed immediately by single-party laughter (Line 3,

Frame 5.1). Following her laughter, Nora recalibrates her initiation (Lines 6–8). Like the tease in Excerpt 4, the one in Excerpt 5 reuses the students' responses with transformation involving smiling and laughter. The tease in Excerpt 5 is followed by Nora initiating a subsequent IRF that does not mobilize a response, further indicating that the students are struggling to respond (Lines 3–5).

In sum, the IRFs in this section overlap with teasing sequences in their second and third turns. Teasable student turns present disaligning responses that are oriented to as humorous. The teases were third-turn repeats (Park, 2014) that modified the preceding responses using lexis, exaggerated and contrastive prosody and laughter. By teasing in third turns, Nora affiliates with humorous stances that the students have displayed while also providing negative assessment of their disaligning turns and projecting a trajectory for a return to the serious business of the class. The negative assessment is clearly oriented to as such by the students, who wait for Nora to reinitiate another IRF.

Noting the inadequacy of response design

Repeating student responses with transformation is not the only practice for teasing in the third turns of IRFs. This section unpacks three IRFs in which Nora teases in third turns by commenting on the inadequate turn design of responses. Excerpt 6 occurs seconds after Excerpt 5. As we have seen in earlier excerpts, the sequence contains student and teacher laughter and smiling.

Excerpt 6: *your answer is in cat*

```
1   NOR:        it's a little bit longer than that. >try it again<.
2   UNK:        xxx
3   NOR:        [@hahahaha
4   STS:        [@hahahaha
5   DAN:        xxx
6   NOR:    →   dan, it sounds like your walther's law is in cat.
7           →   you might wanna think about that. @hhh
```

Frame 6.1

```
8   STS:        ((gaze at DAN, smile))
```

Excerpt 6 starts with Nora's initiation 'it's a bit longer than that. try it again' (Line 1). This initiation turn, unlike the earlier examples, is not a *wh*-question but instead an imperative directing the students back to the action of the prior display question. In the ensuing lines (2–4), the students produce unintelligible responses and Nora and the students laugh. Then Dan produces an inaudible response that becomes the teasable (Line 5). Like the response in Excerpt 5, this one disaligns with Nora's initiation turn by not advancing the instructional project or matching the projected preferred turn design. The tease occurs in Lines 6–7 when Nora says, 'it sounds like your Walther's Law is in cat' and suggests that Dan rethink that, i.e. the design of his response. Again, the tease, which is preceded by shared laughter, provides negative assessment while also displaying a humorous stance. The tease is not designed with exaggerated prosody, but during her tease Nora smiles and laughs (Frame 6.1). Contrasting with the teases in the prior section which mock the design of student responses, the tease in Excerpt 6 categorizes the response as insufficient. In the receipt, students other than the speaker, Dan, who is outside the camera's view, participate in the teasing sequence by smiling and turning their gaze toward him (Line 8).

Prior to Excerpt 7, Nora halts the group work in which the class is engaged and begins guiding the students through a specific problem in the lab as a class. As the sequence opens, Nora draws a diagram and asks the students what they know just by looking at the diagram. A student describes the diagram as confusing, and student laughter ensues. Nora reciprocates the humorous stance by teasing the student.

Excerpt 7: *that's your opinion*

```
1    NOR:      >okay<. (1.2) here's our diagram. (1.0) {what do we
2                                                     {((gaze at STS))
3    NOR:      know:, (.) jus:t from looking at this.
4              (0.8)
5    S01:      [it's confusing.]
6    S02:      [b's on top.    ]
7    S03:      @hhhh.
8    NOR:   →  ((smiles))
```

Frame 7.1

```
 9    NOR:   →   {that's your opinion. i don't think you {#know:#
10                {((tilts head))                          {((rolls eyes))
```

Frame 7.2   **Frame 7.3**

```
11    NOR:       [{#tha:t#.]
12                {((gaze at STS, smiles))
```

Frame 7.4

```
13    S04:       [you       ]have a divergent boundary.
14    NOR:       {you have a divergent bounda↑ry,
15                {((turns toward chalkboard))
16    NOR:       ((writes on chalkboard))
17    NOR:       yes, >n what else<.
```

Nora asks the students what they know about a diagram she has drawn on the chalkboard in Lines 1–3. The initiation, like those in Excerpts 4 and 5, is an open-ended *wh*-display question. Following a gap, two students reply in overlap (Lines 4–6). A student outside the camera view laughs (Line 7). One of the response turns, 'it's confusing' (Line 5), becomes the teasable. This response disaligns in both its delayed delivery and its rejections of the terms and presuppositions of the initiation, i.e. responses should state empirical observations about the diagram. As her tease begins, Nora smiles (Frame 7.1), shifts her gaze slightly left, and contrasts opinion with knowledge (Lines 8–9). The tease is marked by creaky voice, exaggerated falling contrastive stress on the word 'know', and lengthened vowels in the words 'know' and 'that'. While she is speaking, Nora tilts her head slightly back to the right (Frame 7.2), rolls her eyes (Frame 7.3) and continues smiling (Frame 7.4). Like Excerpt 6, this tease notes the inadequacy of the student's response. In an overlapping turn, an unknown student self-selects and provides an answer that Nora positively assesses (Lines 13–17). This receipt provides a candidate response after a negative assessment turn from the teacher, an action reported in past IRF literature, once again illuminating how the IRF and teasing sequences are tightly linked (Hellermann, 2005; Seedhouse, 2004). Excerpt 7 shows that third-turn teases do not only deliver negative feedback while also displaying a humorous stance. They also indicate a transition-relevance place (TRP) (Schegloff, 2007) at which a student may self-select.

While the students may display a humorous stance by smiling and/or laughing before teases, Nora does the teasing in all of the first five excerpts. Her teases do not become teasables for the students who at most smile and laugh, thus displaying affiliation during and following teases. In Excerpt 8 we see the students not only acknowledging Nora's tease but actually taking it up as a teasable.

Excerpt 8: be specific in your pointing

```
1   NOR:    hey: so: (1.0) just another note.
2           (1.0)
3   NOR:    i'm sorry.
4           (0.5)
5   NOR:    u:m (0.5) when you:- which way: (0.8) <do you thi:nk> (1.0)
6   NOR:    the sediment is coming from.
7           (0.5)
8   NOR:    from which direction is the point of origin.
9   UNK:    (xxxx)?
10          (2.2)
11  NOR:    be:: (0.5) be: specific in your pointing.
12          (0.5)
13  UNK:    [top and bottom (of it)?
14  TIM:    [(((crosses arms, points in opposite directions))
15  UNK:    @hhhhhh
16          (0.5)
17  NOR:    no one is pointing.
18  ISA:    ((points upward with BH, puts out BHs palms facing up))
```

Frame 8.1

```
19  NOR:  →  what is tha:t. @hhhh
20  ISA:     ((gazes at Tim, smiles,        ((RH index finger points up))
             LH index finger points up))
```

Frame 8.2   **Frame 8.3**

```
21  JIM:     ((smiles))
22  DYL:     ((smiles))
23  TIM:     ((crosses both arms again, points in opposite directions))
```

Frame 8.4   **Frame 8.5**

```
24  NOR:     alright. so:: (1.2) here we go.
25  NOR:     ((walks to the projector screen))
```

After Nora poses an initial open-ended *wh*-display question, there is a pause (Lines 5–7). Nora then asks another open-ended *wh*-display question which is followed by an unintelligible student response and a significant gap (Lines 8–10). Nora tells the students to be specific when they point and another gap ensues (Lines 11–12). Once again, as this IRF commences over several turns with repeated gaps and successive recalibrations of the initiation by Nora, there is observable interactional difficulty. In Line 13 an unknown student says, 'top and bottom of it', a response that is followed by laughter (Line 15) and another pause (Line 16). While the student is speaking, Tim gestures humorously by pointing in opposite directions but not at the board (Line 14). In Line 17 Nora states that no one is pointing and Isaac points upward with both hands and then puts both hands up (Frame 8.1) in a gestural claim of insufficient knowledge (CIK) (Sert & Walsh, 2012). This response disaligns in both its delayed delivery and its rejections of the explicitly stated terms and presuppositions of the initiation, i.e. students should 'be specific in [their] pointing' (Line 11). As in Excerpts 6 and 7, Nora teases Isaac in Line 19 by noting the unintelligible design of his turn, 'what is that?', and laughing.

Following Nora's tease, two students extend their collaborative response (Ko, 2014) as Isaac turns his gaze to Tim and smiles, first pointing left with his left hand and then right with his right hand (Frames 8.2 and 8.3). Immediately after Isaac's playful gestures, Jim and Dylan both smile (Lines 21–22), and in Line 23 Tim ups the ante on Isaac's playful gestures by crossing his arms and pointing in opposite directions with index fingers before uncrossing his arms and pointing in opposite directions with his thumbs (Frames 8.4 and 8.5). Instead of orienting to the instructional import, i.e. negative feedback, of the third turn by self-selecting to provide a candidate response or account or waiting for a teacher next turn, the students continue pointing in various directions and smiling, thus teasing Nora back by providing further disaligning responses after the third-turn tease. The continued nonverbal responses prompt Nora to approach the projector screen to provide clarification.

In Excerpt 8 the students' humorous stances are indexed almost entirely through embodied resources, i.e. smiling and gesture. Perhaps more than any other data presented in this paper, this excerpt demonstrates the necessity for the analysis of embodied resources for understanding the action and composition of second and third turns and humor. If we analyzed only verbal turn design, it would appear that the students did not respond at all. The student responses again provide a next action, i.e. pointing, but because the students point in different directions they disalign with Nora's first turn and subsequent amendments to her instructions. Nora's follow-up turn affiliates with the humorous stances expressed in the second turns by teasing, smiling and laughing, but once again notes the responses as inadequate. As in Excerpt 4, following her third turn, Nora gives an explicit explanation that addresses her earlier initiation.

A po-faced (disaffiliative) receipt

Thus far, the third-turn teases presented have all been received with at least mild affiliation. That is not always the case, though. Excerpt 9 is an example of a tease that receives a po-faced (disaffiliative) receipt (Drew, 1987). There are two jarring differences between this teasing sequence and the ones analyzed in Excerpts 4–8 in terms of sequence and embodiment. Excerpt 9 occurs while Nora is returning completed assignments to the students. When she returns Tim's assignment, he asks her a question.

Excerpt 9: keep it forever

```
1    TIM:   [what should we do with this quiz (next).
2                                        ((gazes at quiz))
```

Frame 9.1

```
3    NOR:   [hands paper to Jennifer
4    JEN:                      {((receives paper))
5                              {thank you.
6    NOR:   keep it forever.
7                        ((turns body, gazes at TIM))
```

Frame 9.2

```
8    TIM:   ((gazes at his quiz))
9           (0.7)
10   NOR:   treasure it (.) always.
11          (0.7)
12   NOR:   frame it. hang it in your locker.
13                                   ((walks past TIM))
```

Frame 9.3

Frame 9.4

```
14   TIM:    (why does it have) a {dinosaur on it,
15                                 {((gazes left))
16   NOR:    @heh heh.
17                         ((gazes at TIM, gazes away))
```

Frame 9.5   **Frame 9.6**

```
18   STU:    ((removed due to no consent))
19   TIM:    {it's my dinosaur. huh,
20           {((gazes at student left))
```

After receiving his quiz, Tim asks Nora what the students should do with their graded assignments (Line 1, Frame 9.1). In contrast to the teasing sequences in IRF (Excerpts 4–8), this teasable is an open-ended request for information. While walking away from Tim and continuing to distribute completed quizzes, Nora teases him by making ironic suggestions, using extreme lexical choice, simple declarative syntax and falling intonation (Lines 6–12, Frames 9.2 and 9.3). Whereas the teasables in Excerpts 4–8 were disaligning turns, here it is the tease that is disaligning. Nora's tease receives a po-faced (Drew, 1987), i.e. disaffiliative, response from Tim who immediately turns his gaze away from Nora and toward another student (Lines 14–15, Frame 9.4). Nora then turns back toward Tim, smiling and laughing (Line 16–17, Frame 9.5), but by this time Tim has totally turned away from Nora and is speaking with a classmate sitting next to him (Lines 14–20, Frame 9.6).

So, why does this tease mobilize a po-faced receipt whereas the earlier examples engendered affiliation? An answer can be found in sequentiality and embodiment. In regard to sequence, Excerpt 9 is starkly different from the earlier teasing sequences in which the teasables were disaligning student turns followed by student laughter and smiling before Nora joined in on the playfulness by teasing. Here, the teasable is a student turn in which an open-ended interrogative is posed. The question is asked with no indication of playfulness such as smiley voice or laughter. The tease is a disaligning response from Nora because it presents ironic suggestions for what the students should do with the returned assignment. Thus, Nora treats an apparently serious request for instruction in a non-serious manner. Additionally, the tease in Excerpt 9 is delivered as Nora is walking away from the teased. In all the earlier teasing sequences, Nora faces the students. As Nora walks away, Tim turns his head away from Nora and is not smiling, clearly disaffiliating with the tease. When contrasted with earlier excerpts, this teasing sequence illuminates the importance of body position in the delivery of a tease that is acknowledged or taken up by recipients. Thus, we see that sequence and embodied action are integral to receipts that teases mobilize. This is a topic further research should pursue.

Conclusion

To summarize, in IRFs that overlap with teasing sequences, teachers playfully provide negative assessment to responses that disalign (Stivers, 2008) with the prior initiation turn. In contrast to follow-up turns that deliver negative assessment seriously, third-turn teases are designed using a variety of resources including exaggerated intonation, voice quality, facial expression and laughter to display a humorous stance. The analysis above unpacks two practices for teasing in third turns of IRFs – third-turn repeats with transformation and noting the inadequate design of responses. Our analysis produced three major findings with implications for teachers, teacher preparation and classroom researchers:

(1) Third-turn teases are contingent actions in which teachers manage disaligning student responses.
(2) Third-turn teases engender fourth turns that look similar to those that follow serious negative assessment.
(3) Third-turn teases are embodied actions composed of an ensemble of verbal and nonverbal resources.

Third-turn teases do not arise out of nowhere but are contingent actions which are often preceded by student smiling and laughter. Teasing is a sequential and embodied practice that participants accomplish along with the IRF in the university geosciences lab. One similarity that Excerpts 4–8 share is that they are sequences in which an IRF overlaps with a teasing sequence composed of a teasable, a tease and a receipt. The disaligning student responses are the teasables and the follow-up turns are the teases. Students sometimes provide answers that are 'received as a joke of some sort' (Berge, 2017; Roth *et al.*, 2011; Waring, 2016: 114). This is the case in our data. Third-turn teases do not necessarily initiate humor but instead perpetuate it by affiliating with a humorous stance already taken by other interlocutors.

Interestingly, when IRFs overlap with teasing sequences, they do not lose their instructional import. The students do not usually tease back, smiling and laughing at most. Instead, they wait for Nora to initiate another sequence (Excerpts 4, 5, 6, 8) or self-select to offer another candidate response or account for the prior response (Excerpt 7). These actions are commonly cited in the fourth turns of IRFs in which teachers give negative assessments without teasing. In only one example, Excerpt 8, do the students tease back, and even this tease is short-lived and terminated when Nora self-selects to give explicit instruction. This demonstrates that participants are keenly aware that teasing sequences, while effervescent moments of mirth, are fleeting and situated in a larger instructional project.

Another significant contribution the analysis makes is to our understanding of the IRF and classroom teasing as embodied social accomplishments. While past studies have shown that sequence, lexicosyntactic turn design and prosody matter in both teasing sequences and playful classroom sequences, none puts features such as gaze, body position, facial expression or gesture at the forefront of the analysis. Dismissing the roles that visual resources play as part of embodied actions severely underplays the critical role that visual cues play in classroom, and more generally speaking human, interaction. At times, it is through the decomposition and reuse with transformation, involving lexis, prosody and nonverbal resources, that teases are designed (Goodwin, 2013, 2018). At other times, teases point out the inadequacy of prior turn designs and are spoken while smiling and perhaps moving the head. In addition to unpacking the intricacy of turn design in teasing, examining embodied actions highlights the distributed nature of teases, i.e. receipts involve participants who are not the teaser or the teased.

Additionally, this analysis has added to our understanding of the complexity and situatedness of the interactional work that students and teachers do in the IRF (Lee, 2007). The third-turn teases presented in this paper are composed of dualistic actions that display humorous stances and provide negative assessment in follow-up turns. While this dualistic nature is characteristic of teases in everyday interaction, the teases analyzed here do not attribute deviant identities such as being a cheater, phony or sexual deviant (Drew, 1987; Glenn, 2003). At the same time, they do not index any level of personal familiarity between Nora and the students. Instead, third-turn teases are tightly wrapped up in the unfolding instructional project of the classroom and orient directly to the content of prior turns. That is, the work of these teases tends to the incorrect or inadequate nature of student responses while also affiliating with affective stances already displayed by the students. They do not invoke taboo or personal topics or identities because such topics are not relevant to the here and now of these interactions. Thus, third-turn teases are locally situated actions that differ from teases in everyday interaction in terms of their precise actions and design. Future research should continue to investigate teasing as embodied action in the accomplishment of teaching and learning and how such actions differ from or are similar to those in non-institutional interaction. Additionally, IRF are commonly reported sites for humor (Lehtimaja, 2011; Lin, 1999; Piirainen-Marsh, 2011; Poveda, 2005; Roth et al., 2011). As collections continue to grow, we may begin to be able to generalize that routine classroom sequences are exceptionally susceptible spaces for teasing and, more broadly speaking, humor.

Finally, our findings have implications for teacher education. Teachers will inevitably encounter moments in which students produce disaligning or dispreferred responses. By tending to cues like smiling and laughter, teachers may notice sequential positions in which they can affiliatively manage students' disaligning responses. Managing these moments in a lighthearted manner can help teachers cultivate and maintain an environment in which students produce responses even when they are unsure of their epistemic status. Nonetheless, we want to reiterate that teasing is not a frequent occurrence in our data and it may be taken up disaffiliatively (Excerpt 9). Teases may not always be understood in the same way by all participants. When teasing is taken poorly by some participants, it can work disaffiliatively in interaction. It is thus equally important for teachers in training to recognize how such disaffiliative moments, as well as the affiliative ones, unfold and influence subsequent interactions. Our study demonstrates the potential for using CA as a methodology for teacher training. By paying fine-grained attention to how teachers manage responses in third turns of IRFs, teachers in training can expand their understanding of the multivocality (Waring, 2016) of instructional talk and the intricate work accomplished in follow-up turns, and in turn incorporate such practices into their own instruction.

Acknowledgement

Excerpts 4, 7 and 8 appeared in an earlier publication (Looney & Kim, 2018) and are reproduced here with permission.

References

Berge, M. (2017) The role of humor in learning physics: A study of undergraduate students. *Research in Science Education* 47 (2), 427–450.

Corpus of English for Academic and Professional Purposes (2014) Corpus of videos and accompanying transcripts from educational contexts. Unpublished raw data.

Drew, P. (1987) Po-faced receipts of teases. *Linguistics* 25 (1), 219–253.

Glenn, P. (2003) *Laughter in Interaction*. New York: Cambridge University Press.

Glenn, P. and Holt, E. (2017) Conversation analysis of humor. In S. Attardo (ed.) *The Routledge Handbook of Language and Humor* (pp. 295–308). New York: Routledge.

Goodwin, C. (2000) Action and embodiment within situated human interaction. *Journal of Pragmatics* 32 (10), 1489–1522.

Goodwin, C. (2013) The co-operative, transformative organization of human action and knowledge. *Journal of Pragmatics* 46 (1), 8–23.

Goodwin, C. (2018) *Co-Operative Action*. New York: Cambridge University Press.

Hall, J.K. (1997) Differential teacher attention to student utterances: The construction of different opportunities for learning in the IRF. *Linguistics and Education* 9 (3), 287–311.

Hellermann, J. (2003) The interactive work of prosody in the IRF exchange: Teacher repetition in feedback moves. *Language in Society* 32 (1), 79–104.

Hellermann, J. (2005) The sequential and prosodic co-construction of a 'quiz game' activity in classroom talk. *Journal of Pragmatics* 37 (6), 919–944.

Hutchby, I. (1992) Confrontation talk: Aspects of 'interruption' in argument sequences on talk radio. *Text (The Hague)* 12 (3), 343–372.

Jefferson, G. (1979) A technique for inviting laughter and its subsequent acceptance/declination. In G. Psathas (ed.) *Everyday Language: Studies in Ethnomethodology* (pp. 79–96). New York: Irvington.

Jucker, A.H. (1993) The discourse marker well: A relevance-theoretical account. *Journal of Pragmatics* 19 (5), 435–452.

Ko, S. (2014) The nature of multiple responses to teachers' questions. *Applied Linguistics* 35 (1), 48–62.

Lee, Y.A. (2006) Respecifying display questions: Interactional resources for language teaching. *TESOL Quarterly* 40 (4), 691–713.

Lee, Y.A. (2007) Third turn position in teacher talk: Contingency and the work of teaching. *Journal of Pragmatics* 39 (6), 1204–1230.

Lehtimaja, I. (2011) Teacher-oriented address terms in students' reproach turns. *Linguistics and Education* 22 (4), 348–363.

Lin, A. (1999) Resistance and creativity in English reading lessons in Hong Kong. *Language Culture and Curriculum* 12 (3), 285–296.

Looney, S.D. and Kim, J. (2018) Humor, uncertainty, and affiliation: Cooperative and co-operative action in the university science lab. *Linguistics and Education* 46, 56–69.

Macbeth, D. (2004) The relevance of repair for classroom correction. *Language in Society* 33 (5), 703–736.

Margutti, P. and Drew, P. (2014) Positive evaluation of student answers in classroom instruction. *Language and Education* 28 (5), 436–458.

Matsumoto, Y. and Dobs, A.M. (2017) Pedagogical gestures as interactional resources for teaching and learning tense and aspect in the ESL grammar classroom. *Language Learning* 67 (1), 7–42.

Mehan, H. (1979) *Learning Lessons.* Cambridge, MA: Harvard University Press.

Mortensen, K. (2008) Selecting next speaker in the second language classroom: How to find a willing next speaker in planned activities. *Journal of Applied Linguistics* 5 (1), 55–79.

Mortensen, K. (2009) Establishing recipiency in pre-beginning position in the second language classroom. *Discourse Processes* 46 (5), 491–515.

Mortensen, K. and Hazel, S. (2011) Initiating round robins in the L2 classroom – preliminary observations. *Novitas-ROYAL* 5 (1), 55–70.

Nassaji, H. and Wells, G. (2000) What's the use of 'triadic dialogue'? An investigation of teacher–student interaction. *Applied Linguistics* 21 (3), 376–406.

Park, Y. (2014) The roles of third-turn repeats in two L2 classroom interactional contexts. *Applied Linguistics* 35 (2), 145–167.

Piirainen-Marsh, A. (2011) Irony and the moral order of secondary school classrooms. *Linguistics and Education* 22 (4), 364–382.

Pomerantz, A. (1984) Agreeing and disagreeing with assessments: Some features of preferred/dispreferred turn shapes. In J. Maxwell Atkinson and J. Heritage (eds) *Structures of Social Action* (pp. 57–101). Cambridge: Cambridge University Press.

Poveda, D. (2005) Metalinguistic activity, humor and social competence in classroom discourse. *Pragmatics* 15 (1), 89–107.

Psathas, G. (1995) *Conversation Analysis: The Study of Talk-in-Interaction.* Thousand Oaks, CA: Sage.

Reddington, E. and Waring, H.Z. (2015) Understanding the sequential resources for doing humor in the language classroom. *Humor* 28 (1), 1–23.

Roth, W.M., Ritchie, S.M., Hudson, P. and Mergard, V. (2011) A study of laughter in science lessons. *Journal of Research in Science Teaching* 48 (5), 437–458.

Sacks, H. (1974) An analysis of the course of a joke's telling in conversation. In R. Bauman and J. Sherzer (eds) *Explorations in the Ethnography of Speaking* (pp. 337–353). Cambridge: Cambridge University Press.

Sacks, H. (1992) *Lectures on Conversation, Vols I and II.* Oxford: Blackwell.

Sahlström, J.F. (2002) The interactional organization of hand raising in classroom interaction. *Journal of Classroom Interaction* 37 (2), 47–57.

Schegloff, E.A. (1996) Turn organization: One intersection of grammar and interaction. *Studies in Interactional Sociolinguistics* 13, 52–133.

Schegloff, E.A. (2007) *Sequence Organization in Interaction: A Primer in Conversation Analysis.* New York: Cambridge University Press.

Seedhouse, P. (2004) Conversation analysis methodology. *Language Learning* 54 (S1), 1–54.

Sert, O. (2015) *Social Interaction and L2 Classroom Discourse.* Croydon: Edinburgh University Press.

Sert, O. and Jacknick, C.M. (2015) Student smiles and the negotiation of epistemics in L2 classrooms. *Journal of Pragmatics* 77, 97–112.

Sert, O. and Walsh, S. (2012) The interactional management of claims of insufficient knowledge in English language classrooms. *Language and Education* 27 (6), 542–565.

Sinclair, J.M. and Coulthard, M. (1975) *Towards an Analysis of Discourse: The English Used by Teachers and Pupils.* London: Oxford University Press.

Stivers, T. (2008) Stance, alignment, and affiliation during storytelling: When nodding is a token of affiliation. *Research on Language and Social Interaction* 41 (1), 31–57.

Stivers, T., Mondada, L. and Steensig, J. (2011) Knowledge, morality and affiliation in social interaction. In T. Stivers, L. Mondada and J. Steensig (eds) *The Morality of Knowledge in Conversation* (pp. 3–24). New York: Cambridge University Press.

Thonus, T. (2008) Acquaintanceship, familiarity, and coordinated laughter in writing tutorials. *Linguistics and Education* 19 (4), 333–350.

Waring, H.Z. (2008) Using explicit positive assessment in the language classroom: IRF, feedback, and learning opportunities. *The Modern Language Journal* 92 (4), 577–594.

Waring, H.Z. (2016) *Theorizing Pedagogical Interaction: Insights from Conversation Analysis.* New York: Routledge.

Zemel, A. and Koschmann, T. (2011) Pursuing a question: Reinitiating IRE sequences as a method of instruction. *Journal of Pragmatics* 43 (2), 475–488.

5 A Tale of Two Tasks: Facilitating Storytelling in the Adult English as a Second Language Classroom

Elizabeth Reddington, Di Yu and Nadja Tadic

This chapter offers an account of how participants in one adult English as a second language (ESL) class constitute a storytelling task, with a focus on the role(s) adopted by the teacher. Using the framework of conversation analysis (CA), we show how the teacher utilizes both linguistic and embodied resources to engage with the learners, and we examine how shifts in the nature of her participation shape opportunities for student participation. Juxtaposing two cases, we find that while the teacher generally takes on a supporting role, when the opportunity arises she becomes a co-teller who competes for the floor, prompting the student teller to do the same. We present these two different realizations of the 'same' storytelling task as a starting point for considering options available to the language teacher in facilitating communicative activities and the interactional consequences of exercising those options.

Introduction

As studies of second language (L2) classrooms conducted within the framework of CA have underscored, pedagogical tasks are negotiated by participants in interaction; regardless of what was planned or intended, tasks are what participants make of them (Hellermann & Pekarek Doehler, 2010; Mori, 2002; Seedhouse, 2004). In keeping with this perspective, this chapter offers an account of what participants in one ESL class make of a storytelling task, with a focus on the role(s) adopted by the teacher. Specifically, we show how the teacher utilizes both linguistic and embodied resources (Nevile, 2015) to engage with students as they tell their stories, and consider how shifts in the nature of her participation shape opportunities for student participation. Juxtaposing two cases, we find that while the teacher generally takes on a supporting role, aligning as a story recipient or working to ensure the comprehension of others, when an opportunity arises she also participates as a co-teller who competes for the floor, prompting the student teller to do the same. We present these two different realizations of the 'same' storytelling task in a real classroom as a starting point for considering the options available to the L2 teacher in facilitating communicative activities and the interactional consequences of exercising those options.

Background

In research on classroom discourse generally, much attention has been devoted to how teacher interactional practices can shape student participation and opportunities for learning in the context of the three-part IRF (i.e. teacher Initiation, student Response, teacher Feedback) instructional sequence (e.g. Cazden, 1988; Hall, 1998; Mehan, 1979; Nassaji & Wells, 2000; Sinclair & Coulthard, 1975; van Lier, 1996). Less concerted attention has been devoted to investigating how teachers work with student contributions within other kinds of participation structures or interactional contexts that may be constituted within classrooms, particularly L2 classrooms. One such context is what Seedhouse (2004) refers to as *meaning-and-fluency-focused interaction*, i.e. a context in which topic development, and potentially turn-taking, is open-ended – and thus more akin to 'ordinary' conversation (Sacks *et al.*, 1974) – and communication of students' personal meanings is prioritized over accuracy. Walsh (2006: 79) associates similar features with what he terms *classroom context mode*; the label further acknowledges how such interaction 'emerge[s] from the complex and diverse range of experiences and cultural backgrounds that the learners themselves bring to the classroom'. In such contexts, Seedhouse (2004) and Walsh (2006, 2011) observe, teachers do not generally correct language errors but may instead participate by responding to the content of student turns, collaborating with students to develop topics or ensuring that talk is comprehensible to others.

In addition to discussions in Seedhouse's and Walsh's broader efforts to identify and describe interactional patterns and practices in the L2 classroom, several recent studies have sought specifically to examine how more 'conversational' interaction emerges through microanalysis of teacher–student talk. Drawing on CA, Walsh (2002) describes how an English as a foreign language (EFL) teacher facilitated a whole-class 'conversation' by offering personal reactions, extending wait time and withdrawing from the interaction. As a result, Walsh (2002) argues, students were able to take longer, more complex turns, and their turns were characterized by features normally associated with ordinary conversation, such as self-selection, overlap and latching. Through close examination of interaction in several

L2 classrooms, Richards (2006) found that shifts to more conversational talk occurred with shifts in orientation to participant identities – i.e. when students and teachers positioned themselves and others as nature lovers or sports fans – arguing that measured self-revelation on the part of the teacher can have a facilitative effect. In a more recent CA study, Waring (2014) describes how one ESL teacher embedded a conversational frame within the institutional frame of the classroom by asking personal questions and responding to contributions with appreciations instead of assessments. Waring (2014) argues that through their participation in more symmetrical exchanges, learners are afforded opportunities to expand their language use. Given that implementing open-ended communicative activities and responding to learner contributions – in ways that promote participation and learning – poses a challenge (Bannink, 2002; Walsh, 2002), particularly for novice teachers or teachers-in-training (Fagan, 2012), it is worth continuing these efforts to uncover how instructors facilitate such activities in the real-time unfolding of classroom interaction.

In addition, studies of L2 classroom interaction have only recently begun to examine how teachers use aspects of bodily conduct to accomplish actions such as allocating turns and eliciting student talk (Käänta, 2012; Sert, 2015), displaying engagement (Majlesi, 2015; Reddington, 2018) and explaining grammar or vocabulary (Matsumoto & Dobs, 2017; Waring *et al.*, 2013). In an effort to extend this line of work, in the current study we take a holistic approach to examining teacher and student participation, giving close consideration not only to features of talk but also to the use of embodied resources, including gesture, gaze, facial expressions and body movements (see Mondada, 2016; Nevile, 2015).

Data and Method

This study is conducted within the framework of conversation analysis, an approach to examining naturally occurring interaction, in minute detail, that aims to uncover the tacit practices through which participants accomplish social actions (see ten Have, 2007), including teaching and learning (see, for example, Markee, 2015; Sert, 2015; Waring, 2016). Data include a video-recording and accompanying transcript, produced in accordance with conventions adapted from Jefferson (2004), of a three-hour ESL conversation class in a community language program at a graduate school of education in the United States. The participants are five adult learners and their teacher, a student in the school's MA program in Teaching English to Speakers of Other Languages who had prior teaching experience. Participants are identified by pseudonyms in all transcripts.

For this study, we focus on a whole-class speaking activity in which students were asked by the teacher to share something that had happened to them during the week. In her instructions, delivered at the start and subsequently reiterated for latecomers, the teacher refers to the activity as 'storytelling', and it precedes a teacher-led discussion of the components of good storytelling. It is worth recognizing, however, that the tellings are shaped by the participants' orientations to the constraints and affordances of the institutional, i.e. classroom, setting. Unlike in episodes of storytelling common in ordinary conversation (Sacks *et al.*, 1974), in our data one interactant – the teacher – exercises the right to select speakers; as a result, storytellers do not need to negotiate for space to launch extended tellings. In other words, every student in the group is granted, and must take in order to comply with the task instructions, the opportunity to tell a story.

From the teacher's perspective, as observable in her instructions and general pattern of participation, one purpose of this activity is to provide space for individual students to engage in extended, meaningful talk. Given this purpose, we became interested in those instances in which the teacher's participation goes beyond minimal displays of listenership (e.g. nodding and offering continuers) that align with the continuation of the telling (Goodwin, 1986; Schegloff, 1982; Stivers, 2008) and the impact of these turns on student participation. In other words, when and how does the teacher intervene in the students' stories? We proceeded to conduct turn-by-turn analysis of the tellings, examining how turns were produced, received and acted upon (Schegloff, 2007). In the following we juxtapose our analyses of what turn out to be two quite different realizations of the storytelling task, illustrating how the teacher's varying participation leads to different kinds of participation opportunities for the students – and hence, we argue, different kinds of learning opportunities.

Analysis and Findings

In the unfolding of the first student telling (Ana's story), we trace how the teacher moves from simply aligning as a recipient of the telling to offering linguistic assistance to the teller and, subsequently, to checking the understanding of other recipients, actions that support the successful production of the telling. In the unfolding of the second telling (Nina's story), we describe a different sort of shift in the teacher's participation as she moves from story recipient to competitive co-teller. In this latter case, the teacher's actions prompt the student to undertake additional interactional work to regain control of the telling. Throughout the analysis, we examine both the linguistic and embodied resources employed by the participants to accomplish these actions.

Task 1: Ana's story

We join the participants as Ana is in the middle of her telling about an outing with friends in New York City. The outing included a visit to Roosevelt Island, which is accessible from the city via elevated tramway. As shown in Figure 5.1, the teacher, May, and the students are seated

Figure 5.1 Classroom setup and participants

around several tables that have been pushed together. May sits in front of the whiteboard, and students Ana and Yoshi sit across from each other. Lina sits across from May. Nina, who arrives during Excerpt 2, takes a seat between Lina and Yoshi. Another student, Kara, who is not shown here, arrives during Excerpt 5. May keeps a small notebook open in front of her on the table and writes in it from time to time during the tellings. She makes use of her notes in the subsequent discussion of the stories.

In Excerpt 1 we first observe May's minimal participation as she aligns with the in-progress telling as a story recipient by bypassing opportunities to launch turns at possible completion points in Ana's talk (see Mandelbaum, 2013; Sacks *et al.*, 1974), even when Ana attempts to recruit her assistance with a word search.

Excerpt 1

```
1    ANA:        ((gaze to Y)) i really enjoy it. my friends took
2                pictures, a::nd then? [i take the- tsk-
3    YOS:                             m[hm?
4    ANA:        {i don't know the name it is.
5                {(((turns to M))
6    MAY:        {(((gaze to A, covering mouth))
7    ANA:        (must) {figure out.
8                        {(((retracts gaze, points at temple))
9                it was not {boat? u:h-
10                          {((Nina walks in, others turn to look))
11   NIN:                  {hi.
12   ANA:        it was {some thing that you can go insi:de? and see-
13   MAY:    →          {(((leans to left, writes, returns gaze to A))
14   ANA:        {have a view (of high-)          {you know?
15              {(((raises hand, moves from right to left))}{((gaze to M))
16   MAY:    →   {((nodding))
17   ANA:        {in the- it's u:h Roosevelt {(.)square.
18              {((gaze to Y))                {((gaze to M))
19   YOS:        roo{sevelt square?
20   MAY:           {(((tilts head, gaze to A))
21   ANA:        {yes.
22              {((gaze to Y))
23   YOS:        °roosevelt square,  [(  )]°
24   ANA:                            [[stat]ion.
25              {((gaze to M))
26   MAY:                            {(((straightens head, opens mouth))
27   ANA:        °so- station, you have a (.) really nice view,°
28   MAY:    →   o↑::h. okay,
29   ANA:        {yes.
30              {((gaze to Y))
31   YOS:        [uhuh?
```

In Line 2 Ana begins to display trouble locating a word; she interrupts her telling-in-progress to initiate a word search (note the cut-off on *the*, followed by a *tsk*, which is also cut off). She then turns from Yoshi, whom she has been facing and addressing, to May as she states, *I don't know the name it is* (Lines 4–5). She thus formulates the trouble as a lack of (L2) knowledge of the word rather than as a momentary lapse in memory (Koshik & Seo, 2012). While this formulation, coupled with her turning toward May, may constitute an appeal to the teacher, the recipient with greater epistemic authority (Heritage, 2012) on matters of linguistic form, for assistance, May does not offer a candidate solution or attempt to elicit other information from Ana that might help with clarification. As Ana proceeds to offer other formulations of the trouble source word (Lines 9, 12, 14–15), using gesture to support her description of the 'something' that offers a view, May either writes in her notebook (Line 13) or signals alignment as a story recipient by nodding (Line 16) as Ana adds more detailed description. Since May does not intervene in a more substantive way (i.e. as a language expert) in response to Ana's display of linguistic difficulty, Ana is afforded the interactional space to engage in circumlocution and attempt to make her description comprehensible to her recipients. After receiving only nonverbal responses from May, she shifts her gaze back to fellow student Yoshi when she adds further, specific detail about the location, introducing the term Roosevelt Square (Line 17). May treats Roosevelt Square as a recognitional, responding with a high-pitched o↑::h, a change-of-state-token (Heritage, 1984) that displays new understanding (Line 28).

Although May's *oh*, as well as Yoshi's *uhuh* in Line 31, show recognition, Ana does not treat her own description as satisfactory. Immediately after, in Excerpt 2, she re-initiates her word search (note the cut-off on *is* in Line 2, followed by additional cut-offs within the same turn) and offers further formulations, supported by gesture (Lines 3–5, 7–12, 14) until she elicits the sought-after assistance.

Excerpt 2

```
1    YOS:      [uhuh?
2    ANA:      [it is- i- i don't know- it's rai:l-
3              ((gaze to M)) high- rail::- >i don't know.<
4              {it's like that- you can stay-
5              {((gestures square shape))
6    MAY:      ((tilts head, gaze to A))
7    ANA:      {it's hi:gh,      {they go this way
8              {((raises hand))  {((moves hand from right to left))
9              and you have a view. {really nice view.
10                                  {((gaze to Y))
11             it's cheap. it's- u:h how can i say- you don't need
12             to pay for- °it is cheap. so,°
13   MAY:  →   [is that-                        {((gaze to Y))
14   ANA:      [(i had)to:-{i don't know the name {because (   )
15   YOS:                  {now she's explaining her (   )
16                         {((leans to N))
17             (            )
```

```
18    NIN:        o:h.
19    MAY:        {((gaze to N))
20                {we're talking about one story (.) that happened
21                to you (.) during the week.
22    NIN:        mhm. ((nods))
23    ANA:        and it's really nice- you don't needed to pa:y,
24                and you saw uh seeing landscapes. i needed to:
25                take [(   )
26    MAY:   →        [is ↑it a helicopter? like-
27    ANA:        it's not like helicopter.
28                Bu:t {it's like that.
```

May's first possible attempt to assist in the word search comes at Line 13, but the beginning of her turn, *is that-* is produced in overlap with Ana's continuation of her turn (Line 14) and is cut off before a candidate solution is proposed; in other words, May suspends her talk while Ana continues to address Yoshi. After a side sequence (Jefferson, 1972) in which Yoshi and May bring Nina up to speed (Lines 15–22), it seems that Ana may have moved past the trouble source word and on with her telling again (Lines 23–24). She offers a positive assessment of this part of the outing and adds new details about what she did and saw. However, the following *I needed to: take* (Lines 24–25) may signal a return of focus to the problematic term for the mode of transport. In response, May begins, in turn-incursive overlap, to offer *helicopter* as a candidate solution (Line 26). The proposal is delivered in interrogative format with final rising intonation, indicating uncertainty, and Ana responds by rejecting it (Line 27).

As shown in Excerpt 3, Ana's next step toward a solution involves using non-linguistic resources.

Excerpt 3

```
1     ANA:        Bu:t {it's like that.
2                      {((retracts gaze, looks down, picks up pencil))
3                      ((assumes writing posture, draws)) °now °
4     MAY:        @huh huh
5     LIN&MAY:    @huh huh huh huh
6     MAY:   →    $yeah. draw it for us.$=
7     YOS:        =$uhuh,$
8     ANA:        ((drawing in notebook)) °(something) like tha:t- °
9     MAY:   →    O:h.
10    ANA:        ((continues drawing)) you have thi:s- and you- it's like
11                this- ((picks up notebook, runs pen left to right))
12    MAY:        yeah.
13    ANA:        and you were {((gaze to M, raises right arm)) going-
14    MAY:   →                 {it's the: (um)-
15    YOS:        u:huh?
16    MAY:   →    the cable (.) car.
17    ANA:        {yeah.
18                {((nods))
```

Ana proceeds to draw the item (starting in Line 3), an action which May affirms by responding with the agreement token *yeah* and a verbal formulation, *draw it for us*, of what Ana has already begun to do (Line 6). May's *o:h* in Line 9 displays new understanding of the trouble source word. After slight hesitation (note the sound stretch on *the:* and the cut-off), she offers a new solution, *the cable (.) car*, with greater certainty than her original proposal of *helicopter* (note the declarative syntax and final falling intonation) (Lines 14, 16). Ana accepts this solution in Lines 17–18.

Considering Excerpts 1–3 together, we observe the teacher – along with other students – primarily in the 'passive' role of story recipients. They align with Ana's telling by giving her the space to complete it. As a result, Ana has the opportunity to engage in extended talk and use cir-cumlocution to describe the mode of transport for which she seems to lack a term in her L2. May does not initially take up Ana's attempt to involve her in the word search; she treats Ana's description of the cable car as adequate early in the telling. It is Ana's persistence in topicalizing the term by initiating and reinitiating the word search that finally brings about more substantive participation from May. By responding to Ana's orientation to getting the term 'just right', May adds further specificity to the telling.

Once the word search is concluded, and May and Ana both treat 'cable car' as satisfactory, May shifts her attention to other story recipients, as shown in Excerpt 4.

Excerpt 4

```
1    ANA:        {yeah.
2                {((nods))
3    MAY:        [so you took- [roosevelt
4    YOS:        [(seeing)      [roosevelt island.
5    MAY:        yeah. roose[velt is[land.
6    ANA:                   [yes::.
7    YOS:                          [uhuh?
8    MAY:        that station.
9    YOS:        uhuh?
10   MAY:    →   {((gaze to N & L while pointing to A's drawing))
11               {do you all ↓know th[at?
12   LIN:                           [no.
13   NIN:        ((looks up from writing))
14   MAY:    →   so: there's a metro- there's- do you know like between
15               manhattan and uh (.) queens? there's a roosevelt island.
16   ANA:        they [have a bri:dge,
17   LIN(&NIN?):      [O:::::h yeah.
18   MAY:    →   yeah. [and you can take the {cable (.)
19                                           {((sweeps arm up))
20   NIN:              [yeah.
21   MAY:    →   {to:-                  {the island.
22               {((moves arm to right)) {((points down))
23               {and you can (.)        {have a good view.
24               {((retracts arm, points down)){((lowers arm))
25   LIN:        {in the sky?
26               {((raises arm))
27   MAY:    →   yeah in the [sky.
28   ANA:                    [yeah.
29   LIN:        [>o(h)h.<
30   YOS:        [yeah yeah.
31   MAY:        yeah. {°in the sky.°
32   ANA:              {it's really nice. {°i did (it) that (also). it was-
33                     {((gaze to Y))      {((retracts gaze))
34               {(    ). it was very good. °
35               {((gaze to M))
```

Figure 5.2 May's 'cable car' gesture Line 18 MAY: cable

Figure 5.3 May's pointing to the 'island' Line 22 MAY: ((*points down*))

In her turn in Line 3, May seems to be on the path to offering a (re)formulation of how Ana got to Roosevelt Island (*so you took-*), but she halts this turn constructional unit to respond to Yoshi and confirm his use (Line 4) of the recognitional Roosevelt Island (Line 5) (a slight revision of Ana's Roosevelt *Square*), partly in overlap with Ana's own confirmation (Line 6). May then shifts her attention to the other two story recipients, Nina and Lina, who have not signaled recognition of Roosevelt Island or verbally displayed understanding of the telling, as Yoshi has; Nina also arrived late in Ana's telling. While pointing to Ana's drawing, May initiates a side sequence (Jefferson, 1972): she shifts her gaze to Nina and Lina, who are seated across the table from her, and asks *do you all ↓know that?* (Lines 10–11). This understanding check is accomplished through coordinated use of verbal and embodied resources: while directing her gaze, and the question, to her addressees, May also points to Ana's drawing, specifying the *that* which has been the topic of talk.

In response to Lina's *no* (Line 12), May elaborates, offering her own formulation of how to travel to Roosevelt Island (Lines 14–15, 18–19, 21–24). Her use of specific place names not included in Ana's telling (e.g. Queens and Manhattan) suggests that she is drawing on her own, independent knowledge of the tourist attraction. Her description is coupled with iconic gestures that seem to trace the movement of the cable car to the island and back (see Figures 5.2 and 5.3), and Lina and Nina display recognition verbally (Lines 17, 20). While it is May who initiates the side sequence, note that Ana also participates. She adds a clarifying detail in Line 16, and both she and May respond to Lina's confirmation question, *in the sky?* (Line 25), in Lines 27–28. May also repeats some of Ana's own phrasing, *have a good view*, in Line 23. Clarifying for recipients who are not familiar with the place described in the story is thus a collaborative effort. Following additional displays of recognition from Lina and Yoshi (Lines 29–30), Ana directs her gaze to Yoshi as she offers another overall positive assessment of the experience (Lines 32–33). By engaging with another recipient in this way, Ana resumes control of the telling and begins to move it toward closure (Lines 34–35). May's more substantive turns are thus produced, and treated, as supporting the successful completion of the story, rather than as 'taking over'.

Thus, in Excerpts 3–4, we see May shifting the nature and focus of her verbal and embodied participation as she orients to potential needs of the recipients: she moves from helping the teller with a relevant lexical item to initiating a side sequence to help others comprehend the telling or, to put it another way, to ensure that they are engaged as story recipients. She thus contributes in a supportive manner to the overall success of Ana's telling – achievement of mutual understanding.

Task 2: Nina's story

We turn now to a second student telling in which a different pattern of teacher participation can be found. Note first that, at the start of Nina's telling about her visit to an 'amazing' Chinese restaurant in Excerpt 5, May's participation resembles her early participation in Ana's telling: she aligns as a story recipient with the progression of the telling, even when a focus on linguistic form is initiated by the student teller.

Excerpt 5

```
1    NIN:         ((gaze to M)) nothing like (.) ehm (.) ((circle gestures))
2                 extravagant or {something=
3    MAY:    →                   {↑yeah.
4                                 {((nods))
5    NIN:         =happened to me (0.2) this weekend, but yesterday, (.)
6                 i:: met {with a fr↑iend,
7    MAY:    →            {((picks up pen, gaze to notes)) {°mm-hm,°
8                                                          {((gaze to N))
9                 {((gaze to notes, writes))
10   NIN:         {a:::nd with a:: a: american friend and she: (0.3) e::hm
11                (.) {she(m)-
12   MAY:             {((gaze to N))
13   NIN:         >i don't know how to say< but she (0.5)
14                {eh (0.5)
15   MAY:         {((gaze to notes, writes))
16   NIN:         ehm (.) {brought me,
17                        {((gesturing to M))
18   MAY:    →    {((gaze to N, nods))
19   YOS:         {((gaze to N))
20   NIN:         but not {to me
21                        {((gestures to self))
22                {y(eah)- s(ame)- eh instead of a place he brought me
23                {((gesturing to M))
24                {or he:(0.6)
25   MAY:    →    {((nods))
26   NIN:         we went to {a chinese place {i:n chinatown,
27   MAY:    →               {((nods))         {((nods))
28                °mm-hm,°
29   NIN:         {e:h a chinese restaurant {and
30                {((gaze to Y))             {((gaze to M))
31   YOS:                                    {((nods))
32                {it was          {really amazing we ate a: (.)
33   MAY:    →    {((gaze to notes)) {((gaze to N))
34                                  {((Kara walks to seat))
```

Nina prefaces her story by stating that *nothing like* [...] *extravagant* happened to her (Lines 1–2). In response, May simultaneously produces a high-pitched ↑*yeah* and nods (Lines 3–4); she both aligns with the telling's launch and affiliates with the teller's stance (Stivers, 2008), that is, with her characterization of the events to come as not *extravagant* but nevertheless tellable. As Nina proceeds, May looks down and begins to write (Line 7). She continues to switch between the task of taking notes, which is relevant to her pedagogic agenda of leading the class in a discussion of the stories, and aligning as a story recipient. In Lines 7–9, for example, she looks up at Nina and offers a continuer before returning to the note-taking.

In Line 10 Nina begins to display some linguistic difficulty; note the sound stretch on *she*, the subsequent pause and *e::hm*, followed by a micro-pause. May orients to the trouble by looking up (Line 12) as Nina initiates repair with a cut-off on *she* (Line 11). Similar to Ana, as she gazes at the teacher, Nina claims a lack of (L2) knowledge: *I don't know how to say* (Line 13). Having suspended her telling to launch a word search, she pauses again while continuing to gaze at May (Lines 13–14), soliciting the teacher's assistance on this question of form. As she did when Ana initially sought to involve her in a word search, May bypasses the opportunity here to collaborate in the search, orienting instead to her note-taking (Line 15). She looks up again as Nina supplies her own solution (Line 16) and nods, treating 'brought me' as adequate and aligning with the continued progression of the telling (Line 18). Nina, however, does not initially treat this phrase as satisfactory; as her gaze remains directed at May, she provides another, longer formulation in Lines 20–23, repeats 'brought me' (Line 22), and finally replaces 'she brought me' with 'we went' (Line 26). She then moves past her focus on a particular phrasing and begins to add further detail to her telling (starting in Line 26). May continues to align as a story recipient by nodding or offering continuers while occasionally orienting to her notes (Lines 25, 27, 33).

As she proceeds with the telling in Excerpt 6, Nina announces that she has the menu of the restaurant with her and produces it to show the group (Lines 18–19). From this point on, May's independent knowledge of and first-hand experience with the restaurant enable her to participate in Nina's telling in a different manner from Ana's. See also Figures 5.4–5.5, which illustrate changes in May's body positioning and facial expression. (Note that *LL* in the transcript refers to talk from multiple, unidentifiable learners.)

Excerpt 6

```
((10 lines of description of the first dish omitted))
1    NIN:       it was (.) prepared very good.=i have never tried
2    YOS:       {mhm?
3               {((nods))
4    NIN:       that be↑fore,(.) a:nd {it was a very:{crowded place,
5    MAY:                             {((gaze down)) {((gaze up))
6               {((nods))
```

```
 7   NIN:        {she
 8               told me tha:t e::hm: ((gaze down)) she told me that (.)
 9               like (.){fifteen years ago, only japane-
10                        {((gaze up))
11               {>uh-< only chines:e           {knew this place,
12               {((closes eyes, shakes head))  {((gaze to Y))
13   YOS:        {mhm?
14               {((nods))
15   NIN:        {but now it's very {tourist,
16               {((gaze to M))     {((gaze down))
17   MAY:        {((nods))          {((gaze down))
18   NIN:        {((searching in bag))  {((takes out, holds up menu))
19               {i have here the °name {because°  {I ha(h)ve the: the menu?
20   MAY:   →                                      {((gaze up, opens mouth))
21   LL:         [@hhhhhhhh
22   MAY:   →    [↑O::h i think it's {my f-
23   NIN:                            {shang hai
24                                   {((gaze to front of menu))
25               {cafe.
26               {((gaze to M, turns front of menu to class))
27   MAY:   →    that's my (very) favorite restau{rant.
28   LL:                                         {((light laughter, talk))
29   NIN:                                        {it's grea::t.
```

Figure 5.4 May 'doing listening' Line 1
NIN: it was (.) prepared

Figure 5.5 May displaying recognition
Line 20 MAY: ((gaze up, opens mouth))

After Nina removes the menu from her bag, May displays recognition, nonverbally in Line 20 (she opens her mouth wide, as shown in Figure 5.5) and verbally in Line 22 with the high-pitched ↑O::h. May begins to expand in Line 22, but her turn occurs in overlap with laughter from others in response to Nina's holding up the menu and with continued talk from Nina, and she aborts the turn. After Nina shows off the menu and states the full name of the restaurant (Lines 23–25), May announces, in the clear, that it is her favorite restaurant (Line 27). With this assessment, she endorses Nina's positive stance, an affiliative move on the part of a story recipient. As Stivers (2008) has shown, however, recipient assessments produced *mid-telling* may also be seen as disaligning; since they are 'too strong, too soon', they interrupt the progression of the telling. In addition, May is here sharing from her own perspective, as opposed to taking on the teller's perspective; note that she uses the formulation *that's my (very) favorite restaurant* instead of a more general assessment such as *that's a great restaurant*. Nina is now recipient of May's assessment, and she responds with a second, positive assessment (Line 29).

As Nina begins to build up to a possible climax in her story in Excerpt 7, she finds herself in competition with May for the floor. (See also Figures 5.6–5.7, which illustrate changes in May's body positioning, use of gesture and facial expression.)

Excerpt 7

```
1    LL:         {((light laughter, talk))
2    NIN:        {it's grea::t. rea:lly great
3                a:nd (.) when {it cames
4                              {((arm out to M))
5                the:: ((circling gesture)) m- the:: check,
6    MAY:        {>mm-hm.<
7                {((nods))
8    NIN:        (i)/(it) wa{s ama:::z(ed),
9    MAY:    →             {it's s::uper cheap
10                         {((smiles, leans forward))
11               [right? [@heheheh
12   NIN:        [it's   [super cheap.
13   YOS?:              [oh ↑really.
14   MAY:    →   it's {>really really< cheap.=
15                    {((hand up, waves back and forth))
16   NIN:        =we {a:te
17                   {((gaze to menu))
18               {(an-)
19   MAY:    →   {>it's (.) my {favorite<=
20               {((smiles, arm out to N))
21   NIN:                      {((gaze to M))
22               =Yeah. [it's very cheap,=
23   MAY+LL?:           [@heh heh heh heh
```

Figure 5.6 May smiling and leaning forward Line 9 MAY: it's s::uper cheap

Figure 5.7 May waving hand Line 14 MAY: >really really< cheap

Nina projects an upcoming climax in Lines 3–5 with *when it cames the:: (.) m- the:: check*, (when the check came), reporting that she was *ama:::z(ed)* (Line 8). It is May, however, who supplies the upshot in Lines 9–11, *it's s::uper cheap*, using marked prosody (note the stress and vowel elongation). She simultaneously leans forward and smiles, physically inserting herself into the telling (see Figure 5.6). She ends this assessment with a *right?*, seeking confirmation from Nina, who provides it by repeating the assessment in overlap with May's laughter (Line 12). At this point, May is doing something other than being a recipient – she has become an animated and involved co-teller. She goes on to offer similar positive assessments in Lines 14–15 and 19–20 in partial overlap with Nina, even waving her hand back and forth while delivering one assessment in an apparent bid for attention (see Figure 5.7), a noticeable contrast with her previous body positioning (compare Figure 5.4 from earlier in Nina's telling).

May continues to disalign from the telling-in-progress by producing substantive turns that constitute a parallel 'informing' or telling from her

perspective. In addition to her independent, first-hand experience, there is
another basis for her entitlement to tell about the Shanghai Cafe, as
becomes clear at the start of Excerpt 8.

Excerpt 8

```
1    MAY+LL?:            [@heh heh heh heh
2    MAY:    →    =i highly recommend.
3    NIN:         y{eah. ((gaze to menu))
4    MAY:    →    {i'm from shanghai
5    NIN:         {And i ate,
6                 (((holds up menu, gaze to menu, points))
7    MAY:    →    {and (it's) (they) have shanghai food.
8    NIN:         {and i ate (.) those things,
9    YOS:         {((gaze to N))
10   MAY:    →    {((leans back))
11                yeah. {soup dumplings.=
12   NIN:              {((gaze to M))
13   YOS:         =s{(h)oup dumplings.
14   MAY:           {gaze to Y
15   NIN:            {yeah, and she t{ells me (how)
16   MAY:    →                       {XIAO LONG BAO.
17   YOS:                             {gaze to M
18   MAY:    →    xiao {long
19                     {((gaze to LL, then down))
20   YOS:             {((nods, gaze to N))
21   MAY:    →    {bao.
22   NIN:         {yeah.
23                {((gaze to Y, nods))
24                {yea:h,=
25                {((gaze to menu in hands))
26   YOS:         =soup dumpling.
27                {((nods))
28                {o:{:h,
29   NIN:            {and very good,
30                  {((gaze to Y))
31   MAY:    →    {we're changing into (a) chinese class
32                {((smiles))
33                {now.
34   NIN:         {((gaze to M))
35   MAY+LL:      @HA HA HA
36   MAY:         (okay.) ve:r{y {good.
37                            {((gaze down))
38   NIN:                     {and very good, and uh
39                            {((gaze to menu, points to menu))
40                {she taught me (.) how to eat it {because they're
41                {((gaze to Y))                    {((gaze to menu))
42                (.) [they have
43   YOS:            [>yeah yeah yeah.<
44   NIN:         steam inside so ((continues))
```

After personally recommending the restaurant in Line 2, May states
that she is from Shanghai (Line 4), accounting for her ability to assess the
quality of the food, and perhaps also for her continuing intervention in the
telling. It is not only the case that the restaurant is her favorite; by invoking the category 'Shanghai native', a category in which Nina cannot claim
membership, May positions herself as specially qualified to evaluate the
restaurant. Arguably, May temporarily 'steals the spotlight' from the

student whose experience should, according to the pedagogic goals of the task, be the focus of talk.

As a result of May's competitive participation, Nina must engage in extra interactional work to maintain a claim to the floor and to move her telling forward, and she employs both linguistic and embodied resources to do so. At various points, she launches turns in overlap with May (e.g. Lines 22, 29, 38); she makes use of a recycled turn beginning (Schegloff, 1987) when the start of one turn is absorbed in overlap (Line 8); she raises and points to the menu as a bid for attention (Line 6); and she shifts her gaze to recruit or maintain the attention of other recipients (e.g. to Yoshi in Line 23). More subtly, she also shifts from assessing the restaurant to attempting to describe what she ate during her visit – not, in theory, something that May could contribute to reporting on. May, however, correctly supplies the menu item that Nina points to in Line 11, *soup dumplings*. After Yoshi apparently repeats the term (Line 13), May directs her gaze to him and provides the Chinese name at a louder volume (Lines 14, 16).

As May repeats the Chinese name of the dish at a regular volume, she directs her gaze first to the other students and then down to her notebook (Lines 18–19, 21). Perhaps orienting to her own participation as disaligning or 'off-task', May says with a smile in Lines 31–33 that the class has become a Chinese class. After this, there is a clearer withdrawal from the telling as she utters the positive assessment *ve:ry good* (Line 36), signaling the closing down of her own participation (although it may not be clear to participants exactly what she is assessing: the restaurant/dishes or the students'/Nina's participation). Nina, who has displayed her interactional competence as a storyteller in maintaining her claim to the floor and pursuing her topic, is able to continue her report of how she was taught to eat the dumplings (begun in Line 15) in Line 40. In fact, she goes on to further develop her telling, describing a visit to another eatery for ice cream, garnering affiliative responses from recipients and leading May to joke that the whole class should dine out in Chinatown together (not shown in the transcript).

Thus, as shown in Excerpts 6–8, May's grab for the spotlight through more frequent, animated and substantive turns, along with her body movements and animated use of gesture and facial expression, pushes Nina to employ practices that may be necessary in storytelling in multiparty interactional contexts outside the classroom, where multi-unit turns are not typically bestowed on speakers by a single manager of interaction. It is May's verbal and embodied intervention in the telling that enables such interaction to occur in the classroom.

Discussion and Conclusion

In the preceding analysis, we have focused on illuminating how one ESL teacher and her students engage in what turn out to be quite different storytellings. In the two cases examined, we observe the teacher moving in and out of various roles throughout the course of the student tellings, exercising interactional options that lead to differing outcomes for learner participation. 'Facilitation' of classroom interaction, in the data examined here, thus takes different shapes and forms and involves the use of both linguistic and embodied resources.

We might say that by aligning as *recipient* early in the tellings and avoiding the heavy-handed approach of intervening at each sign of trouble in the students' talk, the teacher affords both Ana and Nina the opportunity to practice communication strategies when they find themselves lacking key lexical items in the L2. When the teacher does intervene more substantively in Ana's telling, it is first in the role of *language consultant*, which she takes up in response to the student's own repeated pursuit of a specific term. She also intervenes in Ana's telling in the supporting role of *content mediator*, checking and working to ensure that other recipients remain engaged and that Ana's telling is well received (see also Seedhouse, 2004). In contrast, during part of Nina's telling, the teacher's heightened involvement, her competing for the floor and contributions as *co-* or *competitive teller*, briefly affords the more fluent Nina practice in the kind of storytelling she may participate in outside of class. In both cases, we see the teacher responding, in the moment, to the content, experiences and interactional resources that the students bring to this open-ended activity.

While studies of classroom interaction have tended to foreground the significance of teacher *talk*, the preceding analysis offers evidence of the centrality of the teacher's embodied conduct in enacting these different roles. In our data, we note a progression from more 'minimal' bodily conduct to more animated conduct in parallel with the teacher's verbal participation. For instance, in the role of *recipient*, the teacher nods to display alignment with the telling-in-progress. As a *content mediator*, she uses deictic and iconic gestures to support the comprehension of other recipients. And finally, the teacher's shifts in body positioning and more animated use of facial expression and gesture help to constitute the role of *co-* or *competitive teller*. We thus hope to have shown how verbal and embodied communicative resources may work together in a *gestalt*-like manner, mutually elaborating each other (Mondada, 2014, 2016).

We also hope to have illustrated the complexity of the teacher's task when it comes to working with extended student contributions in the L2 classroom, as well as the flexibility in the deployment of communicative resources that is required to do so (see also Waring, 2016, for a discussion of the principles of complexity and contingency in pedagogic interaction). After adopting an initial 'non-interventionist' role, the teacher works with what individual students are capable of doing; her actions are responsive to the students' own interactional competencies as L2 conversationalists. We also observe that her interventions in student tellings orient not only to the needs of the tellers but also to possible comprehension difficulties on the part of the recipients. How teachers manage to attend not only to an individual student but to the needs of the group is worth further examination as a component of the work of teaching (Fagan, 2015; see also Can Daşkın, 2015; Walsh, 2006, 2011).

Although we cannot claim on the basis of these two cases that the practices observed are generalizable to similar classroom settings, what we hope to have provided is a nuanced view of what may be involved for the teacher in managing or facilitating meaning-and-fluency-focused interaction. Rather than view the roles and resources discussed here as a checklist for teachers to follow (do X first, then do Y, in this way), practices uncovered through CA are best viewed as possibilities (Peräkylä, 2004) or, as Pomerantz (1990: 234) has put it, 'proposals regarding the resources that interactants use and their methods of accomplishing social actions'. We offer these proposals as opportunities for teachers and teacher educators to consider how what is done, or not done, at each point by the teacher shapes subsequent student participation, and how these outcomes relate to the intended pedagogic focus (see also Walsh, 2006, 2011).

In the end, both Ana and Nina were able to engage in practice in the L2 that may have benefited their learning in different ways. We are, however, left wondering to what extent the activity afforded them the opportunity to practice *storytelling*, as was intended. Rather than negotiating story launch, the students were, generally speaking, assigned slots for extended talk. That the teacher could participate more conversationally in parts of Nina's telling was a 'happy accident' (she happened to know the restaurant and had a personal connection to it). This raises the question of if and how opportunities for the kinds of practice Nina engages in can be engineered in the L2 classroom, and with what consequences for individual students who exhibit varying levels of linguistic and interactional competence.

References

Bannink, A. (2002) Negotiating the paradoxes of spontaneous talk in advanced L2 classes. In C.J. Kramsch (ed.) *Language Acquisition and Language Socialization: Ecological Perspectives* (pp. 266–289). New York: Continuum.

Can Daşkın, N. (2015) Shaping learner contributions in an EFL classroom: Implications for L2 classroom interactional competence. *Classroom Discourse* 6 (1), 33–56.

Cazden, C.B. (1988) *Classroom Discourse: The Language of Teaching and Learning*. Portsmouth, NH: Heinemann.

Fagan, D. (2012) Dealing with unexpected learner contributions in whole group activities: An examination of novice language teacher discursive practices. *Classroom Discourse* 3 (2), 107–128.

Fagan, D. (2015) Managing language errors in real-time: A microanalysis of teacher practices. *System* 55, 74–85.

Goodwin, C. (1986) Between and within: Alternative sequential treatments of continuers and assessments. *Human Studies* 9, 205–217.

Hall, J.K. (1998) Differential teacher attention to student utterances: The construction of different opportunities for learning in the IRF. *Linguistics and Education* 9, 287–311.

Hellermann, J. and Pekarek Doehler, S. (2010) On the contingent nature of language-learning tasks. *Classroom Discourse* 1 (1), 25–45.

Heritage, J. (1984) A change-of-state token and aspects of its sequential placement. In J. Maxwell Atkinson and J. Heritage (eds) *Structures of Social Action: Studies in Conversation Analysis* (pp. 299–345). Cambridge: Cambridge University Press.

Heritage, J. (2012) Epistemics in action: Action formation and territories of knowledge. *Research on Language and Social Interaction* 45 (1), 1–29.

Jefferson, G. (1972) Side sequences. In D.N. Sudnow (ed.) *Studies in Social Interaction* (pp. 294–338). New York: Free Press.

Jefferson, G. (2004) Glossary of transcript symbols with an introduction. In G. Lerner (ed.) *Conversation Analysis: Studies from the First Generation* (pp. 13–31). Amsterdam: John Benjamins.

Käänta, L. (2012) Teachers' embodied allocations in instructional interaction. *Classroom Discourse* 3 (2), 166–186.

Koshik, I. and Seo, M.-S. (2012) Word (and other) search sequences initiated by language learners. *Text & Talk* 32 (2), 167–189.

Majlesi, A.R. (2015) Matching gestures: Teachers' repetitions of students' gestures in second language learning classrooms. *Journal of Pragmatics* 76, 30–45.

Mandelbaum, J. (2013) Storytelling in conversation. In J. Sidnell and T. Stivers (eds) *The Handbook of Conversation Analysis* (pp. 492–507). Oxford and New York: Wiley-Blackwell.

Markee, N. (2015) CA-for-SLA studies of classroom interaction: Quo vadis? In N. Markee (ed.) *The Handbook of Classroom Discourse and Interaction* (pp. 425–440). Oxford: Wiley-Blackwell.

Matsumoto, Y. and Dobs, A.M. (2017) Pedagogical gestures as interactional resources for teaching and learning tense and aspect in the ESL grammar classroom. *Language Learning* 67 (1), 7–42.

Mehan, H. (1979) *Learning Lessons: Social Organization in the Classroom.* Cambridge, MA: Harvard University Press.

Mondada, L. (2014) The local constitution of multimodal resources for social interaction. *Journal of Pragmatics* 65, 137–156.

Mondada, L. (2016) Challenges of multimodality: Language and the body in social interaction. *Journal of Sociolinguistics* 20 (3), 336–366.

Mori, J. (2002) Task design, plan, and development of talk-in-interaction: A study of a small group activity in a Japanese language classroom. *Applied Linguistics* 23, 323–347.

Nassaji, H. and Wells, G. (2000) What's the use of 'triadic dialogue'? An investigation of teacher–student interaction. *Applied Linguistics* 21 (3), 376–406.

Nevile, M. (2015) The embodied turn in research on language and social interaction. *Research on Language and Social Interaction* 48 (2), 121–151.

Peräkylä, A. (2004) Reliability and validity in research based on naturally occurring social interaction. In D. Silverman (ed.) *Qualitative Research: Theory, Method, and Practice* (2nd edn) (pp. 283–304). London: Sage.

Pomerantz, A. (1990) On the validity and generalizability of conversation analytic methods: Conversation analytic claims. *Communication Monographs* 57 (3), 231–235.

Reddington, E. (2018) Managing participation in the adult ESL classroom: Engagement and exit practices. *Classroom Discourse* 9 (2), 132–149.

Richards, K. (2006) Being the teacher: Identity and classroom conversation. *Applied Linguistics* 27 (1), 51–77.

Sacks, H., Schegloff, E.A. and Jefferson, G. (1974) A simplest systematics for the organization of turn-taking for conversation. *Language* 50 (4), 696–735.

Schegloff, E.A. (1982) Discourse as an interactional achievement: Some uses of 'uh huh' and other things that come between sentences. *Analyzing Discourse: Text and Talk* 71, 93.

Schegloff, E.A. (1987) Recycled turn beginnings: A precise repair mechanism in conversation's turn-taking organization. *Talk and Social Organisation* 1, 70–85.

Schegloff, E.A. (2007) *Sequence Organization in Interaction: A Primer in Conversation Analysis, Vol. 1*. Cambridge: Cambridge University Press.

Seedhouse, P. (2004) *The Interactional Architecture of the Language Classroom: A Conversation Analysis Perspective*. Malden, MA: Blackwell.

Sert, O. (2015) *Social Interaction and L2 Classroom Discourse*. Edinburgh: Edinburgh University Press.

Sinclair, J.M. and Coulthard, M. (1975) *Towards an Analysis of Discourse: The English Used by Teachers and Pupils*. London: Oxford University Press.

Stivers, T. (2008) Stance, alignment, and affiliation during storytelling: When nodding is a token of affiliation. *Research on Language and Social Interaction* 41 (1), 31–57.

ten Have, P. (2007) *Doing Conversation Analysis* (2nd edn). Thousand Oaks, CA: Sage.

van Lier, L. (1996) *Interaction in the Language Curriculum: Awareness, Autonomy and Authenticity*. New York: Longman.

Walsh, S. (2002) Construction or obstruction: Teacher talk and learner involvement in the EFL classroom. *Language Teaching Research* 6 (1), 3–23.

Walsh, S. (2006) *Investigating Classroom Discourse*. New York: Routledge.

Walsh, S. (2011) *Exploring Classroom Discourse: Language in Action*. Abingdon: Routledge.

Waring, H.Z. (2014) Managing control and connection in an adult ESL classroom. *Research in the Teaching of English* 49 (1), 52–74.

Waring, H.Z. (2016) *Theorizing Pedagogical Interaction: Insights from Conversation Analysis*. New York: Routledge.

Waring, H.Z., Creider, S. and Box, C.D. (2013) Explaining vocabulary in the second language classroom: A conversation analytic account. *Learning, Culture and Social Interaction* 2, 249–264.

6 Teacher Embodied Responsiveness to Student Displays of Trouble within Small-group Activities

Drew S. Fagan

While much work has uncovered what 'teaching' entails in whole-class settings, investigations into what this looks like in small-group activities remains minimal. The current conversation analytic (CA) study addresses this quandary by examining the embodied achievement of teaching that one English for speakers of other languages (ESOL) teacher accomplishes when responding to student troubles within small-group activities. Specifically, it focuses on how such responsiveness is systematically accomplished in teacher self-selected turns, or those turns that the students have not overtly invited her to take. Stemming from 10 hours of small-group interactional video data, two overarching findings emerged, highlighting the actions that are done in those turns. First, when orienting to student displays of trouble with activity content, the teacher's embodied actions *mark the path* for students to work through those troubles and continue toward the activity's final product. Secondly, when orienting to student displays of trouble with interactional expansion, the teacher's embodied actions *mobilize elaboration*. The findings suggest that doing 'teaching' in small groups is indeed complex, where the teacher directly and succinctly addresses students' trouble sources while simultaneously ensuring that the small-group activity remains a student-led, student-responsible interactional space.

Introduction

Doing 'teaching' is viewed as intricate and complex due to the high levels of coordination needed to address multiple and simultaneous actions moment to moment. As examples of this, Ball and Forzani (2009) highlight that teachers:

> keep track of [all] students as they move through content, keep their eye on the learning goals, attend to the integrity of the subject matter, manage

individual student behavior and maintain a productive learning environment, pose strategically targeted questions, interpret students' work, craft responses, assess, and steer all of this towards each student's growth. (Ball & Forzani, 2009: 501)

Researchers have focused on how such diverse actions are succinctly accomplished in classroom interactions through teachers' embodied actions; these actions, as found in the literature, are based on teachers' orientations to students' embodied actions in prior turns-at-talk. Examples include eliciting student talk (e.g. Fagan, 2018; Lee, 2006; Toohey, 2000), giving feedback (e.g. Fagan, 2015; Thoms, 2014; Waring, 2008) and responding to student initiations (e.g. Ishino, 2017; Sert, 2017).

It is not surprising that the majority of this scholarship stems from whole-class, teacher-led interactions, where teacher and student are jointly viewed as having overt participatory roles in the interactive construction of the talk (Wells, 1993). In contrast, the research investigating small-group activity interaction has focused on students' interactions, given that these activities allow for student-led, student-responsible engagement with various tools as they work through a task, characteristics which are perceived[1] as limited in whole-class sequences-of-talk (Hellermann & Cole, 2009). Examinations of teachers' interactions in connection to such activities, however, are minimal (Hofmann & Mercer, 2016). Within the education literature, looking into teacher engagement with small-group activities has been mostly relegated to examining the different roles teachers play in promoting student interactions and task collaboration (Gillies & Khan, 2009). On the one hand, teachers are viewed as stage setters who compose groups, mark student roles and frame the purpose of the small-group work prior to activity commencement (Corden, 2001; Webb *et al.*, 2017). One the other hand, teachers are also viewed as guides during the activity, asking for elaboration, providing feedback to encourage further interaction and promoting connections to students' own lives outside of the activity (Gillies, 2004; McIntyre *et al.*, 2006; Rainer Dangel & Durden, 2010).

While this work highlights potential teacher roles in connection to small-group activities, it does not uncover 'how language is actually used by teachers … to orchestrate learning within [these] activities' (Bloome, 2015: 138). In other words, there is a lack of empirical evidence detailing the highly specialized, intricate work that is accomplished by teachers taking part in student-led, student-responsible small-group interactions. To address this, this chapter examines the embodied achievement of teaching that one ESOL teacher does when self-selecting turns in small-group interactions to respond to what she orients to as student troubles with the activity. This includes investigating: (1) the embodied actions done by students which the teacher orients to as displays of trouble; (2) the embodied actions accomplished in the teacher's turns-at-talk when responding to those student displays of trouble; and (3) the effects of the teacher's actions on subsequent student interaction.

Background

In contrast to turns in whole-class activities, those in small-group activities are largely student driven through self-selection, nomination of another for next turn and response to another's nomination. To situate how and why a teacher enters this student-dominated interactional space, three areas of research are presented: soliciting and responding vis-à-vis summons–answer sequences, marking recipiency for solicitations and displaying epistemic stance in talk-in-interaction.

Instances of student initiations which solicit teacher assistance often surface in summons–answer (SA) sequences (Cekaite, 2009). Minimally, this sequence consists of a summons turn incorporating attention-getting devices designed to get the recipient's attention and an answer turn illustrating the recipient's orientation to the first-turn summons (Schegloff, 1968). SA sequences hold specific properties that illustrate a clear connection between the two turns. For example, the non-occurrence of an answer turn leads to the summons turn being repeated until an answer is provided. In addition, a turn cannot be labeled a summons unless the next turn is constructed in a way that shows the recipient's orientation to the prior turn as being a summons. The proximity of the two turns is also restricted in that 'an item that may be used as an answer to a summons may not be heard to constitute an answer to a summons if it occurs separate from the summons' (Schegloff, 1968: 1084).

SA sequences-of-talk are also nonterminal; in other words, the interaction does not end with this sequence but continues in some form with both interlocutors taking part. The original summoner continues the interaction by doing something in the interaction with the answer provided, even if it entails abandoning the original course of action (e.g. Summoner: 'Hey!'; Recipient: 'Yes?'; Summoner: 'Forget it.'). Continued interaction is also the responsibility of the recipients in that, by virtue of answering the summons, 'they commit themselves to staying with the encounter' (Schegloff, 1968: 1083).

Bridging the work on SA sequences with classroom discourse, Cekaite (2009) identifies two tasks that students must do in order to solicit teachers vis-à-vis summonses: establish the teacher's attention and clearly indicate what it is they want to share so that student and teacher have a mutual understanding of what is being addressed. To achieve these tasks, students utilize a multitude of embodied actions which include verbal cues (e.g. teacher address turns, increased intonation signaling question, loudness), nonverbal conduct (e.g. proximity to teacher, body torque toward teacher) and use of physical artifacts (e.g. putting a textbook in front of teacher) (Gardner, 2015). Once teachers orient to learners' actions as summonses, how they choose to address them varies depending on the teachers' orientations to the summonses as being relevant to the content at hand (Shepherd, 2012), occurring within activities or at activity boundaries (Jacknick, 2011) or following the activity's planned progression (Waring *et al.*, 2016).

Identifying student solicitations and teacher responses also entails understanding how solicitation recipiency is constructed and oriented to. Often, the intended recipient is clearly identified in the summons turn through direct addressing (e.g. 'Teacher, I need help.') (e.g. Cekaite, 2009; Lehtimaja, 2011). In other cases, recipiency is identified vis-à-vis actions in prior turns such as the intended recipient being the only other interlocutor in the talk or being the one who provided information about which the solicitor needs further information (Lerner, 2003). Conversely, various cues used by recipients in their turns show that they have oriented to the prior summons as meant for them, including redirection of eye gaze toward the summoner and quick self-selection of the next turn following the summons to provide an answer (Mortensen, 2009; Schegloff, 2007).

While establishing that recipiency is, more often than not, already understood through the various means presented above, Schegloff (2007) cautions that neither overt marking of a recipient nor a recipient overtly interacting in the prior talk are requisites for someone to take on the role of recipient. As found through the use of retrospective inferencing, any interlocutor involved in the interaction in some way who has oriented to the prior turn as a summons can take on the role of recipient. It is this understanding of recipiency from the recipient's perspective, not the summoner's, that allows for further in-depth analyses of what actions constitute solicitations for assistance.

One final point in understanding student solicitations and teacher responses is the notion of epistemic displays. Defined as 'the knowledge claims that interactants assert, contest, and defend in and through turns-at-talk and sequences-of-interaction' (Heritage, 2013: 370), epistemics have been investigated in terms of what cues are both used and oriented to by interlocutors to display knowing and unknowing stances in interaction. These cues and the orientations to them play a significant role in constructing action formation within and across sequences-of-talk. Heritage (2012) further highlights how displays of unknowing epistemic stance invite elaboration from others, thus leading to sequence expansion. This can be initiated by the unknowing interlocutor through what Jakonen and Morton (2015) call *epistemic search sequences* (ESSs). In ESSs, interlocutors display their unknowing stances by overtly soliciting information from others. Through solicitation, the unknowing interlocutor places the recipient in the position of knowing and makes the recipient accountable for their knowledge claim.

In other instances, it is another participant in the interaction who, in their orientation to the cues displayed by the first interlocutor, self-selects turns to address the unknowing stance of that first person. Sert (2013), in looking at teacher–student interactions in whole-class settings, examines the communicative cues used by students that teachers orient to as displays of their epistemic stance. He shows how teachers orient to student response delays as displays of unknowing, leading the teachers to self-select the next turn and do what he labels *epistemic status checks* (ESCs), which include teachers verbalizing their interpretation of the student's state of knowledge (e.g. 'You don't know?') for the purposes of pursuing a pedagogical goal. Similarly, Kääntä (2014) shows the systematicity with which students self-select turns to initiate correction of what they perceive to be potential errors made by the teacher, thus displaying not only their knowing stance but also the teacher's unknowing stance.

The literature presented here contextualizes various factors that could affect how and why a teacher would enter student-centered small-group interactions; specifically, teacher interactional entrance into these spaces is dependent on student prior actions that may or may not include overtly soliciting the teacher to address a trouble source. In connecting these research areas to teacher entry into small-group activity interaction, two points can be extrapolated: the various embodied actions students do in their turns-at-talk in small-group activities that teachers orient to as solicitations for assistance; and the way in which teachers construct their turns-at-talk within small-group activities as a reaction to how they have oriented to students' prior actions. Taking these into account, the current study looks into one ESOL teacher's self-selected turns in small-group activities (i.e. when she has *not* been overtly nominated by the students to enter the talk), by uncovering the discursive factors affecting her in-the-moment decisions to self-select turns, the embodied actions done within those turns and the effects of the actions in those turns on students' subsequent interaction.

Data and Method

The data for this study stem from 26 hours of video-recorded classroom interactions from an adult ESOL community program course associated with a university in the United States; 10 of those hours were of small-group work and were the data source used here. This community program caters to the university's local neighborhood and focuses on helping the students understand everyday interactions needed for living in the United States, whether oral or written. Each course has 50 hours of classroom contact per semester.

The teacher participant, Ann,[2] was a master teacher in the program. The role of a master teacher is twofold: to provide high-quality instruction for students and to model and guide effective instructional strategies for the novice teachers in the program, all of whom are teachers-in-training within the university's Teaching English to speakers of other languages

(TESOL) education program (Program Director, personal communication). At the time of the study, Ann had over 30 years of language teaching and teacher education experience and was a doctoral student in applied linguistics. The course she taught was the most advanced in the program. Aggregate scores from an entrance examination that covers the four language skills (listening, speaking, reading and writing) are used for placement; thus, students who are strong in some language skills but slightly weaker in others may still be placed in this highest level. At the time of the study, 11 students were in Ann's course, all of whom varied in age, educational backgrounds, English learning experiences, careers, days in attendance and language skill strengths and weaknesses.

Conversation analysis (CA) was utilized to examine the transcribed video data. Central to CA examinations is addressing why a specific action is being done in a specific way at a specific point in time, i.e. 'why that now' (Schegloff & Sacks, 1973: 299). Doing this entails performing line-by-line microanalyses of the discourse data from which recurring patterns begin to emerge, illustrating how the interlocutors construct their turns-at-talk based on how they have oriented to others' prior turns. Through the lens of CA, the 10 hours of small-group video-recordings were transcribed using Jefferson's (2004) system. Following transcription, initial line-by-line analyses were done on the discourse data from which all instances where Ann self-selected turns were identified. For each instance, students' prior turns leading up to Ann's self-selected ones, as well as student turns following Ann's, were extracted and put into their own data set. Subsequent line-by-line analyses of this data set were then done, from which distinct actions used by Ann in those self-selected turns began to emerge and were then separated from one another. Further analyses of the excerpts in these separate groups revealed the factors found to influence the varied embodied actions used by Ann when responding to what she oriented to as students' displays of trouble in need of assistance.

Findings

In examining Ann's self-selected turns during small-group activities, two overarching findings emerged. The first focused on Ann's turn construction when orienting to students' displays of trouble with an activity's content. In response to these student displays, Ann's embodied actions in her self-selected turns accomplished what I call *marking the path* toward activity completion. The second focused on the construction of Ann's turns when orienting to students' displays of interactional trouble within activities whose intended goals were interactional practice as opposed to completing a specific product. When such displays emerged, Ann's embodied actions accomplished what I call *mobilizing elaboration* among group members. In the following sections – excerpts illustrating the factors affecting Ann's in-the-moment decisions to *mark the path* and *mobilize elaboration* – the varied constructions of these actions and their effects on subsequent student talk are presented. In each excerpt, → marks Ann's embodied action turns.

Marking the path

Within Ann's self-selected turns, the embodied actions of *marking the path* surfaced when she oriented to evidence in the interaction of student troubles with the content of the activity potentially preventing them from completing the activity's final product (e.g. a worksheet). This is exemplified in Excerpt 1, where *marking the path* directs students toward a part of the activity that they have overlooked. Here, the students were first asked to individually guess the states on an empty map of the United States. They were then put into pairs to compare their answers before returning as a whole class to review the map. Ann has been listening in on Clara and Arata who have been reviewing the northern middle part of the map; Arata had identified a few states there while Clara had not identified any.

Excerpt 1

```
1    CLA:        {for minnesota where did you put-
2                {(((uses finger to circle around northern part of map))
3                (0.4)
4    ARA:        i chose {it here. for me.          {but i do(hh)n't know.
5                        {(((points to Clara's sheet)) {(((puts hand up))

             ((lines omitted- Ann jokes about being from Minnesota))

6    CLA:        {and i don't remember any of these.
7                {(((points to sheet))
8                (0.4)
9    ARA:        {it's called (0.2) lakes.
10               {(((gazing at Clara's sheet))
11   CLA:        {oh yeah?
12               {(((waves hand in air))
13   ARA:        @haha.
14               {(4.2)
15               {(((Arata and Clara gaze at sheets not marking them))
16   ANN:  →     now (.) you have to remember {canada (0.2) is up here.
17         →                                  {(((points to Clara's sheet))
18   CLA:        {uh-huh?
19               {(((nods to her sheet))
20   ARA:        {yes.
21               {[(((looks at Clara's sheet and nods))
22   ANN:  →     {right here.
23         →     {(((points to map))
24               {(2.8)
25               {(((all three gaze at Clara's sheet))
26         →     {canada is really (.) comes over to about here.
27         →     {(((moves finger over map))
28   CLA:        <mhm? {and here's maine?
29                    {(((points to map))
30   ANN:        {yeah. that's very good.
31               {(((takes finger off map, nods, and steps back))
32               [well done. yeah. yeah.
33   CLA:        [°yes.°
34   ARA:        [(((nods at Clara's sheet and writes on his))
35   CLA:        and massachussetts is {near here too.
36                                     {(((points near Maine))
```

Lines 1–15 show Clara's and Arata's various displays of epistemic stance. First, Clara in Lines 1–2 asks Arata where he put Minnesota, potentially in reference to a comment Ann made earlier about being from Minnesota and its being in the north. Clara's turn puts Arata into the position of knowing and makes him accountable for his claim (Jakonen & Morton, 2015). This is evident when Arata points to Clara's map and says what he chose (Lines 4–5), although he mitigates this with two *post-expansions* (Schegloff, 2007), 'For me' and 'But I don't know', accompanied by *metaphoric gesture* (McNeill, 1992) with his hand, all of which appear to be done to exonerate himself from accountability. Clara continues to display her unknowing epistemic stance in Lines 6–7 as she points to a specific part of the map. Looking at where Clara is pointing, Arata takes the next turn to clarify: 'It's called lakes.' Clara orients to this response as new information as shown by the cues used in Lines 11–12: the use of discourse marker 'oh' (Heritage, 2002) followed by 'yeah' with increased intonation (Couper-Kuhlen, 2001). In Lines 14–15 both students gaze back to their maps for 4.2 seconds without marking them or initiating further talk.

Although Arata displays knowledge about the lakes (Lines 9–10), many of these turns are displays of not knowing (Lines 1–2, 6–7, 11–12) or, at most, mitigated knowing (Lines 4–5). Orienting to these displays as solicitations for assistance, Ann self-selects the turn in Lines 16–17 to provide the students with information that they have yet to discuss or mark on their maps. She emphasizes that they 'have to remember that Canada is up here' while simultaneously pointing to Canada on Clara's worksheet. Notice Ann pointing to Clara's sheet in all of her turns, the same artifact used as a reference by both students in Lines 1–15. Throughout Ann's turns (Lines 16–17, 22–23, 26–27) neither Clara nor Arata gaze up at Ann; instead, they follow her finger on Clara's map (Figure 6.1).

Figure 6.1 Excerpt 1, Lines 16–17, 22–23, 26–27

Ann's finger movement in Line 27 is what Clara responds to by pointing out Maine's location, the first time she displays a knowing stance in the activity; Maine is also a state neither she nor Arata had focused on in their earlier interaction. In response to this, Ann provides Clara with *explicit positive assessments* (EPAs) (Waring, 2008) in Lines 30 and 32, while also removing her finger from Clara's map and stepping back from the group in Line 31. These uses of sequence-closing EPAs and the changes in nonverbal conduct display Ann's interactional disengagement from the group. The excerpt ends with Arata and Clara continuing the activity by moving to the eastern part of the map.

In addition to providing students with points they overlooked in their activity, *marking the path* also provides students with a new perspective on a particular activity item with which they display struggles in understanding. Taking place 30 seconds following the previous excerpt, Ann continues to stand off to the side listening in on Clara and Arata as they discuss the eastern half of the map:

Excerpt 2

```
1      CLA:          {and washington de:ce: <i think> is somewhere ove::r-
2                    {((makes circular motion on eastern half of map))
3      ANN:    →     {<w↑ashington dc [[is like <this big.>
4              →     {(((steps closer))[{((forms small hole with fingers))
5      CLA:                            [((gazes at Ann))
6      ARA:          [((gazes at Ann))
7      ANN:    →     [[it's ti:ny.
8              →     [[(((continues forming small hole with fingers))
9      CLA:          ye:ah.
10     ARA:          a:h.
11     ANN:    →     it's ti:ny tiny.
12     CLA:          {then i don't know where is washington dc.
13                   {((to Arata while looking at her sheet))
14     ARA:          {maybe this is it.
15                   {((points to sheet))
16     CLA:          ((looks at Arata's sheet and nods))
17     ANN:          ((looks at group while walking away))
```

In Lines 1–2 Clara displays some knowledge of the task at hand, i.e. Washington's general vicinity, as shown by her circling over the eastern portion of the map. Simultaneous to doing this, she verbalizes her knowledge of Washington's general location, although this is mitigated with 'I think'. Throughout her turn, Clara also uses slow speech and sound elongation, two verbal cues which signal current speaker maintaining speakership while doing a search (Couper-Kuhlen, 2001) – in this case, searching for Washington, DC.

Although Clara displays a searching stance through her use of slow speech and sound elongation, these cues can also be oriented to by others as displays of unknowing, allowing those others to self-select the next turn (Clark & Schaefer, 1989). This is what Ann does in Lines 3–4 where she begins *marking the path* for Clara and Arata by providing a new perspective on their search for Washington: focusing on size.

Figure 6.2 Excerpt 2, Lines 3–5

In addition to verbalization, Ann incorporates *iconic gesturing* (McNeill, 1992) in her turn to emphasize Washington's size. Ann's actions in Lines 3–4 are done in overlap with Clara changing gaze to focus on Ann's gesture (Line 5) (Figure 6.2). Arata also does this in Line 6 in overlap with Ann's turn in Lines 7–8 where she uses verbal cues in the form of sound elongation with the word 'tiny' to further emphasize smallness (Figure 6.3).

In response to Ann's embodied actions in Lines 3–4 and 7–8, Clara and Arata provide acknowledgement markers in Lines 9 and 10, respectively, marking receipt of the information. Following Ann's further use of cues to emphasize Washington's size (Line 11), Clara responds to this new-found information in Lines 12–13 with a change in her epistemic stance to one of unknowing. Arata, however, takes Ann's information and proceeds to guess where it is on the map (Lines 14–15), to which Clara then provides nonverbal agreement (Line 16) as Ann continues looking at the group but begins walking away to another group (Line 17).

As shown in the first pair of excerpts, Ann's embodied actions of *marking the path* are done when she orients to students' actions in prior turns as displays of trouble with the activity's content. It is this

Figure 6.3 Excerpt 2, Lines 6–8

orientation, as opposed to any overt soliciting from the students, that leads Ann to enter the discourse by self-selecting turns to address these displayed troubles. When the students display unknowing epistemic stances over the course of numerous turns, Ann *marks the path* by noting points they may have overlooked in the activity. When they display some form of knowledge of a particular task item, although not full knowledge, *marking the path* entails providing a different perspective on that particular item not previously noted by the students. Specific characteristics of *marking the path* are consistent across its different manifestations. First, Ann's actions include a multitude of cues beyond simple verbalization of ideas. With Excerpt 1, Ann simultaneously verbalizes the importance of considering Canada while also marking it on the map, thus using the same physical artifact in her turns that the students themselves used in their earlier turns. With Excerpt 2, the combined use of verbal prosodic cues (e.g. sound elongation) and nonverbal conduct (e.g. iconic gesturing) put emphasis on the size of Washington, DC, a perspective the students did not display realization of in their earlier turns. Secondly, *marking the path* does not include the teacher providing answers to the activity but rather guiding the students through their difficulties with the content; in this way, the students are still responsible for completing the activity. Finally, the embodied actions done when *marking the path* do not end until there is evidence from the students of activity continuation. It is only then that Ann displays disengagement with the interaction both verbally and nonverbally.

Mobilizing elaboration

While *marking the path* surfaced within small-group activities the goals of which were to complete a specified final product, such as filling in a map, the embodied actions of *mobilizing elaboration* occurred in activities the goals of which were interaction in the target language, i.e. interaction for the sake of interaction. To clarify, in these instances there was already evidence of some student interactional engagement. The focus here is on Ann self-selecting turns when she oriented to evidence of students struggling with *elaborating* on their interactional engagement, as illustrated in Excerpt 3. This excerpt takes place during Day 7's warm-up activity. Ann has reiterated throughout the semester that the purpose of warm-up activities is to get students into 'English mode' after most of them had been speaking in another language throughout the day; therefore, she verbally emphasizes equal speaking time for everyone and elaborated talk without worrying about accuracy. Here, the groups have been asked to discuss what common things they did during the day and to make a list. Tetsu, Arata and Hiro are discussing their ideas while Ann is some distance away at the front of the room looking at and listening to this group.

Excerpt 3

```
1    TET:    i woke up. then (0.4)}{brush the teeth?
2                               {((makes circular motion))
3    HIR:    °yes.°
4            {(3.2)
5            {((Tetsu writes))
6            {(0.2)
7            {((Tetsu look to his colleagues))
8    TET:    {put on clothes?
9            {((makes gesture over shoulders))
10   ARA:    [{ye(hh)s.
11           [{(((nods))
12   HIR:    [((nods))
13           {(1.8)
14           {((Tetsu writes))
15   TET:    uh- did you took- did you take (0.2) subway?
16   ARA:    <ye:ah.
17   TET:    ((gestures to Hiro))
18   HIR:    {°yes.°
19           {((nods))
20   TET:    okay?
21           {(0.2)
22           {((Tetsu looks at paper))
23           {good.
24           {((writes on paper))
25           {(5.2)
26           {((Testsu writes; Ann moves closer))
27   TET:    did you have a (0.2) breakfast? i didn't. so,
28   HIR:    i didn't.
29   ARA:    i di(hh)dn't. {sorry. hehehe.
30                         {((shrugs shoulders))

             ((lines omitted- Tetsu asks Ann a grammar question))
31   TET:    u:hm did you take lunch?
32   ARA:    yes.
33   TET:    {yes.
34           {((writing on sheet))
35   ANN: →  <you all had lunch.
36   ARA:    °yes.°
37   HIR:    ((nods))
38   ANN: →  ah. okay. maybe the time was the same?= i don't ↑know.
39           find the details.= maybe: (0.4) something- maybe you had
40           {(0.2) one of the things you had was the ↑same.
41           {((looks at Tetsu and puts up index finger))
42           {for ↑all of you. >i don't know.<
43           {((gestures to all three))
44           ((Ann begins to move to another group))
45           {i don't know.
46           {((looks back while walking away))
47           (0.6)
48   ARA:    what time did you have lunch?
49   TET:    around two pm. {i think. not su(hh)re
50                          {((tilts head back and forth))
51   HIR:    [((nods))
52   ARA:    [@haha. that's about the sa(hh)me.
53           {(1.0)
54           {((Tetsu writes))
55   HIR:    what did you eat.
56           (0.4)
57   TET:    snack. @haha.
58   HIR:    a:h. ↑just (.) snack.
59   TET:    just snack. @haha[haha.
60   ARA:                     [@haha. really?
61   TET:    chi(hh)ps.
62   ARA:    @haha.
63   HIR:    {oh.
64           {((nodding))
65   ARA:    (            ).
```

```
66    TET:        no. i don't think so.
67    HIR:        actually i [(0.2)u::h(0.4)soup.
68    ANN:                   [((looks over at group from a distance))
69                [((continues looking over at group))
70    ARA:        [only soup?
71    HIR:        [yup.    well i - u:h  (0.4)    [have a coffee.
72    ANN:        [((continues looking at group))[((looks away))
```

Lines 1–5, 8–14, 15–26, 27–30 and 31–34 illustrate the students following the same sequential pattern: Tetsu initiates a yes/no interrogative first pair part, sometimes accompanied by a gesture; Hiro, Arata or both give a type-conforming affirmative second pair part response; Tetsu provides a post-expansion third turn either verbalizing acknowledgement, writing down the answer or doing both. The sequences themselves are constructed in ways that restrict student-elaborated interaction. Tetsu's first pair parts, for example, restrict what is sequentially feasible for his partners to say in the second pair part. Although there is the potential for sequence expansion in the case that Hiro or Arata provide a negative response, here all responses are in agreement with Tetsu. In alignment with the literature on adjacency pair agreements (cf. Schegloff, 2007), Tetsu's post-expansion third turns are oriented to by all three students as sequence closing.

While the group is technically following the instructions for this specific activity, they are not following the macro guidelines that have been established over the previous six days of class: warm-ups are for the purpose of all group members elaborating on their interaction. As such, Ann orients to their sequences-of-talk as trouble sources in being able to achieve the macro purpose of this type of activity. Following the fifth iteration of this sequential pattern (Lines 31–34), Ann hurriedly takes up the turn in Line 35 by repeating (with grammatical correction) the idea just initiated by the students in the previous sequence ('lunch'), including incorporating the same emphasis that Tetsu used in Line 31. In using the students' own ideas and communicative cues in her turn, Ann not only is able to enter the discourse by linking to a topic just initiated by the students but also is able to use the students' topic as a foundation to do her mobilization.

Over the course of Lines 38–46, Ann accomplishes multiple actions simultaneously in order to *mobilize elaboration*. First, she provides potential outlets for the students to consider in elaborating on their 'lunch' idea (Lines 38–41), although she is careful to mark the students as the final decision makers in deciding what to do with her information. This is accomplished by using communicative cues which reduce her perceived role as knowledge holder of the interaction. Case in point, following each suggestion she immediately latches on to the next turn with either 'I don't know' or 'maybe' (Lines 38–39), commonly used to mitigate one's own display of knowledge in the interaction (Heritage, 2012).

Secondly, Ann incorporates different cues into her turns to signal that all three students are responsible for changing the sequential

Figure 6.4 Excerpt 3, Lines 40–41

patterns. When she suggests in Lines 40–41 that they may have 'one of the things that was the same', she emphasizes the importance of 'one of the things' using gesture, and focuses her gaze on Tetsu, the prominent initiator of the previous sequences (Figure 6.4). In Lines 42–43 Ann changes gaze to Hiro and Arata and emphasizes through gesture and higher pitch the importance of 'all of you' needing to do this (Figure 6.5). It is at this point that Ann begins to disengage from the group physically by walking away but leaving them with one more 'I don't know' (Lines 45–46).

Following Ann's departure, the three students continue, although with different interactional patterns. Arata for the first time in the activity initiates a sequence in Line 48, following Ann's suggestion from Line 38. His initiation is not phrased as a yes/no interrogative, and indeed there is some sequence expansion in Lines 49–54 compared to the prior sequences. Hiro then initiates a sequence for the first time in Line 55, and it is from this initiation that an elaborated sequence begins and continues through the end of the excerpt. Note that even though Ann physically moved away from the group, she continues to listen even from a slight distance in Lines 68–69 and 72 (Figure 6.6). At the end of Line 72 she changes gaze to

Figure 6.5 Excerpt 3, Lines 42–43

Figure 6.6 Excerpt 3, Lines 68–69

another group and does not return to this initial group for the remainder of the activity, thus displaying that she has oriented to their interaction as no longer needing assistance.

While Excerpt 3 demonstrates how Ann *mobilizes elaboration* when orienting to displays of struggle with the entire group, Excerpt 4 illustrates Ann mobilizing when orienting to group members' difficulties in entering the interaction due to one member not relinquishing speakership. Here, the groups have been given a list of 10 statements and they are to justify their opinions about each sentence. The current group consists of Clara, Hiro, Arata and Bae. Ann has been sitting with them since their discussion of the previous sentence and has remained quiet the entire time. Now Arata is self-selecting the next turn to begin discussing the sentence, 'Older people should move into nursing homes':

Excerpt 4

```
1    ARA:    i think- yes. in their home they feel alone.
2            {but in this home (0.2) {many people share same
3            {((looks at paper))     {((looks at group))
4            situation. {and people can find the same types
5                       {((rolls hand))
6            of people. {yeah.
7                       {((nods))
8            {(0.4)
9            {((groups continues looking at Arata))
10   ARA:    i think (0.2) this is a (.) positive aspect of the
11           {(0.2) of these people's home.
12           {((looks down and points to sheet))
13   BAE:    yeah. i think it is too.
14   ARA:    [.hh-
15   CLA:    [but in brazil we have this- these homes. but they are
16           are not really that common,
17           (0.2)
18           especially because of the price,
19           (0.2)
20   HIR:    {mhm.
21           {((nodding))
22   CLA:    <in the end what people do is like- (0.4)
23           {one (0.4) is like    {live everybody together?
24           {((points finger up)){[((makes circle with hand))

             ((lines omitted- Clara maintains speakership for
             next two minutes ten seconds))

25   CLA:    people don't like these houses in general.
26           (0.4)- ((colleagues nodding towards her))
```

```
27   CLA:        my mother don't like those houses.= she always tell me
28               $do't go in there.$
29   BAE:        [hhh.
30               (0.2)
31   ANN:   →    [{.hh-
32               {((gestures to Arata))
33   ARA:        [((gazes to Ann))
34   HIR:        [((gazes to Ann))
35   CLA:        [i don't know where i go when i'm old.
36   ANN:   →    {<what you said was interesting.{sometimes older=
37               {((to Arata)).                  {((to others))
38               =people get really isolated?
39   ARA:        mhm?
40   ANN:   →    and they don't really have anybody?
41   CLA:        <yeah. i agree [with this.
42   ARA:                       [yeah. i don't think we know much
43               their living in an apartment?
44               (0.2)
45   HIR:        [uh-hu:h?
46   BAE:        [((nods))
47   ARA:        so- u:h- (0.4) i really [think the community network
48                                       [((makes circle with hands))
49               [is an important place to help each other.
50   ANN:        [((looks down at pad for rest of interaction))
```

Over the course of Lines 1–12, Arata makes the argument for why nursing homes could be beneficial for older people, namely, so that older people are not alone. Following Bae's agreement in Line 13, Arata proceeds to take the next turn in Line 14 as indicated by his use of an in-breath. In overlap with this, though, Clara self-selects the turn in Line 15, starting her turn with the discourse marker 'but', signaling that the discourse segment that follows will somehow contrast with the previous segment. She spends the next two minutes relaying to the group why she disagrees with having older people go into nursing homes. Lines 15–24 and 25–28 exemplify the diverse communicative cues Clara uses to maintain speakership over the course of her time talking: using non-final intonation (e.g. Lines 16 and 18); quickly taking up a turn following a colleague's acknowledgement turn (Line 22); and using latching to link two successive turns together (e.g. Line 27).

As illustrated, Clara's communicative cues restrict other interlocutors from entering the talk. Orienting to this, Ann self-selects the turn in Lines 31–32 following a brief gap in the talk where she gestures toward Arata and begins to talk. In response, both Arata and Hiro orient to Ann's turn as a potential change in interaction, for both change their gaze from Clara to Ann in that moment (Figure 6.7). Even though Clara overlaps with Ann in Line 35 and continues speaking, Ann quickly takes over the next turn in Lines 36–38, returning the focus of the talk to Arata's original content. By asking Arata for confirmation and elaboration of what he said two minutes prior (Lines 36–38, 40), Ann allows him to regain the floor that he lost in Line 14. Once Arata proceeds to take the speakership and elaborate on his ideas, Ann begins to disengage from the interaction by changing her gaze from Arata (and the rest of the group) to her notepad and leaning back in her chair. She remains silent for the rest of the time she is with the group.

Figure 6.7 Excerpt 4, Lines 31–35

These last two excerpts exemplify Ann's embodied actions when *mobilizing elaboration*, which occurs when she orients to students' embodied actions in prior turns as displays of trouble with interactional elaboration. Such actions that Ann orients to as trouble sources can include all group members using sequential patterns that restrict opportunities for sequential expansion. In these instances, *mobilizing elaboration* is accomplished by Ann providing potential ideas for varying the sequential patterns, although her ideas are presented in ways that reduce her perceived role as knowledge holder and leave the final interactional decisions to the group members. In cases where the trouble sources are identified as an individual group member's use of various communicative cues that restrict other group members from interactional entrance, Ann reorients the talk to allow other group members entry in subsequent turns-at-talk. Across both examples are commonalities. First, Ann's actions incorporate the students' previously discussed ideas as a foundation to build on, as was the case with 'lunch' in Excerpt 3 and 'older people being alone' in Excerpt 4. Secondly, Ann's embodied actions, which include the use of varied verbal cues and nonverbal conduct, are succinctly done over the course of only a few turns, keeping her interaction to a minimum. Finally, Ann remains engaged with the group in some manner until she sees evidence of elaborated interaction, at which point she displays disengagement with the group.

Discussion and Conclusion

The current study examined the use of embodied actions done by one ESOL teacher, Ann, when responding to what she oriented to as student displays of trouble within small-group activities. Specifically, it focused on how such responsiveness was accomplished in the teacher's self-selected turns as opposed to turns that the students had nominated her to take. From the analysis, two overarching findings emerged. When orienting to students' actions in prior turns as displays of trouble with the content of an activity, Ann's actions would *mark the path* toward working through those troubles and continuing toward the activity's final product. In cases where students displayed unknowing epistemic stances over the course of numerous turns, Ann *marked the path* by highlighting factors in the activity that the students overlooked. When students displayed some, although not full, knowledge of a particular task item, *marking the path* enabled them to look at that item from a new perspective.

When students displayed trouble with being able to elaborate on their interaction within small-group activities, Ann's actions *mobilized elaboration*. In cases where the trouble source was the restrictive nature of the sequences-of-talk used by the group members (e.g. initiating a sequence with a yes/no interrogative), *mobilizing elaboration* was done by providing potential ideas for the group members to consider in order to change the sequences being used, thus enabling the potential for sequence expansion. When the trouble source was identified as an individual group member who, through the use of varied communicative cues, held on to the speakership of the turns, Ann would *mobilize elaboration* by reorienting the construction of the talk to allow other group members entry in subsequent turns.

Although they manifest differently in the discourse, *marking the path* and *mobilizing elaboration* shared characteristics. First, both consistently incorporated specific actions done by the students in their prior turns, the same turns that Ann oriented to as displays of trouble. This included using the topics initiated by the students as a foundation and source for Ann's subsequent actions (Excerpts 2, 3, 4), the artifacts the students used and focused on in their turns (Excerpt 1), and the verbal communicative cues that the students used when formulating their turns (Excerpt 3). In this way, Ann marked the actions in her self-selected turns as extensions of what the students had done immediately prior. Secondly, Ann's actions consisted of a multitude of simultaneous cues beyond simple verbalization of ideas, including paralinguistic cues (e.g. speed, loudness, pitch and intonation changes), nonverbal conduct (e.g. gesturing, body torque changes, shifts in eye gaze), and the use of activity artifacts (e.g. pointing on a map). As evident in subsequent turns-at-talk, it was the combination of these cues that the students oriented to as guiding them through the trouble sources. Thirdly, Ann's actions kept her involvement in the discourse minimal while clearly marking the students as responsible for activity continuation. *Marking the path* guided the students through their trouble sources but never provided them with answers to the activity; *mobilizing elaboration* provided suggestions for changing the sequential construction used in the interaction, although these were never overtly formed as mandatory directives. Finally, Ann's interaction with the small groups continued until she oriented to the students' turns as displays of overcoming the trouble sources. It was only then that Ann disengaged with the interaction, as displayed by ending her talk, stepping back from the artifacts, shifting eye gaze and body torque from the group members and physically moving away from the groups.

These findings detail the intricate and complex work teachers accomplish when choosing to enter small-group activity. Given that small-group interaction construction is meant to be student-led and student-responsible (Hellerman & Cole, 2009), teacher self-selection of turns may appear on the surface to contradict that purpose. The current study's findings, though, confirm that teacher self-selected turns are in fact contingent upon prior student actions, where the teacher orients to the varied embodied actions that students do in prior turns as solicitations for assistance even when no overt solicitations are given. Two points support this. First, the findings align with Schegloff's (2007) assertion that the key to marking a turn as a summons is to look at the recipient's orientation to that turn as a summons regardless of whether the summoner overtly marked the recipient as such or the recipient overtly took part in prior turns. Ann's self-selected turns are not random; they only surface immediately following what she perceives as evidence of student solicitations for assistance. This evidence often consisted of students' uses of varied communicative cues displaying unknowing (or mitigated knowing) epistemic stance in terms of doing the activity. In alignment with prior research (e.g. Käänta, 2014; Sert, 2013), Ann chose to self-select turns to address those displayed epistemic stances. What is unique with the current findings is that her self-selected turns are constructed not as overt changes to the discourse but rather as expansions of what the students had done previously, reducing the perception of teacher-led sudden shifts in interaction while still guiding the students beyond the trouble sources.

That these teacher turns are based on students' prior actions is further supported when examining the actions that follow the teacher's turns. As Schegloff (1968) originally noted, SA sequences are nonterminal, i.e. the interaction must continue beyond the answer turn with both the original summoner and the answerer taking part in the continued interaction in some way. Based on the perspective argued here that teacher self-selected turns in small-group activities are in fact responses (or answers) to students' covert solicitations (or summonses), it is not surprising that the students (or original summoners) do something with the teacher's responses, nor that the teacher (or answerer) remains engaged with the activity until there is clear evidence that the students have addressed their trouble sources.

For teachers, it is important to understand that their actions within small-group activities are quite different from but just as complex as those in whole-class settings. There is a perceived conundrum about the teacher's role within small-group activities. On one side, these activities are used for the purpose of being student-centered, with the students themselves taking charge of constructing the interaction; on the other side, teachers in their role as teacher are expected to continuously oversee and monitor all classroom interactions across activity types (Ball & Forzani, 2009). While these may appear to be contradictory, they are not. Teachers entering into small-group interactions do so based on their perception of student progression with the activity. They must understand that student displays of activity progression or non-progression can take many forms and incorporate various verbal and nonverbal cues simultaneously. It is necessary for teachers prior to entering the interaction to consider why their entry is necessary and how it will benefit the students' continued interactional management and leadership within these activities. As shown in this study, Ann's entry into the interaction was based on evidence gathered from student displays of difficulties with doing the small-group work; Ann was careful not only to gather that evidence before entering the talk but also to use it in her own turns to help the students work through their troubles. In so doing, Ann's entry was viewed as an expansion of what the students had already initiated, as opposed to being an overt teacher-initiated change to the interaction. At the same time, her actions clearly marked the students, not her, as being the ones to continue the activity. This is central to small-group work in classroom settings. What may be quite difficult for teachers, particularly novice teachers, to do is to be cognizant *in-the-moment* of ensuring that their actions within small-group activities do not highlight them as interactional directors or sole knowledge holders of the activity. Instead, they are there to directly and succinctly address the students' trouble sources, thus ensuring that the students not only can continue with the activity but, more importantly, continue being responsible for leading the interaction.

Notes

(1) See Fagan (2018) for a discussion on the (mis)perceptions of student interactional restriction within the initiation-response-feedback (IRF) sequence commonly found in whole-class interactions.
(2) All names are pseudonyms.

References

Ball, D.L. and Forzani, F.M. (2009) The work of teaching and the challenge for teacher education. *Journal of Teacher Education* 60, 497–511.
Bloome, D. (2015) The role of talk in group-based activity in classrooms. In N. Markee (ed.) *The Handbook of Classroom Discourse and Interaction* (pp. 128–141). Malden, MA: Wiley Blackwell.
Cekaite, A. (2009) Soliciting teacher attention in an L2 classroom: Affect displays, classroom artefacts, and embodied action. *Applied Linguistics* 30, 26–48.
Clark, H.H. and Schaefer, E.F. (1989) Contributing to discourse. *Cognitive Science* 13, 259–294.
Corden, R. (2001) Group discussion and the importance of a shared perspective: Learning from collaborative research. *Qualitative Research* 1, 347–367.
Couper-Kuhlen, E. (2001) Interactional prosody: High onsets in reasons-for-the-call turns. *Language in Society* 30, 29–53.
Fagan, D.S. (2015) Managing language errors in real-time: A microanalysis of teacher practices. *System* 55, 74–85.

Fagan, D.S. (2018) Addressing learner hesitancy-to-respond within initiation-response-feedback sequences. *TESOL Quarterly* 52, 425–435.

Gardner, R. (2015) Securing turns: The business of securing turns in a busy classroom. In C.J. Jenks and P. Seedhouse (eds) *International Perspectives on ELT Classroom Interactions* (pp. 28–48). New York: Palgrave MacMillan.

Gillies, R.M. (2004) The effects of communication training on teachers' and students' verbal behaviours during cooperative learning. *International Journal of Educational Research* 41, 257–279.

Gillies, R.M. and Khan, A. (2009) Promoting reasoned argumentation, problem-solving and learning during small-group work. *Cambridge Journal of Education* 39, 7–27.

Hellermann, J. and Cole, E. (2009) Practices for social interaction in the language learning classroom: Disengagements from dyadic task interactions. *Applied Linguistics* 30, 186–215.

Heritage, J. (2002) Oh-prefaced responses to assessments: A method of modifying and agreement/disagreement. In C. Ford, B. Fox and S. Thompson (eds) *The Language of Turn and Sequence* (pp. 196–224). New York: Oxford University Press.

Heritage, J. (2012) Epistemics in action: Action formation and territories of knowledge. *Research on Language and Social Interaction* 45, 1–29.

Heritage, J. (2013) Epistemics in conversation. In J. Sidnell and T. Stivers (eds) *The Handbook of Conversation Analysis* (pp. 370–394). London: Blackwell.

Hofmann, R. and Mercer, N. (2016) Teacher interventions in small group work in secondary mathematics and science lessons. *Language and Education* 30, 400–416.

Ishino, M. (2017) Subversive questions for classroom turn-taking traffic management. *Journal of Pragmatics* 117, 41–57.

Jacknick, C.M. (2011) Breaking in is hard to do: How students negotiate classroom activity shifts. *Classroom Discourse* 2, 20–38.

Jakonen, T. and Morton, T. (2015) Epistemic search sequences in peer interaction in a content-based language classroom. *Applied Linguistics* 36, 73–94.

Jefferson, G. (2004) Glossary of transcript symbols with an introduction. In G. Lerner (ed.) *Conversation Analysis: Studies from the First Generation* (pp. 13–31). Amsterdam: John Benjamins.

Kääntä, L. (2014) From noticing to initiating correction: Students' epistemic displays in instructional interaction. *Journal of Pragmatics* 66, 86–105.

Lee, Y.A. (2006) Respecifying display questions: Interactional resources for language teaching. *TESOL Quarterly* 40, 691–713.

Lehtimaja, I. (2011) Teacher-oriented address terms in students' reproach turns. *Linguistics and Education* 22, 348–363.

Lerner, G. (2003) Selecting next speaker: The context-sensitive operation of a context-free organization. *Language in Society* 32, 177–201.

McIntyre, E., Kyle, D.W. and Moore, G.H. (2006) A primary teacher's guidance toward small-group dialogue. *Reading Research Quarterly* 41, 36–66.

McNeill, D. (1992) *Hand and Mind*. Chicago, IL: University of Chicago Press.

Mortensen, K. (2009) Establishing recipiency in pre-beginning position in the second language classroom. *Discourse Processes* 46, 491–515.

Rainer Dangel, J. and Durden, T.R. (2010) The nature of teacher talk during small-group activities. *Faculty Publications from CYFS* 15, 74–81.

Schegloff, E.A. (1968) Sequencing in conversational openings. *American Anthropologist* 70, 1075–1095.

Schegloff, E.A. (2007) *Sequence Organization in Interaction, Vol. 1*. Cambridge: Cambridge University Press.

Schegloff, E.A. and Sacks, H. (1973) Opening up closings. *Semiotica* 8, 289–327.

Sert, O. (2013) 'Epistemic status check' as an interactional phenomenon in instructed learning settings. *Journal of Pragmatics* 45, 13–28.

Sert, O. (2017) Creating opportunities for L2 learning in a prediction activity. *System* 70, 14–25.

Shepherd, M.A. (2012) A quantitative discourse analysis of student-initiated checks of understanding during teacher-fronted lessons. *Linguistics and Education* 23, 145–159.

Thoms, J.J. (2014) An ecological view of whole-class discussions in a second language literature classroom: Teacher reformulations as affordances for learning. *The Modern Language Journal* 98, 724–741.

Toohey, K. (2000) *Learning English in School: Identity, Social Relations and Classroom Practice* (1st edn). Clevedon: Multilingual Matters.

Waring, H.Z. (2008) Using explicit positive assessment in the language classroom: IRF, feedback, and learning opportunities. *The Modern Language Journal* 92, 577–594.

Waring, H.Z., Reddington, E. and Tadic, N. (2016) Responding artfully to student-initiated departures in the adult ESL classroom. *Linguistics and Education* 33, 28–39.

Webb, N.M., Franke, M.L., Ing, M., Turrou, A.C., Johnson, N.C. and Zimmerman, J. (2017) Teacher practices that promote productive dialogue and learning in mathematics classrooms. *International Journal of Educational Research.* doi:10.1016/j.ijer.2017.07.009

Wells, G. (1993) Reevaluating the IRF sequence: A proposal for the articulation of theories of activity and discourse for the analysis of teaching and learning in the classroom. *Linguistics and Education* 5, 1–17.

7 Gaze Shifts as a Resource for Managing Attention and Recipiency

Hansun Zhang Waring and Lauren B. Carpenter

With the surge of interest in the study of multimodality in social interaction (Streeck *et al.*, 2011) and that in second language (L2) acquisition and classroom research (McCafferty & Stam, 2012), scholars have become increasingly attuned to those resources that structure and drive interaction beyond the logocentric focus on talk (Goodwin, 2007). Based on 36 hours of video-recorded interaction from an adult ESL class, our analysis shows how gaze shifts can be used to manage attention and recipiency. In particular, upon accepting an individual contribution, the teacher shifts his gaze: (1) to call attention to what needs to be treated as important information relevant to the entire class; and (2) to return to a wider participation framework where the class as a collective becomes the addressed rather than the unaddressed recipient. Findings of this study contribute to the growing work on multimodality by specifying how gaze shifts constitute a powerful resource for maneuvering the complexity of teaching.

Introduction

Scholars of language and social interaction have become increasingly attuned to those resources that structure and drive interaction beyond the logocentric focus on talk (Arnold, 2012; Goodwin, 2003, 2007; Raymond & Lerner, 2014; Streeck *et al.*, 2011). In the classroom context in particular, various embodied resources such as gesture, body movement, facial expression, haptics and eye gaze have been deemed viable for scaffolding understanding problems or managing classroom logistics (Cekaite, 2015; Eskildsen & Wagner, 2013, 2015; Jakonen, 2015; Käänta, 2015; Mortensen, 2016; Sert, 2015; Zwiers, 2007). Teachers tend, for example, to produce more gestures than usual to resolve problems raised by students (Alibali *et al.*, 2013a). They use iconic and metaphoric gestures coupled with talk, facial expression and body movement to explain the meaning of unfamiliar vocabulary words (Lazaraton, 2004; Morton,

2015; van Compernolle & Smotrova, 2017; Waring *et al.*, 2013) and to teach tense and aspect (Matsumoto & Dobs, 2017). Most pertinent to our project, teachers rely heavily on eye gaze to implement turn-allocation – by first scanning the class and then using head nods as well as pointing gestures once mutual gaze has been established (Käänta, 2012; Mortensen, 2008). In this chapter, we further explore the use of eye gaze in the specific context of an adult ESL classroom. More specifically, we are interested in those moments when the teacher shifts his gaze away from an individual who is the current speaker during or at the possible completion of his/her talk, and we ask: what do those shifts do?

Background

Existing work on classroom discourse has produced convincing evidence of how embodied resources can be mobilized to facilitate understanding and manage participation. In math classrooms, for example, teachers use pointing gestures to 'ground' instructional language to real-world referents (Alibali & Nathan, 2007), to link or connect different mathematical concepts (Alibali *et al.*, 2014), and to address students' problems of understanding with visual scaffolding that speech alone lacks (Alibali *et al.*, 2013).

In the L2 classroom where language constitutes both the means and the goal of learning, on the other hand, gesture has been documented as a useful resource for teaching various aspects of language such as tense, aspect and, most notably, vocabulary. Based on video-recorded interactions from a beginner- and an advanced-level grammar classroom in an intensive English program at a US university, for example, Matsumoto and Dobs (2017) found that the teachers used abstract deictic gestures to contrast tenses and metaphoric gestures to represent aspectual concepts. The employment of gestures in the teaching of vocabulary seems to be tied specifically to that of unplanned vocabulary. Based on a detailed analysis of a teacher's use of a wide variety of gestures, Lazaraton (2004: 109) was perhaps the first to argue for the importance of gestural input in unplanned vocabulary explanation. The author also notes that when the teacher uses or does not use certain gestures is 'perhaps the most intriguing question' that her study could not answer. A partial answer to Lazaraton's question may be found in Waring *et al.* (2013: 262), where two approaches that may assume 'a division of labor' of unplanned vocabulary explanation are identified – *analytic* and *animated*. While the *analytic* approach conveys more of the definitional information, the *animated* approach, which involves the use of *gesture, environmentally coupled gesture* (e.g. pointing to something in the environment such as a pictorial depiction on the blackboard) or *scene enactment* (also see Morton, 2015), is particularly useful for communicating contextual information. The superiority of gesture in delivering contextual information is further confirmed in van Compernolle and Smotrova's (2017: 15) study, where gesture in conjunction with speech is shown to highlight 'the most relevant, contextualized meaning of the target words' in unplanned vocabulary explanations.

In addition to facilitating students' understanding, embodied practices have also been shown to organize participation. Gaze can be used, for example, to identify and indicate willingness to participate (Mortensen, 2008), to allocate turns along with head nods and pointing gestures (Käänta, 2012), and, in conjunction with the use of the body, to 'exploit the instructional benefit' of student questions through 'dual addressivity' as teachers respond to questions in such ways that 'meet both individual *and* collective accountabilities' (St. John & Cromdal, 2016: 252). Finally, a 'hand to ear' gesture may be used to signal a problem with hearing, which would prompt the speaker to reorient his/her gaze and body toward the recipients (Mortensen, 2012), and an ensemble of nonverbal resources may be engaged to secure the smooth progression of the initiation-response-evaluation (IRE) sequence (Käänta, 2012).

In this chapter, we further explore the role of embodied resources in facilitating understanding and organizing participation in the classroom by examining how gaze shifts are deployed by the teacher in an adult English as a second language (ESL) classroom to manage attention and recipiency. After all, while attention is a baseline requirement for understanding, recipiency figures prominently in the configuration of participation frameworks.

Data and Method

Our data consist of 36 hours of interaction from an advanced-level adult ESL class video-recorded over the course of a semester at a community English program (CEP) in the United States in Spring 2009. Designed to help students develop integrated English skills, the class met three times a week, from 10 to 12 o'clock on Monday, Wednesday and Thursday mornings, for 10 weeks. For various reasons (e.g. quizzes, exams, conference travel), not every class was recorded, and a total of 18 two-hour classes constitute the entire data set for this course.

As a lab school for a TESOL (teaching English to speakers of other languages) MA program at a major graduate school of education on the East Coast of the United States, CEP served the adult immigrant and international population in the neighborhood surrounding the university, typically represented by a mixture of stay-at-home moms, spouses of international students, immigrants who held full-time jobs, and international students who sought to improve their English. The teachers included MA students who were taking a TESOL practicum course as well as master teachers who acted as models for the MA students and fulfilled the staffing needs of the program.

The class was taught by a master teacher who is a native speaker of English and an experienced language teaching professional with over 15 years of English language teaching experience, both in the United States and abroad in Spain, Mexico, Japan, China and Slovakia. Fourteen students were enrolled, representing a variety of first-language backgrounds, including Chinese, Japanese, Korean, Italian, Spanish, Polish, German, Russian, Persian and Serbian-Croatian. Of the 14, 13 were female and only one male. Their length of residence in the United States ranged from 'just arrived' to 15 years, and their history of learning English ranged from one year and three months to 15 years. In many ways, the class composition reflected the heterogeneity typically found in adult ESL classes.

Both the teacher and his students gave consent to being video-recorded. The teacher also agreed to manage the recording himself using a single camera with no additional microphones. The video-recordings were transcribed in their entirety using Jeffersonian conventions with some slight modifications to accommodate the timing of nonverbal conduct as well as features of the classroom context (e.g. T = teacher; S = students). The analysis is conducted within a conversation analytic framework.

The class was conducted in a flexible, facilitative format in which the teacher, at times, guided learners into pair or group activities, during which time he circulated the room to listen in and provide on-the-spot feedback. The focus of our analysis, however, is on those segments where the teacher leads whole-class discussions around various topics and language issues. Assuming that ensuring student engagement in this wider participation framework would require a great deal of teacher expertise, our interest is in specifying the role of gaze shifts in this expertise and, in particular, in managing the tension between attending to an individual and to the class as a whole.

As such, we began the analysis by watching the video files repeatedly to identify instances during whole-class interactions where the teacher shifts his gaze away from an individual who is the current speaker during or at the possible completion of his/her talk. A total of 131 instances emerged from that initial scanning, where 35 instances of the gaze shifts were found in the environment of responding to student questions, and 96 in the environment of addressing student responses to teacher elicitations. We then took a closer look at the 96 instances and selected 76 for further analysis, excluding cases where the camera angle does not allow for an accurate view of the gaze recipients, where the teacher shifts his gaze toward the board or other material objects (e.g. handout or book) rather than the larger class, and where the gaze shift is clearly warranted by the talk that requires a new addressee (e.g. when the teacher turns to the class or another individual with 'What did Ana just say?'). Among the 76 instances, 59 involve gaze shifts when the student's response was treated as adequate and 17 when the student's response was treated as less than adequate. For the current project, we focus specifically on the 59 instances where the teacher shifts his gaze away from the student to the larger class as he accepts the latter's response, and we ask: 'Why that now?' (Schegloff & Sacks, 1973).

Before we proceed, it is important to clarify what seem relevant but are not included in our collection in order to delineate the boundary of our cases (Schegloff, 1997). Unlike the 59 cases where the teacher engages in gaze shifts upon acceptance of student responses, there are times when the teacher maintains his gaze on the individual students upon acceptance of the response without any shifts and, invariably, the students in those cases are responding to questions of a personal nature. In receiving the students' responses to his inquiry about weekend activities at the beginning of Monday classes, for example, the teacher often oscillates his gaze between his attendance sheet and that individual student, and upon completion of the account, he simply moves on to the next student without addressing the class as a whole.

Gaze Shifts and Acceptance of Learner Talk

Our analysis shows that as the teacher accepts the learner response, he shifts his gaze to others in the room in two slightly different sequential environments – either during or immediately after his initial acceptance, which is typically followed by some elaboration or directives. What we have roughly glossed as 'elaboration' would include further talk about the accepted response, ranging from simple repetitions and reformulations, to further specifications, and our 'directive' would include follow-up questions or instructions for an activity. In what follows, we show six instances representative of our data set, beginning with three instances where the teacher essentially addresses his acceptance to the rest of the class via gaze, and ending with another three instances where the teacher shifts his gaze away from the individual immediately after his initial acceptance of the latter's response as he embarks on further affirmation and/or a follow-up directive. As will be argued, such gaze shifts appear to rally attention to important information and recalibrate the participation framework.

Gaze shift during acceptance

In Excerpt 1 below, the class has been working in small groups on a set of tongue twisters that involve difficult sound pairs such as /r/ versus /l/. As the segment begins, the teacher selects Sato to read aloud the first tongue twister, and he looks down at the handout during Sato's reading (Lines 2–3).

Excerpt 1: *032309 2530–2601 fruit flies*

```
1    TEA:      >°go ahead sato.°<
2    SAT:      f::-few (.) free (.) fruit (.)
3              fli:es, fly (.) from. flames.
```

Sato

Figure 7.1 Excerpt 1, Lines 2–3

```
4        TEA: →      ((gaze up from handout with nod
5                    and extended arms to Ss))
```

Figure 7.2 Excerpt 1, Lines 4–5

```
6                    pronunciation was ↑good?
7                    (0.2)
8                    pronunciation >was good< .h now.
9                    what are the sou:nds. that we're
10                   focusing on (or off.) here.
```

As can be seen, in response to Sato's carefully and perfectly enunciated delivery, the teacher looks up from the handout as he nods and gesturally treats her performance as satisfactory (Lines 4–5) before proceeding with the explicit assessment of *pronunciation was good* (Line 6). Notably, this verbal and nonverbal acceptance (or positive assessment more precisely) is directed, via his gaze, not to Sato individually, but to the larger class. By momentarily reconfiguring the participation framework as such, the class is now the addressed recipient (as opposed to an overhearer) (Goffman, 1981) of the teacher's assessment of Sato's delivery – an assessment that serves to inform the entire class what is worthy of public attention: the correct pronunciation of this particular tongue twister. At the same time, this gaze shift away toward the class has also paved the way for the teacher to re-engage the larger group as he addresses his follow-up directive to the latter, thereby reactivating the wider participation framework (Lines 9–10).

In the next slightly more extended segment (Excerpt 2), the teacher's gaze shift is followed by an elaboration rather than a directive. The class is trying to figure out the meaning of the noun *produce*. As the excerpt begins, the teacher offers a clue to the word (Lines 1–3) and then selects Ana to respond (Lines 6–9).

Excerpt 2: *021109–1 001614–001642 produce*

```
1      TEA:        i can tell y- every single person
2                  in this class does know this word.
3                  °you've all seen this wo:rd,
4                  in supermarkets.°
5                  (0.5)
6                  {ana?
7                  {((leans towards ana))
8                  (0.8)
9                  {((hand extends to ana))
10     KAR:        {it's agricultural products?
11     TEA:        {ah-
12                 {((turns to KAR and points))-ye[ah.
13     ANA:                                        [vegetables,
14                 a[nd
15     TEA:        {[a::nd?
16                 {((gaze shift to ana with inducing gesture)
```

Direction of Ana

Figure 7.3 Excerpt 2, Lines 15–16

```
17     ANA:        °frui:t.°=
18     TEA:    →   ={yes
19                 {((nods/retrieves arm/gazes away))
```

Figure 7.4 Excerpt 2, Lines 18–19

```
20          ((nods)) {((to ana direction))
21                   {°mhm?°
22          ((underlines 'produce' on board))
22          ((nods to class))
23          PROduce. >vegetables and fruits.<
24          ((gazes and gestures to kara))-or
25          agricultural products °
26          {((to STU))
27          {°like kara said.°
```

Note that in accepting Ana's response of *vegetables* (Line 13) and *fruit* (Line 17), the teacher's affirming *yes* is produced with his gaze away from Ana to the rest of the class, thereby momentarily reconfiguring the participation framework wherein the class is the addressed recipient rather than the over-hearer (Goffman, 1981). By directing his positive assessment to the class as such, the teacher treats the answer *vegetables and fruit* as official and rele-vant information worthy of attention for the entire class, thereby doing informing (the class) and evaluating (Ana) at the same time. Both the evalu-ating and the informing are then extended into the next few lines as the teacher nods (Lines 19, 20), utters in *sotto voce* a *mhm* in Ana's direction (Line 21), underlines 'produce' on the board (Line 22), repeats the word along with its definitions (Line 23), and extends the definition to include what Kara said earlier: *or agricultural products* (Lines 24–25). Aside from doing informing and evaluating simultaneously then, the teacher's gaze shift also appears to widen the participation framework as he solidifies the mean-ing of *produce* with further affirmation, moving from the individual to the larger class and re-engaging those who failed to be engaged earlier.

In the final case of this section (Excerpt 3), we observe both elabora-tion and a directive after the gaze shift. The teacher is leading a discussion on figuring out the meaning of *disposable diaper* (Line 1), and his accep-tance of Ting's explanation is done visibly via quick nods along with a gaze shift to the rest of the class (Line 8).

Excerpt 3: 040209 004317–004337 disposable diaper

```
1    TEA:        but ↑what's a dispo::sable diaper.
2    TIN:        °use {and throw it away.°
3    TEA:             {((gazes toward and arm out to ting))
4    STU:             {((various similar responses))
```

Figure 7.5 Excerpt 3, Line 3

```
5    TEA:        {ah. ting.
6                {((gazes at ting))
7    TIN:        you use and then, you throw away.
8                [°after using it.°
9    TEA:   →    [((quick repeated {nods to STU))
10   STU:                           {oh ok.
```

Figure 7.6 Excerpt 3, Line 9

```
11      TEA:            so after one use? >throw it away.<
12                      .hh {((gaze to ting direction))
13                          {↑what's the traditional type of diaper.
14                      (0.2)
15                      {((gaze to rest of class))
16                      {befo::re we had dis-.=>disposable diaper<
17                      only maybe thirty: thirty-five years
18                      old. what-
```

Ting's initial response is done in *sotto voce*, which quickly draws the teacher's attention soon after its beginning (Line 2) amidst other similar responses (Line 4). The teacher then explicitly nominates Ting as the next speaker along with his gaze, which remains on Ting as she repeats her earlier answer in a louder voice (Line 7). Immediately upon her completion of *throw away*, the teacher turns to the class with quick nods (Line 9), thereby visibly accepting the explanation as correct and doing so in overlap with the Ting's *sotto voce* continuation of *after using it* (Line 8).

Again, by addressing his visible acceptance to the rest of the class, the teacher officially informs the class, via Ting's explanation, the meaning of *disposal diaper*, which is received as such as we hear *oh okay* from the class (Line 10). The teacher then further affirms the meaning by repeating Ting's response with a slight adjustment, replacing her *use* and *using* with *one use*, thus highlighting the disposable quality of the diaper. This public informing is then followed by a directive that elicits the term for diapers before 'disposal diapers' (Lines 13–16). Note that the teacher addresses the first turn construction unit (TCU) of his question to Ting's side of the room and then shifts his gaze to the rest of the class after the brief gap (Line 14) as he delivers the adverbial increment (*before we had …*) that specifies *traditional* (Line 16). Although the gaze shift is not exercised upon the acceptance of student response, it displays a similar sensitivity to the wider participation framework as we have documented so far.

In all three cases, then, as the teacher shifts his gaze to the rest of the class while accepting or positively assessing an individual student's response, which typically involves a relatively simple and straightforward task such as reading aloud a tongue twister or explaining a vocabulary item, he accomplishes the dual task of both evaluating and informing. At the same time, the gaze shift also constitutes a delicate move of shifting between the various participation frameworks that teacher has to constantly manage in an actual classroom, allowing him to smoothly transition to addressing the subsequent elaboration and/or directives to the entire class.

Gaze shift post-acceptance

Sometimes the teacher's gaze shift is done not during but immediately after his initial acceptance of the student's response, and we show three such cases in this section. As in the prior section, the first excerpt is followed by a directive, the second by elaboration and the third by both. In the transcripts below, we use the regular (as opposed to block) arrow to high-light 'initial acceptance' and the block arrow for 'gaze shift'. In Excerpt 4 the teacher is leading a discussion on why English is difficult to learn (Lines 1–3). Yoshi volunteers and is selected as the next respondent (Lines 4–5).

Excerpt 4: *0211091 000237–000311 what makes English difficult*

```
 1    TEA:        {((to class))
 2                {any other comments.
 3                {°what makes English difficult.°
 4    YOS:        {((hand up swipe gesture))
 5    TEA:        ((points to YOS))
 6    YOS:        uh for me I have no: (.) no (real)
 7                chance to: (0.2) uh °speak.
 8                {and to: listen.°
 9    TEA:   →    {((nods with gaze on YOS))
10                ((continues nodding))
11    YOS:        °and (      )°
12    TEA:   →    .HHH ↓ah
13    YOS:        {°(      )°
14    TEA:   →    {((nods))
15           →    very true as well. very true °also.°
```

Figure 7.7 Excerpt 4, Line 14

```
16           →    {((gaze to rest of class))
17                {ALL these are very very good points.=
```

Figure 7.8 Excerpt 4, Lines 16–17

```
18              =>what we're going to do right now is
19              we're going to have a little PRActice.
20              ((walks back to board)) what makes english
21              (.)difficult. °for different types of
22              people.° what ↑i would like you to do,
```

Note that Yoshi's response is produced with some difficulty, as evidenced in the elongations, pauses and *uh*s (Lines 6–7), and the teacher carefully attends to this response (even as Yoshi's volume decreases as early as *speak* in Line 7 and becomes partially and then completely inaudible at least for the overhearing analyst) with sustained gaze, nods (Lines 9–10, 14) and what may be heard as an understanding claim (.*HHH ↓ah*) (Line 12). While nodding displays both listening and visible acceptance of Yoshi's very personal explanation, the verbal acceptance comes in Line 15 as the teacher twice claims the veracity of Yoshi's account with *very true*. Unlike the cases we have observed so far, both the visible and verbal acceptance are done with the benefit of the teacher's sustaining gaze, which Yoshi's personal account appears to warrant. Just as story recipients display affiliation through nodding (Stivers, 2008), the teacher's affiliation with Yoshi's account here is conveyed at least in part through his gaze.

Immediately thereafter, however, with a jumpstart and at a louder volume, the teacher shifts his gaze to the rest of the class with a positive assessment of what everyone (including Yoshi) has contributed on the topic, thereby wrapping up the discussion so far (Lines 16–17). This is followed by a directive involving what the class is about to do next (Lines 18–22) – an activity involving homonyms that evidence the difficulty of the English language (not shown). This gaze shift co-occurs with a transition to the next activity for which the entire class, not just Yoshi, is the addressed recipient. The shift is, therefore, at least a partial resource for achieving such a transition, which requires the widening of participation framework from the individual to the class.

Immediately before the next segment (Excerpt 5), Tara had reported that she did not understand, in response to a reading, how someone can fall into the sewer. As the excerpt begins, the teacher redirects the question to the class and nominates Cindy as the next speaker.

Excerpt 5: *022609 001256–00140 fall into a sewer*

```
1       TEA:    {((to STU))
2               {hh how can you fall into a sewer
3               (0.8)
4               {((gaze to CIN))
5               {Cindy.
        ((Lines omitted that contain a brief joking sequence))
6       CIN:    it's- when it's maybe: u:h (0.2)
7               sometimes you have big (.) uh ho:le
8               in the: u:m (0.5) on the road?
9       TEA:    mm [hm?
10      CIN:       [so and and sometimes onl:y
11              covered with so:me (.) wood? >°and
12              then you can fall down.°< =
```

```
13     TEA:   →      ={(((to CIN))-
14                    {.hh ((nods)) exactly.
```

Figure 7.9 Excerpt 5, Lines 13–14

```
15            →      {(((gaze shift to class))
16                    {so, in the street, sometimes you see
17                     the ho:le? and there's (.) a to[p?
18     JAC:                                          [yeah.
19     TEA:           if you pick it up, ((continues))}
```

Figure 7.10 Excerpt 5, Lines 15–16

Cindy's explanation of falling into the sewer is a relatively complicated one and is delivered, like Yoshi's in the prior excerpt, with some difficulty as evidenced in the cut-offs, *uh*s, pauses and elongations (Lines 6–8), which is supported by the teacher's continuer (Line 9) as she presses on to bring the account to its completion with *then you fall down* (Lines 11–12). Immediately thereafter, the teacher produces a positive assessment *exactly*, along with nodding, with his gaze maintained on Cindy, as he does in the prior excerpt. Again, this sustained gaze appears to be warranted by the 'specialness' of Cindy's response given the complexity of the process she is describing and Cindy's successful management of such complexity. It may also be, as observed in an earlier excerpt, similar to the nodding done by story recipients to convey affiliation (Stivers, 2008).

At the same time, the in-breath (Line 14) at the beginning of the teacher's turn that projects a multi-unit turn (Schegloff, 1996) is borne out by his subsequent reformulation of Cindy's response as Jackie displays recognition of the *hole* and *top* one sees in the street (Lines 16–19). The need for reformulation may also constitute evidence for the complicated nature of the question and its response. As he embarks on this reformulation, the teacher also shifts his gaze to the class, thereby ostensibly offering this recount as done for the wider participation framework of the larger group, not just for Cindy.

In our final segment, the class is discussing the difference between *very* and *too*. As Excerpt 6 begins, the teacher tries to elicit the different meanings between *New York is very dangerous* and *New York is too dangerous* (Lines 1–8).

Excerpt 6: *0212094 003658–003758 too dangerous for what*

```
 1    TEA:          new york is very da:ngerous.
 2                  new york is too dangerous.
 3                  (0.8)
 4                  those are very different
 5                  senten[ces.
 6    SAT:                [°mhm°
 7                  (0.2)
 8    TEA:          {((to STU))
 9                  {tell me the meaning of those sentences.
10    SAT:          when {you say TOO dangerous,=
11    TEA:               {((gaze shift to SAT))
12    SAT:          = uh- you have expla:in something
13                  °else.° too dangerous for wha:t.
14    TEA:   →      {(('body nod' to SAT))
15                  {↓A↑A:H. a:h
```

Figure 7.11 Excerpt 6, Lines 14–15

```
16        →      {((gaze to Ss, to bb, and back to Ss))
17               {something has to come afterward.=
```

Figure 7.12 Excerpt 6, Lines 16–17

```
18   SAT:      =>yeah.<
19   TEA:      it is TOO dangerous (.) for me to
20             go there.
21             (0.8)
22             >but if i: say,< New York is very
23             dangerous, .h (0.5) [period.
24   SAT:                          [okay.
25   TEA:      end of sentence, (0.8)°you don't
26             have to say anything else. °
27             {((walks to board))
28             {.HHH↑let's cha:nge this.
29             ((erases 'very' and 'too' near 'multicultural'))
30             new york i:s, ((writes 'so'))
31             SO multicultura:l, ((stares at class))
32             period. is that a sentence?
```

Immediately after Sato volunteers to *tell the meaning* of the two sentences, the teacher shifts his gaze to her (Line 11). As Goodwin (1980) shows, one of the gaze rules is that *recipient* should be gazing at *speaker* when being gazed at by the speaker. As soon as Sato completes her response, the teacher signals his acceptance with a big 'body nod' (see Figure 7.8) along with an *a:h* delivered at a loud volume and with sharp prosodic shifts. This is followed by a second elongated *a:h*. In so doing, the teacher highlights the enlightening quality of Sato's just completed explanation as if it had just unlocked the 'mystery' relationship between *so* and *too* (Line 15). One gets the sense that the teacher is treating the question as one not easily answerable and is 'impressed' by Sato's answering, and the dramatic rendering of his acceptance along with the sustained gaze is perhaps one way of making that stance public.

This prosodic headline is then immediately followed by a gaze shift to the rest of the class (see Figure 7.9) as the teacher reformulates Sato's explanation: *something has to come afterward*, thereby cementing his acceptance of the latter as important and relevant information for all – again doing both evaluating and informing. This gaze shift to the wider participation framework also ensures that his subsequent elaboration of the explanation (Lines 19–20, 22–23, 25–26) is clearly done for the entire class, and the follow-up directive that introduces the use of *so* into the mix is clearly directed toward the entire class (Lines 27–32).

In all three cases here, then, unlike what we have observed in the previous section, the teacher's gaze remains on the individual as he produces his initial acceptance (or appreciation) of the student's response, similar to what story recipients do as they display alignment or convey affiliation, and this added attention may be attributed to the 'specialness' of the various individual contributions given their personal or challenging qualities. Nevertheless, this 'individual attention' is not lavished excessively but is followed by a disciplined reconfiguration of the participation framework, in part achieved through gaze, to ensure that the larger pedagogical project of learning various aspects of the English language (e.g. pronunciation, vocabulary, syntactic structure) is implemented with efficacy with the entire class on board.

Discussion and Conclusion

In this chapter, we have described one teacher's practice of deploying gaze shifts, while accepting an individual contribution, as a resource for: (1) calling attention to what needs to be treated as important information relevant to the entire class; and (2) shifting back into a wider participation framework where the class as a collective becomes the addressed rather than the unaddressed recipient. In other words, we have shown how gaze shifts are used by this particular teacher in this particular classroom to manage what we have roughly glossed as attention and recipiency. More specifically, these shifts are found in two major sequential environments: *during* and *post-* acceptance. While the shifts implemented during acceptance perform the double duty of evaluating the individual response and informing the larger class, those exercised post-acceptance manifest a particular sensitivity toward the 'specialness' of the student's response, be it personal or challenging. Perhaps not by pure coincidence, then, the responses accepted with gaze shifts tend to involve simple and straightforward tasks such as explaining what a 'disposal diaper' is, and those accepted with sustaining gaze, on the other hand, appear to feature greater complexity such as explaining why English is difficult. In either case, the shift itself launches a departure from the participation framework wherein the individual student alone is the addressed recipient and a return to the wider participation framework that extends addressed recipiency to the rest of the class. Such shifts appear to be designed for the benefit of accomplishing larger pedagogical projects (e.g. learning pronunciation, vocabulary and grammar) for which the attention and participation of the class as a collective is crucial. Similar to 'the artful addressivity work' engaged by the teachers in St. John and Cromdal (2016: 257) in response to student questions, the teacher in our study also accomplishes 'dual addressivity' (St. John & Cromdal, 2016: 252), but does so while accepting student responses.

It is important to note that we are by no means claiming that such monumental tasks as managing attention and recipiency are accomplished by gaze shifts alone, the utility of which is necessarily activated in conjunction with other verbal and visible means. Simply shifting the gaze away from the individual toward the class is unlikely in and of itself to achieve any reconfiguration of the participation framework without, for example, the accompanying verbal evaluation of *All these are very good points*. In addition, we are not claiming that what this teacher does is generalizable to other teachers in similar contexts. What we have shown, however, is that engaging gaze shifts in these particular ways is a culturally available and analytically describable resource that is 'possibly (and probably) reproducible' (Psathas, 1995: 50). It is this potential reproducibility that enables our subsequent discussion on the pedagogical implications of these findings.

Before launching that discussion, however, we briefly note that our findings on gaze shifts in the classroom may extend the growing work on how multimodality constitutes a powerful instrument for maneuvering the complexity of teaching. In particular, while relevant work on embodied resources in the classroom has shown how such resources are engaged to either facilitate understanding or manage participation, the gaze shifts we describe attend to both dimensions of the teacher's pedagogical work simultaneously. In addition, while conversation analytic work on multimodal analyses of the L2 classroom has mostly concerned vocabulary explanation and turn allocation, by foregrounding attention and recipiency, we hope to have broadened the scope of multimodality as an object of investigation within the context of the L2 classroom, showing in particular how embodied resources are integral not just to determining the next speaker, but also to shaping the next recipient, and not just to facilitating understanding through enhanced explanations, but also to recruiting the attention required for any understanding in the first place.

In a classroom where the teacher is constantly negotiating the challenge of meeting the needs of the individual and the group, the choreography of one's gaze seems to be a crucial tool for navigating such a challenge or to resolve what Reddington (2018) calls the 'participation paradox' – the necessity of *engaging in* and *disengaging from* interactions with individual students to promote extended as well as even participation. By shifting his gaze to the class during or immediately after initial acceptance of an individual student's response, the teacher is able to simultaneously mark his acceptance and its subsequent elaboration as informative and relevant for the group, thereby re-establishing the larger participation framework that allows for any follow-up work to be addressed to the larger group. As such, one might argue that the kind of gaze shift we have documented here is an important teacher resource for multitasking and doing being inclusive in the classroom.

Admittedly, compared to such macro tasks as lesson planning and activity designs in language teacher education, gaze shifts seem hopelessly trivial. No teacher education program, to our knowledge, has included gaze deployment as part of the pedagogical practices for which novice teachers are trained. Yet, teacher trainers are not unfamiliar with certain peculiar gaze patterns that novice teachers tend to exhibit, such as talking with sustained gaze at the board, the textbook, the handout, a single student or one side of the classroom (Wagner, personal communication, 17 July 2017). While we are intuitively aware that teaching requires multitasking, and creating an inclusive classroom is often a stated goal of (language) teacher education (e.g. van Lier, 2007), how such multitasking and inclusion are achieved in the micro-moments of actual teaching remains a largely unexplored terrain. It seems hard to believe that monumental undertakings like multitasking and inclusion can at least in part be achieved through such interactional 'minutiae' as gaze shifts. We hope to have provided a glimpse, with evidence from the actual classroom, into how small gestures can indeed matter for big ideas and are in fact the stuff that big ideas are built from. Doing evaluating and informing at the same time via gaze shifts and adjusting the timing of such shifts contingent upon the nature of learner contributions, for example, are concrete, teachable practices that novice teachers can emulate, adapt and build upon. As a matter of fact, we believe that mere exposure to such practices would be instrumental in cultivating a critical appreciation for the complexity and contingency of teaching (Hall, 2019; Hall & Smotrova, 2013; Waring, 2016) and in providing novice teachers with some assurance that such complexity and contingency are manageable in the very specificity of teacher conduct.

References

Alibali, M.W. and Nathan, M.J. (2007) Teachers' gestures as a means of scaffolding students' understanding: Evidence from an early algebra lesson. In R. Goldman, R. Pea, B. Barron and S.J. Derry (eds) *Video Research in the Learning Sciences* (pp. 349–365). New York: Routledge.

Alibali, M.W., Nathan, M.J., Church, R.B., Wolfgram, M.S., Kim, S. and Knuth, E.J. (2013) Teachers' gestures and speech in mathematics lessons: Forging common ground by resolving trouble spots. *ZDM Mathematics Education* 45 (3), 425–440.

Alibali, M.W., Nathan, M.J., Wolfgram, M.S., Church, R.B., Jacobs, S.A., Johnson Martinez, C. and Knuth, E.J. (2014) How teachers link ideas in mathematics instruction using speech and gesture: A corpus analysis. *Cognition and Instruction* 32 (1), 65–100.

Arnold, L. (2012) Dialogic embodied action: Using gesture to organize sequence and participation in instructional interaction. *Research on Language and Social Interaction* 45 (3), 269–296.

Cekaite, A. (2015) The coordination of talk and touch in adults' directives to children: Touch and social control. *Research on Language and Social Interaction* 48 (2), 152–175.

Eskildsen, S.W. and Wagner, J. (2013) Recurring and shared gestures in the L2 classroom: Resources for teaching and learning. *European Journal of Applied Linguistics* 1, 139–161.

Eskildsen, S.W. and Wagner, J. (2015) Embodied L2 construction learning. *Language Learning* 66, 268–297.

Goffman, E. (1981) *Forms of Talk*. Philadelphia, PA: University of Pennsylvania Press.

Goodwin, C. (1980) Restarts, pauses, and the achievement of a state of mutual gaze at turn beginning. *Sociological Inquiry* 50 (3–4), 272–302.

Goodwin, C. (2003) Pointing as situated practice. In S. Kita (ed.) *Pointing: Where Language, Culture and Cognition Meet* (pp. 217–241). Mahwah, NJ: Lawrence Erlbaum.

Goodwin, C. (2007) Participation, stance, and affect in the organization of activities. *Discourse and Society* 18 (1), 53–73.

Hall, J.K. (2019) An EMCA approach to capturing the specialized work of L2 teaching: A research proposal. In M. Haneda and H. Nassaiji (eds) *Perspectives on Language as Action* (pp. 228–245). Bristol: Multilingual Matters.

Hall, J.K. and Smotrova, T. (2013) Teacher self-talk: Interactional resource for managing instruction and eliciting empathy. *Journal of Pragmatics* 47, 75–92.

Jakonen, T. (2015) Handling knowledge: Using classroom materials to construct and interpret information requests. *Journal of Pragmatics* 89, 100–112.

Kääntä, L. (2012) Teachers' embodied allocations in instructional interaction. *Classroom Discourse* 3 (2), 166–186.

Kääntä, L. (2015) The multimodal organisation of teacher-led classroom interaction. In C.J. Jenks and P. Seedhouse (eds) *International Perspectives on ELT Classroom Interaction* (pp. 64–83). London: Palgrave Macmillan.

Lazaraton, A. (2004) Gesture and speech in the vocabulary explanations of one ESL teacher: A microanalytic inquiry. *Language Learning* 54 (1), 79–117.

Matsumoto, Y. and Dobs, A.M. (2017) Pedagogical gestures as interactional resources for teaching and learning tense and aspect in the ESL grammar classroom. *Language Learning* 67, 7–42.

McCafferty, S.G. and Stam, G. (2012) *Gesture: Second Language Acquisition and Classroom Research*. New York: Routledge.

Mortensen, K. (2008) Selecting next speaker in the second language classroom: How to find a willing next speaker in planned activities. *Journal of Applied Linguistics* 5 (1), 55.

Mortensen, K. (2012) Visual initiations of repair- some preliminary observations. In K. Ikeda and A. Brandt (eds) *Challenges and New Directions in the Micro-analysis of Social Interaction* (pp. 45–50). Osaka: Division of International Affairs, Kansai University.

Mortensen, K. (2016) The body as a resource for other-initiation of repair: Cupping the hand behind the ear. *Research on Language and Social Interaction* 49 (1), 34–57.

Morton, T. (2015) Vocabulary explanations in CLIL classrooms: A conversation analysis perspective. *The Language Learning Journal* 43 (3), 256–270.

Psathas, G. (1995) *Conversation Analysis: The Study of Talk-in-Interaction*. Thousand Oaks, CA: Sage.

Raymond, G.T. and Lerner, G.H. (2014) A body and its involvements: Adjusting action for dual involvements. In P. Haddington, T. Keisanen, L. Mondada and M. Nevile (eds) *Multiactivity in Social Interaction: Beyond Multitasking* (pp. 227–245). Amsterdam: John Benjamins.

Reddington, E. (2018) Managing participation in the adult ESL classroom: Engagement and exit practices. *Classroom Discourse* 9 (1), 1–14.

Schegloff, E.A. (1996) Turn organization: One intersection of grammar and interaction. In E. Ochs, E.A. Schegloff and S.A. Thompson (eds) *Interaction and Grammar* (pp. 52–133). Cambridge: Cambridge University Press.

Schegloff, E.A. (1997) Practices and actions: Boundary cases of other-initiated repair. *Discourse Processes* 23, 499–545.

Schegloff, E.A. and Sacks, H. (1973) Opening up closings. *Semiotica* 7, 289–327.

Sert, O. (2015) *Social Interaction and L2 Classroom Discourse*. Edinburgh: Edinburgh University Press.

St. John, O. and Cromdal, J. (2016) Crafting instructions collaboratively: Student questions and dual addressivity in classroom task instructions. *Discourse Processes* 53 (4), 252–279.

Stivers, T. (2008) Stance, alignment, and affiliation during storytelling: When nodding is a token of affiliation. *Research on Language and Social Interaction* 41 (1), 31–57.

Streeck, J., Goodwin, C. and LeBaron, C. (2011) *Embodied Interaction: Language and Body in the Material World*. New York: Cambridge University Press.

van Compernolle, R.A. and Smotrova, T. (2017) Gesture, meaning, and thinking-for-teaching in unplanned vocabulary explanations. *Classroom Discourse* 8 (3), 194–213. doi:10.1080/19463014.2016.1275028

van Lier, L. (2007) Action-based teaching, autonomy and identity. *International Journal of Innovation in Language Learning and Teaching* 1 (1), 46–65.

Waring, H.Z. (2016) *Theorizing Pedagogical Interaction: Insights from Conversation Analysis*. New York: Routledge.

Waring, H.Z., Creider, S.C. and Box, C.D. (2013) Explaining vocabulary in the second language classroom: A conversation analytic account. *Learning, Culture and Social Interaction* 2 (4), 249–264.

Zwiers, J. (2007) Teacher practices and perspectives for developing academic language. *International Journal of Applied Linguistics* 17 (1), 93–116.

8 Mutual Gaze, Embodied Go-aheads and their Interactional Consequences in Second Language Classrooms

Olcay Sert

The last decade has witnessed an *embodied turn* (Nevile, 2015) in research on language and social interaction, including research on classroom discourse and interaction. Gaze and other embodied resources that interactants deploy have been investigated in content and language classrooms, showing that embodiment is key in the interactional unfolding of learning and teaching events in classrooms. Among different kinds of embodied resources, the investigation of interactants' gazing behaviors has been a research concern over the last few years. Gaze has been shown to be a vital resource to show, for instance, willingness and unwillingness to participate in second language (L2) classrooms (Mortensen, 2008; Sert, 2015). In this chapter I demonstrate how students' attempts to establish mutual gaze with teachers in specific sequential positions and teachers' orientations to these by providing go-ahead responses can become consequential in the unfolding of subsequent student participation. Using transcriptions of video-recorded English as a foreign language (EFL) classroom interactions, I first describe the actions accomplished through a state of mutual gaze, and then explicate the ways in which teachers' embodied go-aheads create space for student engagement. I close the chapter by providing implications for teachers, teacher educators and research on gaze in classroom discourse and interaction.

Introduction

In order to be able to capture the dynamics and building blocks of human sociality, one needs to take into account how the semiotic resources deployed by participants in mundane and institutional interaction 'interact with each other to build locally relevant action' (Streeck *et al.*, 2011: 2). Conversation analytic work on the visual aspects of human interaction has mushroomed recently, and this growing interest brings about opportunities but also challenges for researchers, as 'no transcript can substitute for the data – i.e. a video-recording of the interaction' (Hepburn & Bolden, 2017: 101). Yet researchers have been developing different ways in which to describe multimodality with additional transcription notations that can account for resources including gaze (Goodwin, 1981; Rossano, 2013), and even on-screen behaviors (Balaman & Sert, 2017a, 2017b). Although it is challenging to describe the role of multimodal resources like gaze, systematic investigations carried out on such aspects of interaction have been feeding into the knowledge base of researchers and practitioners alike, particularly in settings where successful interaction becomes *the sine qua non* of effective teaching and learning, e.g. L2 classrooms.

Research in the last decade that has explored multimodal aspects of L2 classroom interaction, including participants' gaze behaviors, has equipped us with micro-level details of key phenomena, e.g. the social organization of turn taking and allocation practices (e.g. Kääntä, 2012; Mortensen, 2008), preference organization (Duran & Sert, 2019) and epistemics (e.g. Sert, 2013), as well as displays of willingness (e.g. Evnitskaya & Berger, 2017) and unwillingness (Sert, 2015) to participate, all of which help us understand participation and engagement at different levels. Conversation analytic accounts of such phenomena not only provide insights into teaching and learning practices, but also inform us on human conduct at a broader level. Participants' gaze behaviors have been found to play a central role that is intertwined with other verbal and embodied aspects of 'learning talk' (Markee & Seo, 2009); however, research that locates gaze as the focal analytic phenomenon in classrooms is scarce.

Against this background, this chapter presents analyses of a particular gaze trajectory found in teacher–student interactions in an L2 English classroom in a European context. The trajectory is observable in sequences in which a student, during a turn-in-progress, gazes toward the teacher to establish mutual gaze ending in a *gaze window* (Bavelas *et al.*, 2002), which is terminated after the teacher provides an embodied go-ahead. The embodied go-ahead functions as a response to the gaze, subsequently granting the rights to the floor to the student. The trajectory thus becomes consequential for student participation and engagement. The findings have direct relevance for research on gaze in classrooms and beyond, and has the potential to inform conversation analytic work on classroom interactional competence and teacher education.

Gaze in (Classroom) Interaction

Gaze has been of interest to researchers from diverse research paradigms, ranging from those applying cognitive theories (e.g. Phelps *et al.*,

2006) and conversation analysis (e.g. Goodwin, 1980) to scholars combining conversation analysis with quantitative methods (Kendrick & Holler, 2017). Although the number of studies that take gaze in everyday interaction as their focal interest is not scarce, studies that analyze the functions of gaze in classroom interaction have been rare. In such studies of classroom discourse and interaction (e.g. Evnitskaya & Berger, 2017; Fasel Lauzon & Berger, 2015; Käänta, 2012, 2015; Mortensen, 2008), however, gaze was described as one of the multimodal resources among other verbal and embodied ones. This is only natural, thinking that one cannot isolate the solitary function of gaze in the interactional unfolding of activities, especially those institutional activities in which the business of teaching and learning is at stake.

Kendon (1967)was one of the first researchers who systematically investigated gaze behaviors, and found that speakers tend to look away from recipients during long utterances, and tend to gaze back to their recipients when approaching the end of the utterances. Researchers have displayed a motivation to come up with norms and rules of gaze behaviors, as has been the case for turn-taking in interaction. Goodwin (1981: 57), for instance, proposed two rules:

(a) A speaker should obtain the gaze of [her] recipient during the course of a turn-at-talk. (b) A recipient should be gazing at the speaker when the speaker is gazing at the hearer.

With these rules, Goodwin emphasized the interrelatedness of participants' gaze behaviors, but he also provided explanations for deviations from these rules, e.g. when there are competing activities. The normative strength of such rules, however, has been questioned by Rossano (2013), as these rules can be relaxed in different conversational activities. Rossano (2013) argued that the analyses of the role of gaze in interaction should bring together different dimensions of such a role, including: (1) its relation to participation; (2) its regulatory functions (e.g. regarding turn-taking); (3) its role in action formation; as well as (4) sequential organization of courses of action.

Gaze can be used as an interactional resource to solicit a response, which is a regulatory function of gaze described previously by Goodwin and Goodwin (1986). A state of mutual gaze can also create *a gaze window* (Bavelas *et al.*, 2002), described as a moment of mutual gaze terminated by the listener's continuers or listenership tokens. Based on their data, Bevales *et al.* (2002) describe a gaze window as follows:

... when the speaker looked at the listener, this started a brief period of mutual gaze, a gaze window, in which we noticed that a listener response was very likely to occur. Moreover, this was not simply a stimulus-response system in which the speaker evoked a response from the listener. Rather, it was the listener's response that seemed to terminate the speaker's gaze and therefore end the gaze window. (Bevales *et al.*, 2002: 570)

A similar pattern will be presented in this chapter: a student looks at the teacher, initiating the gaze window, which is terminated after an embodied go-ahead by the teacher, leading the student to maintain the rights to the floor. This trajectory, as will be demonstrated through the analyses of excerpts, is closely linked to the institutional dynamics in instructed language learning, where epistemic rights and obligations are embodied in the unfolding classroom activities (Lee, 2015).

Classrooms are sites where the role of institutionality and emergent epistemic dynamics in gaze behaviors are observable, especially in the co-constructed asymmetry in turn-taking and allocation practices (Kääntä, 2010, 2012, 2015; Mortensen, 2008). Although the importance of gaze in positions like turn-beginnings has been studied in detail with an emphasis on the actions accomplished in first language (L1) talk (e.g. Goodwin, 1980; Rossano, 2012; Rossano et al., 2009), its relevance to turn-taking practices in L2 talk has only recently been investigated in detail (but see Carroll, 2004). In teacher-fronted classroom interaction, although the role of gaze (and partly gestures) has been briefly referred to in relation to turn-allocation (e.g. Hall, 1998; van Lier, 1994), more thorough, systematic investigations informed by a conversation analytic multimodal paradigm are relatively recent (e.g. Kääntä, 2010, 2012; Mortensen, 2008).

Mortensen (2008) investigated how gaze is systematically used to display willingness to be selected as a next speaker in Danish L2 classrooms. His findings showed that, among other interactional phenomena, by engaging in mutual gaze with the students the teacher displays 'an ongoing monitoring of the students' display of willingness to answer the first pair part as a relevant interactional job prior to the speaker selection' (Mortensen, 2008: 62). Drawing on his findings, it can be argued that the process of turn-allocation and its co-accomplishment through gaze orientations have not only interactional but also pedagogical consequences, as has later been explicated by Sert (2015) in relation to students' disengagement, observable through their gaze behaviors.

In another study within the same L2 context in Denmark, Mortensen (2009) focused on how students claim incipient speakership and establish recipiency with a co-participant before a turn is properly initiated, by using body movements and in-breaths as resources. He showed that, although establishment of mutual gaze is an important component of displaying recipiency, gaze removal and divergent body orientations may be performed due to the existence of different classroom artifacts (also see Carroll, 2004; Goodwin & Goodwin, 1986, for gaze removals in solitary word searches).

With a focus on how interactants orient to the preference structure in university-level writing conferences, Park (2015) documented participants' use of gaze shift as a cue to signal dispreference and showed that the shift allows students to anticipate the teacher's upcoming dispreferred response. Investigating peer group discussions in English as a second language (ESL) settings, Lee (2017: 677) illustrated how gestures can 'solicit the gaze of co-participants who are occupied with other activities, even if the speaker's gaze is not directed at the listeners'. Carpenter (2016), on the other hand, investigated a neglected context: young learners' classrooms. By tracing the gaze behavior of an ESL tutor in a tutoring session with a six-year-old child, she showed that gaze 'is a powerful tool to direct the student's attention and obtain his compliance with teacher directives' (Carpenter, 2016: 27).

Investigating L2 French classrooms, Fasel Lauzon and Berger (2015) documented the role of gaze in the accomplishment of turn allocation and how this is consequential for the subsequent talk. They showed that withdrawing gaze when speaker nomination is recognizably imminent is treated as indicating unwillingness or unavailability to be selected as the next speaker. This is not the only study to refer to the concepts of willingness and unwillingness to participate in relation to gaze behaviors. Evnitskaya and Berger (2017), for instance, investigated multimodal displays of willingness to participate (WTP) in L2 classroom group work and content and language integrated learning (CLIL) classroom whole-class activities. The authors explicated students' reorientation of their gaze to the relevant objects or the current speaker as an indication of WTP as an interactional construct. In a previous study, pointing to the opposite of WTP, namely unwillingness to participate (UTP), Sert (2015) revealed that learners resort to gaze withdrawals to display UTP. Sert concluded with the recommendation that teachers monitor:

> oft-repeated student gaze aversions and withdrawals after initiating a question, especially if these aversions and withdrawals are also combined with other indicators like very long silences. (Sert, 2015: 141)

In this chapter, however, the positive aspects of student and teacher gaze behaviors will be handled, and as opposed to the unwillingness to participate studied in the aforementioned work (Sert, 2015), the engaging, positive and collaborative nature of gaze behavior in EFL classrooms will be documented. The case trajectory explained at the end of the introduction section will illustrate the central role of gaze in co-constructing opportunities for student participation, documenting a micro-analytic case for co-constructing an instance of classroom interactional competence. Before moving on with the analysis and findings, I will now describe the context and the analytic focus in the next section.

Data and Method

The data come from English language classrooms with students in the 10th and 11th grades in a public school in Luxembourg. The video-recordings amount to 16 classroom sessions (each of 45 minutes). Two digital video-cameras were set at the beginning of each session, one focused on the teacher and one focused on the students, in order to capture the details of the embodied behaviors of the participants. The students in both classrooms, with an intermediate level of English, worked with the same course book (New Headway Intermediate, Soars & Soars, 2009) in addition to various materials the teacher brought to the lessons. There was a total of 32 students whose age ranged from 15 to 18 during the time of data collection. All the students, having grown up in Luxembourg, spoke at least three languages other than English. The languages spoken outside the classroom were Luxembourgish, German and French in addition to English due to the multicultural nature of Luxembourg.

There was one teacher for both classrooms, who was also born and raised in Luxembourg. He was multilingual and had a master's degree in TESOL from a British university. The materials used in both classrooms represented a wide range of pedagogical foci, and included short stories and literature books as well as various texts and exercises from the students' course book.

For this chapter, the recordings of the 11th-grade classroom (six classroom hours in total) were selected due to the seating arrangement (U-shape) which made it easier to observe the participants' coordinated gaze behaviors. After each session was transcribed in great detail using the Jeffersonian transcription system, a close analysis revealed the focal phenomenon: students' establishment of mutual gaze with the teacher in a turn-in-progress, which is oriented to by the teacher in a way that enables the student to maintain the rights to the floor and thus facilitate subsequent student participation. Close multimodal analysis of the sequences showed that gaze, and in particular a state of *gaze window* (Bavelas *et al.*, 2002), stands out as a key interactional phenomenon, the repetitive occurrence of which deserves a multimodal analysis. Therefore, using conversation analysis, I closely examined the sequences that include the phenomenon under investigation by focusing not only on the sequential organization of talk, but also on various multi-semiotic resources enacted by the participants, including gaze, gestures, body movements and embodiment of classroom artifacts. This approach to interaction combines the temporally unfolding organization of talk with 'the semiotic structure provided by the historically built material world, and the body as an unfolding locus for the display of meaning and action' (Goodwin, 2000: 1517).

Analysis and Findings

In this section I will present excerpts based on a collection of 18 cases in which students establish mutual gaze with the teacher in a turn-in-progress, and this attempt is oriented to by the teacher in some way (e.g. through what I call embodied go-aheads and its variations) to enable subsequent student participation. It will be argued that the student gaze toward the teacher becomes an important resource to mobilize a response from the teacher; therefore it is an important part of learners' interactional repertoires. Likewise, the teacher's monitoring of and their subsequent response to such behavior is part of their classroom interactional competence. It should be noted that this gaze trajectory, without doubt, is not the only interactional resource participants deploy during these sequences; nevertheless, in all instances we have the same gaze movement pattern which makes gaze the central analytic concern for the present paper.

In Excerpt 1 the class is working on a short story called *My Son the Fanatic*, which describes the life of a Pakistani family living in London. The students were supposed to read the short story before they came to class, so some background knowledge about the story was expected. The topic under focus in the excerpt is the similarities between London and Luxembourg. The analytic focus is on Lines 12, 14 and 17, but an understanding of what comes before and after is necessary. In Lines 1 and 2,[1] already having established an ongoing interaction with DOR, the teacher (TEA) attributes to the student an ability to communicate within her community in Luxembourg. It should be noted here that the Portuguese identity of the student has already been established by the participants before Line 1 (see Sert, 2015: 41), and is then again oriented to by DOR in Lines 7 and 19.

Excerpt 1: prejudice, 04_06_11_07–25

```
1     TEA:  okay so within your com↓munity,
2           you are able to communicate.=
3     DOR:  =yes: but=
4     TEA:  =[very eFFIcient↓ly.=
5     DOR:   [er : : :
6     DOR:  =but not with the luxembourg- only with the
7           (comm- of) people of your country where you are ↑from.
8     TEA:  very goo:{d.=
9                    {((DOR looks down))
10    DOR:  =and=
11    TEA:  =yeah?
12    DOR:  then it gives like.h-{ then >it's the case of the<
13                               {Fig. 8.1((looks at the board))
```

Figure 8.1 DOR looks at the board

```
14→            {<pre-ju-{↑dice>
15            {(((uses a deictic gesture, also moves her finger and hand with
              each syllable))
16                        {Fig. 8.2((looks at the teacher))
```

Figure 8.2 The gaze window

```
17    TEA:   {↑ye:s.
18           {((TEA nods))
19    DOR:   {then (0.4) 'cause >luxembourgers say oh portuguese are<
20           {Fig. 8.3((looks down))
```

Figure 8.3 DOR looks down

```
21            al- all in (one) ↑group and they they don't eh (0.7)mischen.
```

Displaying an orientation to the falling intonation counter that signals
turn completion (to communicate.=), DOR's turn initial and slightly
stretched confirmation token (yes:) in Line 3 latches TEA's utterance,
and is followed by a conjunction (but=) that may mark a stance that is
less than agreement. In Lines 4 and 5 the interactants compete for the
floor: while TEA latches DOR's turn tying his utterance with an adjectival
phrase ([very eFFI]cient ↓ ly.=), DOR in Line 5 produces a stretched
hesitation marker. Repeating the conjunction 'but' turn initially, DOR
explains that she is able to communicate not just with people from her
country of origin, probably referring to the Portuguese community in

Luxembourg as will be evidenced in the last two lines of the excerpt. DOR's turn is responded to with an explicit positive assessment (`very goo:d.=`). Looking down right at the end of TEA's assessment, she uses an additive conjunction (`=and=`) and signals continuation in Line 10, which is oriented to by TEA in the subsequent turn. He offers the floor to the student and encourages further participation.

Using another discourse marker (`then`), DOR keeps her gaze on her notebook, and while producing the second 'then' at the onset of her restart in Line 12 (`then >it's the case of the<`), she looks at the board (Figure 8.1), on which the word 'prejudice' had been written by the teacher 1 minute and 37 seconds ago (see Figure 8.4), before the beginning of this excerpt (see Sert, 2015: 39).

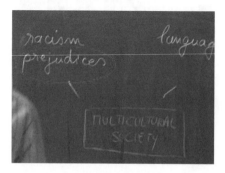

Figure 8.4 The word 'prejudices' on the board

Maintaining her gaze on the board, in Line 15 DOR moves her index finger each time she produces a syllable while producing the word 'prejudice', and establishes mutual gaze (Figure 8.2) with the teacher in producing the final syllable with rising, try-marked intonation. The restart in the previous line, orientation of the gaze toward the board, and suprasegmentally marked production of the word 'prejudice' combined with the mutual gaze between DOR and the teacher indicate that DOR is orienting to the production of this word as problematic at that moment. In particular, the try-marked intonation and gaze together positions TEA as the participant with the epistemic authority, to which the teacher orients in the next turn. In Line 17 TEA, while nodding, produces a confirmation token, which signals to the student to continue her turn, thus forming an embodied go-ahead, positioning himself in K+ (Heritage, 2012a, 2012b). Starting in Line 19, DOR looks down at her notebook (Figure 8.3) and produces a long turn describing her position on Luxembourgers' take on the Portuguese community, thus establishing a relation with the word 'prejudice'.

Locating the gaze behavior of DOR in Lines 16–20 as the main analytic focus, one can argue that she resorts to gaze as an interactional resource to solicit a response, a regulatory function of gaze described previously by Goodwin and Goodwin (1986). We should also note that the mutual gaze represented in Figure 8.2 resembles what Bavelas *et al.* (2002) refer to as a *gaze window*, which I described earlier. The student's embodied request for confirmation is successfully completed in Excerpt 1. TEA's interactional maneuver in Line 17 enables the student to keep participating in interaction and to produce an extended turn in L2 subsequently, something that is desirable in L2 classrooms.

In Excerpt 2 we observe the same gaze trajectory: (1) the student gazes toward the teacher (Line 8); (2) TEA provides a confirmation token enabling the student to go ahead; and (3) the student continues her turn after the gaze window is terminated. However, it will be noted that the pedagogical consequences are not the same in this example although we have the same gaze pattern, which will be discussed after I present the analysis. In this excerpt, one of the students is reading a text aloud and mispronounces the phrase 'the sharp tongue', which is turned into a vocabulary teaching opportunity by the teacher. The teacher tries to elicit a correct description of this idiom from the students, and before JES raises her hand to bid for her turn in turn final position in Line 1, he has provided an explicit negative assessment to another student.

Excerpt 2: *die Zunge 04_06_11_18–16*

```
1     TEA:  er:: >no that's not what it means{:<.
2                                   {((JES raises her hand))
3           (1.3)
4           {you know jessica{?
5           {((pointing at JES))
6                            {((JES looks away))
7  →  JES:  er:: sharp, ehm:: {(da-) {↑schaarf.((Translation:sharp))
8                             {Fig. 8.5((shifts her gaze to TEA))
9                                    {Fig. 8.6((clenches fists, arms upright))
```

Figure 8.5 Looks at TEA   **Figure 8.6** JES clenches fists

```
10    TEA:   {yeah=
11           {((nods))
12    JES:   =dat {heescht= ((LUX))
              that is
13              {((JES looks down))
14    TEA:   =in english?
15           yeah(.)if you have a sharp tongue?
16    JES:   ehm::(0.5)eh:: (0.7) a{gg↑ressive.
17                            {Fig. 8.7((looks at the teacher))
```

Figure 8.7 JES looks at the teacher

```
18    TEA:   YES: okay (.) he has a very aggressive ↑tone when he
19           speaks to his father.
20    TEA:   exactly(.)continue.
```

In Line 4 TEA performs an embodied turn allocation after JES has maintained her gaze toward the teacher for more than one second. In so doing, he uses the student's name in turn final position and formulates a knowledge check question (you know jessica?), at the end of which JES looks away. In Line 7 JES starts her turn with a stretched hesitation marker and produces the first word of the idiom with emphasis (er:: sharp). She then produces another hesitation marker (ehm::) and requests confirmation (↑schaarf) by translating the word 'sharp' into Luxembourgish, flagged suprasegmentally with try-marked intonation and bodily with a shift of gaze to the teacher (Figure 8.5). She also embodies her request as she clenches her fists to illustrate the word (Figure 8.6). This turn, which includes a shift of gaze toward the teacher and the initiation of a state of a gaze window, at the same time positions the teacher as the interactant with epistemic authority, and includes a display of understanding on the part of the student as she is able to translate the word from L2 to L1. TEA provides help by minimally producing a confirmation token in Line 10. Following TEA's confirmation, which also acts as an embodied go-ahead, JES starts off her turn in Line 12 to explain the idiom in Luxembourgish (dat heescht), until the teacher asks her to speak in English (Amir & Musk, 2013; Sert & Balaman, 2018). In Line 16, after a couple of hesitation markers and silences, she provides the meaning of the idiom in English, while again shifting her gaze to the teacher (Figure 8.7). The pedagogical goal of the activity is achieved eventually, that is, to elicit the meaning of the idiom from one of the students. It is clear that there is an interplay between the task of providing the correct answer and the issue of the use of L1 here, conveyed through the request for confirmation. The request brings in the relevance of the epistemic gradient, and it is executed using gaze as the central resource to mobilize the response.

Excerpt 3 represents another instance of the gaze trajectory explained in the analyses carried out thus far. The focus is on the gaze window from Line 10 to Line 12. Immediately before the episode starts, TEA asks a question about the potential problems that the existence of various religions in the same setting (i.e. a multicultural society like London) can bring about. Having received no answer from other students, TEA allocates the turn in Line 1 to SVE, who has made himself available by raising his hand.

Excerpt 3: *War like in Ireland 04_10_10–10*

```
1    TEA:   what do you ↑think [sven?
2    SVE:                      [war like in ireland.
3           (1.7)
4    TEA:   can you exp↓lain (.)you ↑think (.) >it is possible
5           that there will be a war in lon↓don<=
6    SVE:   ={yeah because (the)one religion wants, (0.6) the other
7           {((looks down))
8           to be: (0.6) {same religion as they ↑are.
9                        {((looks up and establishes mutual gaze with TEA))
10   TEA:   ↑yes:, (.)very ↓often (0.3) o↓k[ay
11   SVE:                                  [{and if they (0.4) don't
12                                         {((looks down))
13           reach them with {↑words
14                           {Fig. 8.8((establishes mutual gaze with TEA))
```

Figure 8.8 SVE establishes mutual gaze

```
15    TEA:   {uh huh.
16           {(((T nods))
17    SVE:   {they  take  the  ↑gu{ns.
18           {(((SVE looks down)) {(((establishes mutual gaze with TEA))
```

Figure 8.9 SVE looks down

```
19           (0.8)
20    TEA:   yes very good.
```

In Line 2 SVE provides an answer to TEA's question by categorizing
the case of Ireland as war. A relatively long silence follows this answer
before TEA follows up in Line 4. TEA first requests an explanation (can
you exp ↓ lain), but then initiates a new formulation in turn-in-progress
with declarative syntax (you ↑think (.) >it is possible that
there will be a war in lon ↓ don < =), projecting a confirmation with an elaboration (Seuren & Huiskes, 2017). In Line 6 SVE starts
off his turn with a confirmation token and withdraws mutual gaze with
the teacher at the onset of the token. He then provides an elaboration on
his answer in Lines 6 and 8, arguing that one of the religions may want to
assimilate the other. SVE stops for slightly more than half a second during
the turn-in-progress in Line 8, and establishes mutual gaze with TEA
while formulating the remainder of the turn.

In Line 10 TEA produces a prosodically marked agreement token as a
response to the argument of SVE, and follows up with an extreme case
formulation (very ↓often) to upgrade his agreement. At the end of
TEA's turn, SVE again withdraws mutual gaze and looks down, while
also starting to produce an if-clause statement to build on the topic-in-
progress (Line 9).

Lines 13–18 include a gaze window, initiated by the rising intonation
and gaze toward the teacher (Figure 8.8) and terminated after the embodied go-ahead (Figure 8.9). The gaze window starts at the onset of the final
word of the subordinate clause (if they (0.4) don't reach them
with ↑words) formulated by SVE. Similar to the examples provided in
Excerpts 1 and 2, rising intonation and the establishment of mutual gaze
with TEA elicits an embodied go-ahead (accompanied by a nod) that
stands alone and is minimal (uh huh.) in Line 15. Immediately after this

continuer, SVE terminates the mutual gaze (hence the gaze window) and produces the main clause in his multi-unit turn (they take the ↑guns.). Note that in contrast to the confirmation tokens in the first two excerpts, TEA produces a continuer like 'uh huh' in Excerpt 3, which embodies 'the understanding that extended talk by another is going on by declining to produce a fuller turn in that position' (Schegloff, 1982: 81). With his continuer in Line 15, encouraging the student to continue, the teacher provides the grounds for SVE to maintain speakership and the rights to the floor, enabling him to produce the main clause of his utterance.

The examples depicted in this section have emphasized gaze as a central resource to mobilize a response from the teacher in an EFL classroom in Luxembourg. I believe that the findings presented here have implications for understanding the complexities of teaching and in particular the embodied practices that, while subtle, are significant to the accomplishment of teaching. In addition to this, it has been shown that the institutional nature of interaction and the emerging epistemic imbalance within this gaze trajectory can inform future research on gaze. These will be explained in the final section of the chapter.

Discussion and Conclusion

As the invention and use of the microscope revolutionized our view of the inner workings of biological matter (Scherf & Huisken, 2015), so did the use of conversation analysis enable us to examine the working mechanisms of human sociality. Powerful observation by paying attention to micro-level detail has always provided researchers with rich insights into phenomena under investigation, and a detail like gaze is no exception to this. In this chapter, adopting gaze as the central analytic focus, I have presented analysis of a gaze trajectory which entails students' establishment of mutual gaze with the teacher that elicits a go-ahead, and termination of the mutual gaze following embodied go-aheads by the teacher. The resulting format enables students to maintain the rights to the floor, and deserves close analysis as the interactional resources used by both the teacher and the students are conducive to the progressivity of pedagogical activities and student engagement. Lack of these minimal confirmations, or go-aheads by the teacher, may lead to the interruption of unfolding student turn(s), which is not a desired outcome with regard to student engagement.

The findings have shown that the gaze trajectory and especially the onset of the initial mutual gaze is almost always prosodically marked, mostly with rising intonation. As both of the excerpts analyzed have demonstrated, the gaze behaviors are accompanied by other embodied conduct, including the hand gestures of DOR in Excerpt 1 (Line 15) and JES's clenching of her fists in Excerpt 2 (Line 9). Similar observations have been revealed before by Mortensen (2008, 2016) and Sert (2015) in that gaze movements that are intertwined with frames of participation are coupled with marked body movements, including leaning forward, headshakes, etc.

Rossano (2013: 322) argues that gaze behavior 'is organized with respect to the sequential organization of courses of action' and challenges the already described dimensions of the role of gaze in interaction, as listed in the review of the literature. Likewise, the present chapter also extends this line of research by claiming that, in describing the role of gaze, we need to consider two important elements: institutionality and epistemics in interaction. The institutional fingerprint in relation to gaze was especially clear in Excerpt 2, in which the use of a student's L1 was accompanied by the gaze movement of the student, and the use of the L1 was marked following the termination of the gaze window. The use of the L1 to ask for the confirmation of the teacher represented the interplay between the institutional goal of the use of the L2 in the class and the emerging negotiation and co-construction of such rules through dynamic gaze behaviors.

In addition to the role of institutional context in understanding the role of gaze, epistemics was also important to regulating gaze behavior. Rossano (2013) argues that using gaze to solicit help is a case that can be observed in specific sequential environments, like the one described in this chapter. In soliciting help through mutual gaze with the teacher (in Excerpts 1 and 2), the students at the same time position themselves as the unknowing participant (K-) relative to the teacher, and this claim is supported by the teacher's response to this gaze behavior and his approval/confirmation/go-ahead, assigning himself as the participant with epistemic authority. The epistemic gradient, then, is co-constructed and oriented to by the participants *in situ* visible through their gaze behaviors, thus establishing epistemics as one of the dimensions to understand the role of gaze in interaction. This is also in line with previous research (Sert, 2013; Sert & Walsh, 2013) which defined the role of gaze in negative epistemics (e.g. I don't knows, epistemic status checks).

One of the contributions of this chapter has been to provide further evidence to the concept of gaze window, which was criticized by Rossano (2013), since the coding system for gaze in the original paper describing a gaze window (Bevales *et al.*, 2002) would prevent the analysts from taking into account the actual talk, in addition to the lack of consideration for the existence of communicative behaviors to solicit a response. In this chapter, however, I brought evidence to the findings of the original study on gaze window from a classroom context. Further research could investigate such gaze behavior in other institutional contexts to see if the rights to the floor are managed by the participants in the same manner, resulting in the speakers' gazing away after the listener provides a response.

Previous work on classroom interactional competence (CIC) (Sert, 2015, 2017; Sert & Walsh, 2013; Walsh, 2006, 2011, 2013) has mainly conceptualized the construct from teachers' perspectives (but see Park,

2017). Yet, as the definition clearly suggests, CIC is the 'teachers' and learners' ability to use interaction as a tool for mediating and assisting learning' (Walsh, 2011: 158), since it is a co-constructed phenomenon. This study has hopefully contributed to this line of research by describing a gaze trajectory in which a student successfully mobilizes a response from the teacher and, while doing so, resolves an emergent epistemic issue by being able to embody her request for help in order to be able to provide subsequent utterances in the L2. Maximizing interactional space, use of multimodal resources and managing language alternation have previously been defined as parts of CIC, and the excerpts analyzed here depict all of these interactional phenomena which contribute to enhancing learner participation and engagement at turns-at-talk.

There is also food for thought for teacher education. Integration of episodes in this chapter or videos of teachers' own classrooms into teacher education programs (for an example, see Sert, 2019) can be beneficial for teachers in service and in training. It can help teachers become more aware of how (not) attending to student gaze can have pedagogical consequences and how gaze can become a resource to help students hold the floor for a longer time in L2 classroom interaction, possibly leading to enhanced student engagement. One piece of advice that can be given to teachers is that they should monitor students' attempts to establish mutual gaze in ongoing student turns, and respond with maximum embodiment and minimum talk to encourage the student to speak more. To see examples of how findings from this research can inform teacher education, one can look into teacher education frameworks that include the use of recordings from language classrooms (e.g. Sert, 2015, 2019; Waring, 2019).

Acknowledgements

The data collection, as part of my PhD thesis, was possible thanks to a visiting researcher from Fonds National de la Recherche Luxembourg. This paper was first presented in ARTE symposium in Hanover, Germany in September 2017.

Notes

(1) This excerpt is part of a larger series of episodes that present a 'learning talk analysis' (Markee & Seo, 2009) in Sert (2015, Chapter 3). The part of the excerpt analyzed here has been visually enhanced for this paper to include visual details on the gaze behaviors of the participants.

References

Amir, A. and Musk, N. (2013) Language policing: Micro-level language policy-in-process in the foreign language classroom. *Classroom Discourse* 4 (2), 151–167.
Balaman, U. and Sert, O. (2017a) Development of L2 interactional resources for online collaborative task accomplishment. *Computer Assisted Language Learning* 30 (7), 601–630.

Balaman, U. and Sert, O. (2017b) The coordination of online L2 interaction and orientations to task interface for epistemic progression. *Journal of Pragmatics* 115, 115–129.

Bavelas, J.B., Coates, L. and Johnson, T. (2002) Listener responses as a collaborative process: The role of gaze. *Journal of Communication* 52 (3), 566–580.

Carpenter, L. (2016) Managing the participation of a young learner: A multimodal teacher practice. *Working Papers in TESOL & Applied Linguistics* 16 (2), 24–28.

Carroll, D. (2004) Restarts in novice turn beginnings: Disfluencies or interactional achievements? In R. Gardner and J. Wagner (eds) *Second Language Conversations* (pp. 201–220). London: Continuum.

Duran, D. and Sert, O. (2019) Preference organization in English as a Medium of Instruction classrooms in a Turkish higher education setting. *Linguistics and Education* 49, 72–85.

Evnitskaya, N. and Berger, E. (2017) Learners' multimodal displays of willingness to participate in classroom interaction in the L2 and CLIL contexts. *Classroom Discourse* 8 (1), 71–94.

Fasel Lauzon, V. and Berger, E. (2015) The multimodal organization of speaker selection in classroom interaction. *Linguistics and Education* 31, 14–29.

Goodwin, C. (1980) Restarts, pauses, and the achievement of a state of mutual gaze at turn-beginning. *Sociological Inquiry* 50 (3–4), 272–302.

Goodwin, C. (1981) *Conversational Organization: Interaction Between Speakers and Hearers.* New York: Academic Press.

Goodwin, C. (2000) Action and embodiment within situated human interaction. *Journal of Pragmatics* 32 (10), 1489–1522.

Goodwin, M.H. and Goodwin, C. (1986) Gesture and coparticipation in the activity of searching for a word. *Semiotica* 62 (1–2), 51–75.

Hall, J.K. (1998) Differential teacher attention to student utterances: The construction of different opportunities for learning in the IRF. *Linguistics and Education* 9 (3), 287–311.

Hepburn, A. and Bolden, G.B. (2017) *Transcribing for Social Research.* London: Sage.

Heritage, J. (2012a) Epistemics in action: Action formation and territories of knowledge. *Research on Language and Social Interaction* 45 (1), 1–29.

Heritage, J. (2012b) The epistemic engine: Sequence organisation and territories of knowledge. *Research on Language and Social Interaction* 45 (1), 30–52.

Käänta, L. (2010) Teacher turn-allocation and repair practices in classroom interaction. Doctoral dissertation, Jyväskylä University.

Käänta, L. (2012) Teachers' embodied allocations in instructional interaction. *Classroom Discourse* 3 (2), 166–186.

Käänta, L. (2015) The multimodal organisation of teacher-led classroom interaction In P. Seedhouse and C. Jenks (eds) *International Perspectives on the ELT Classroom* (pp. 64–83). Basingstoke: Palgrave MacMillan.

Kendon, A. (1967) Some functions of gaze-direction in social interaction. *Acta Psychologica* 26, 22–63.

Kendrick, K.H. and Holler, J. (2017) Gaze direction signals response preference in conversation. *Research on Language and Social Interaction* 50 (1), 12–32.

Lee, J. (2017) Multimodal turn allocation in ESL peer group discussions. *Social Semiotics* 27 (5), 671–692.

Lee, Y.A. (2015) Negotiating knowledge bases in pedagogical discourse: Relevance of identities to language classroom interactions. *Text & Talk* 35 (5), 621–642.

Markee, N. and Seo, M.S. (2009) Learning talk analysis. *IRAL – International Review of Applied Linguistics in Language Teaching* 47 (1), 37–63.

Mortensen, K. (2008) Selecting next speaker in the second language classroom: How to find a willing next speaker in planned activities. *Journal of Applied Linguistics* 5 (1), 55–79.

Mortensen, K. (2009) Establishing recipiency in pre-beginning position in the second language classroom. *Discourse Processes* 46 (5), 491–515.

Mortensen, K. (2016) The body as a resource for other-initiation of repair: Cupping the hand behind the ear. *Research on Language and Social Interaction* 49 (1), 34–57.

Nevile, M. (2015) The embodied turn in research on language and social interaction. *Research on Language and Social Interaction* 48 (2), 121–151.

Park, I. (2015) Or-prefaced third turn self-repairs in student questions. *Linguistics and Education* 31, 101–114.

Park, J. (2017) Multimodality as an interactional resource for classroom interactional competence (CIC). *Eurasian Journal of Applied Linguistics* 3 (2), 121–138.

Phelps, F.G., Doherty-Sneddon, G. and Warnock, H. (2006) Helping children think: Gaze aversion and teaching. *British Journal of Developmental Psychology* 24 (3), 577–588.

Rossano, F. (2012) Gaze behavior in face-to-face interaction. Unpublished PhD dissertation, Max Planck Institute for Psycholinguistics.

Rossano, F. (2013) Gaze in conversation. In J. Sidnell and T. Stivers (eds) *The Handbook of Conversation Analysis* (pp. 308–329). Chichester: Wiley-Blackwell.

Rossano, F., Brown, P. and Levinson, S.C. (2009) Gaze, questioning and culture. In J. Sidnell (ed.) *Conversation Analysis: Comparative Perspectives* (pp. 187–249). Cambridge: Cambridge University Press.

Schegloff, E.A. (1982) Discourse as an interactional achievement: Some uses of 'uh huh' and other things that come between sentences. *Analyzing Discourse: Text and Talk* 71, 93.

Scherf, N. and Huisken, J. (2015) The smart and gentle microscope. *Nature Biotechnology* 33 (8), 815–818.

Sert, O. (2013) 'Epistemic status check' as an interactional phenomenon in instructed learning settings. *Journal of Pragmatics* 45 (1), 13–28.

Sert, O. (2015) *Social Interaction and L2 Classroom Discourse*. Edinburgh: Edinburgh University Press.

Sert, O. (2017) Creating opportunities for L2 learning in a prediction activity. *System* 70, 14–25.

Sert, O. (2019) Classroom interaction and language teacher education. In S. Walsh and S. Mann (eds) *The Routledge Handbook of English Language Teacher Education* (pp. 216–238). London: Routledge.

Sert, O. and Balaman, U. (2018) Orientations to negotiated language and task rules in online L2 interaction. *ReCALL* 1–20. doi:10.1017/S0958344017000325

Sert, O. and Walsh, S. (2013) The interactional management of claims of insufficient knowledge in English language classrooms. *Language and Education* 27 (6), 542–565.

Seuren, L.M. and Huiskes, M. (2017) Confirmation or elaboration: What do yes/no declaratives want? *Research on Language and Social Interaction* 50 (2), 188–205.

Soars, L. and Soars, J. (2009) New headway intermediate students' book (4th edn). Oxford: Oxford University Press.

Streeck, J., Goodwin, C. and LeBaron, C. (2011) Embodied interaction in the material world: An introduction. In J. Streeck, C. Goodwin and C. LeBaron (eds) *Embodied Interaction: Language and Body in the Material World* (pp. 1–26). Cambridge: Cambridge University Press.

van Lier, L. (1994) *The Classroom and the Language Learner: Ethnography and Second-language Classroom Research*. London: Longman.

Walsh, S. (2006) *Investigating Classroom Discourse*. New York: Routledge.

Walsh, S. (2011) *Exploring Classroom Discourse: Language in Action*. London: Routledge.

Walsh, S. (2013) *Classroom Discourse and Teacher Development*. Edinburgh: Edinburgh University Press.

Waring, H.Z. (2019) Harnessing the power of heteroglossia in teacher talk. In S. Kunitz, N. Markee and O. Sert (eds) *Emerging Issues in Classroom Discourse and Interaction: Theoretical and Applied CA Perspectives on Pedagogy*. Berlin: Springer.

9 The Use of Embodied Self-directed Talk in Teaching Writing

Innhwa Park

This chapter examines the embodied practices of self-directed talk in the context of college-level writing tutorial. One 60-minute tutoring session between a freshman writer (second language user of English) and a junior writing tutor (first language user of English) is used as data. The data were transcribed and analyzed using conversation analysis methodology. In particular, the study examines: (1) the sequential context in which the writing tutor engages in self-directed talk; (2) the ways in which the thinking process is made visible as an embodied practice; and (3) the ways in which the student joins in the tutor's thinking process. The analyses show how the tutor puts the revision process on display as he produces self-directed talk when dealing with various aspects of writing including grammar and word choice issues. The tutor's self-directed talk is marked with quieter speech that often consists of repetitions and rhetorical questions and is accompanied by various multimodal actions such as gaze shifts, hand gestures and thinking face/posture. Meanwhile, the student contributes to the tutor's thinking process by agreeing/disagreeing, providing clarifications and asking questions for additional thinking. In doing so, the participants arrive at various writing decisions together. The study findings have implications for writing instruction.

Introduction

Self-directed talk, also referred to as private speech (Flavell *et al.*, 1966) and self-talk (Goffman, 1978), has traditionally been characterized as audible speech that is addressed to the self (Berk & Garvin, 1984) and does not anticipate listeners' response (Smolucha, 1992). Its production is distinct from speech that is addressed to others, as self-directed talk is typically delivered at a lowered volume, consists of multiple repetitions and is accompanied by averted eye gaze. In the field of education, self-directed talk has been recognized as the verbalization of thought processes and adopted as an instructional strategy. Teachers use self-directed talk to think aloud and model how a competent person monitors one's own thinking and understanding processes (Baumann *et al.*, 1993; Collins & Smith, 1982; Davey, 1983). Traditionally, the think-aloud strategy has primarily been examined in the context of children's literacy development (Bereiter & Bird, 1985; Olshavsky, 1977; Palincsar & Brown, 1988); it has been depicted as verbally displaying the teacher's cognitive skills for students to mimic.

Recently, there have been an increasing number of studies that are grounded in Goffman's (1978) observation that self-talk may be an integral part of social interaction as one establishes oneself as a competent participant in the interaction. Researchers have examined how self-directed talk is used by learners and teachers in the context of classroom interaction. Examining the use of private speech by second language (L2) learners of English in a problem-solving context (i.e. board game), Smith (2007) finds that private speech reveals the speaker's predicament and facilitates collective thinking, engaging other listeners for joint problem solving. She proposes that private speech has both cognitive and social functions. Focusing on the social functions of self-directed talk, Steinbach Kohler and Thorne (2011) observe how L2 learners of French engage in self-directed talk in small-group interactions and note that this allows the participants to build their actions based on shared knowledge. In the context of writing, Kristiansen (2017) shows how students collectively contribute to the act of composition by demonstrating the process in which they formulate a potential text (i.e. research question); she refers to the practice as using a 'writing aloud voice', which features a quotative construction and marked prosody.

Shifting attention from learner self-directed talk to teacher self-directed talk, Hall and Smotrova (2013) examine how teachers use self-talk in moments of trouble while teaching (e.g. dealing with technology-related issues). Teacher self-talk not only helps students maintain their attention on the main instructional task, but also elicits empathetic responses from them. In addition, Looney *et al.* (2017) find that a teacher's self-directed 'okay' used during math lectures goes beyond marking transitions in instructional activities. It helps the teacher verbalize his thought processes while highlighting the procedural steps in solving a matrix.

In this chapter I examine how self-directed talk functions as an instructional resource in the context of one-on-one writing tutorial, focusing on its embodied display. In particular, the study examines: (1) the sequential context in which the writing tutor engages in self-directed talk; (2) the ways in which the thinking process is made visible as an embodied practice; and (3) the ways in which the student joins in the tutor's thinking process. The analyses show how the tutor's self-directed talk contributes to his teaching as he makes suggestions for revision, explains the rationale behind the suggested revisions and attends to the larger issues of writing (e.g. adhering to the prompt), while eliciting the student to participate in the thinking process.

Data and Method

Taken from a larger data set of approximately 20 hours of video-recorded writing tutoring sessions held at a university undergraduate student writing center in the United States, one 60-minute tutoring session between a freshman writer (L2 user of English) and a junior writing tutor (L1 user of English) is used as data for this study. The student has brought his draft written for his English composition class to the tutoring session. The writing prompt asks students to choose, define, interpret and discuss whether the chosen American myths will or will not continue to influence future generations. The student discusses the myth of individual opportunity and the myth of the melting pot in his paper. This is the student's first visit to the writing center and the tutor's first time reading the student's paper. The data were transcribed and analyzed using conversation analysis (CA) methodology.

Analysis

The analysis section includes three sub-sections in which data excerpts are categorized. In the first set of data excerpts, the participants are concerned with making specific revisions to the student's use of grammar, word form and word choice in writing. The tutor's embodied self-directed talk reveals how he problematizes certain aspects of student writing and considers candidate revisions. In the next section, the tutor's self-directed talk concerns what and how to revise as well as why the revision is necessary. The why-question engenders the tutor's thought process that leads to the justification of the suggested revision. The last section consists of data excerpts in which the tutor engages in tasks that go beyond making and justifying specific revisions. His self-directed talk demonstrates how he keeps track of the writing prompt and the time constraint. Across these different data excerpts, the student responds to the tutor's self-directed talk in distinct ways. Not only does he reveal that he is paying close attention to the tutor's embodied thought process, but he also joins the tutor's thinking process.

Making revisions

In this section, the tutor's embodied self-directed talk reveals the ongoing process of problematizing specific aspects of the student's writing and rehearsing candidate revisions for them. The self-directed talk consists of repetitions, meta-commentaries and rhetorical questions. Also, it is produced at a distinctively lower volume, and accompanied with various nonverbal features such as gaze shift, thinking face and thinking posture (Bavelas *et al.*, 2014; Goodwin, 2000; Goodwin & Goodwin, 1986; Kendon, 2004; Markee, 2006). The embodied self-directed talk engages the student in different ways as the student aligns with the tutor, explains his writing choice, asks questions and displays his own self-directed talk.

In Excerpt 1 the participants are focusing on the following written sentence (emphasis added by the author): 'This notion considers two factors as the precondition *of* success.' The tutor suggests the student change the preposition 'of' to 'for'. Starting in Line 1, after silently reading the student writing, the tutor produces self-directed talk and displays that the use of the preposition 'of' is problematic.

Excerpt 1

```
1  TUT: ->   ((reads)) °.hhh preconditions. preconditions of success.
2       ->   preconditions for success.° {(2.0) °preconditio:ns°
3       ->                               {(((thinking face))
```

Figure 9.1 Excerpt 1, Line 3

```
4  STU:      °for°
5  TUT:      i'm thinking for might be better,
6       ->   °as preconditions {(0.5) of success°
7       ->                      {(((thinking face))
```

Figure 9.2 Excerpt 1, Line 7

```
8             yeah, i think, preconditions for success.
9        ->   instead of, of {(°it's precondition of success°
10 STU:                      {(((thinking face)) °preconditions°
11 TUT: ->   °it's a precondition of success°
12      ->   °it's a precondition for success°
```

Figure 9.3 Excerpt 1, Lines 10–12

```
13 STU:    yeah, i think for would make more sense,
14         because it implies that the second word,
15         as it comes after the first word, [and it suggests
16 TUT:                                       [Mm-hmm,
17 STU:    like the causal result of the preconditions, so:
18 TUT:    ri:ght,
19 STU:    i think it makes sense to use fo:r.
20 TUT:    {(1.0).hh i think either way.
21         {((moves lips))
22         u:m precondition for just sounds better to me,
23         but u:m grammatically and semantically,
24         like it just- it makes sense either way.
25 STU:    °i'll put for°{(2.0)
26                       {((takes notes))
27 TUT:    ((nods))
```

The tutor's self-directed talk begins with an audible in-breath and is produced at a distinctively lower volume than the surrounding talk (Lines 1–3). The turn consists of the repetitions of the problematic phrase, *preconditions of success*, and includes the alternative form, *preconditions for success*. Not only is his self-directed talk audible, but also his thinking face and posture is made visible, constituting the embodied display of his thought process. He gazes down at the paper, resting his index finger on his chin (Figure 9.1).

While the tutor maintains his thinking face, the student quietly repeats the alternative preposition, °*for*° (Line 4). This demonstrates how the tutor's self-directed talk has been made available for the student to use as an interactional resource, a candidate correction (cf. Goodwin, 2013). Subsequently, the tutor moves back and forth between making a suggestion to the student (Lines 5, 8) and producing self-directed talk (Lines 6, 9); the volume of his speech shifts as he engages in these distinct actions. It is noteworthy that the student joins the thinking process by repeating the phrase at a low volume while gazing away (Figure 9.3). In Lines 10–12 the tutor and the student both display embodied self-directed talk. Subsequently, the student directs his turn to the tutor, explaining why he thinks 'for' would be a better choice (Lines 13–19). The tutor acknowledges the student's rationale with acknowledgement tokens (Lines 16, 18). While he does not fully accept the student's rationale, he maintains that he would choose 'for' (Lines 20–24). As the student verbally and visibly accepts the tutor's suggestion (Lines 25, 26), the sequence comes to a close.

In Excerpt 2 the participants are discussing the following written sentence (emphasis added by the author): 'For an illuminating answer, we can *suffice* to our personal experiences.' In particular, they are focusing on the use of the word 'suffice'. Since the excerpt is lengthy with multiple instances of self-directed talk occurring at different sequential positions, it is presented in three separate, consecutive sequences (Excerpts 2a–2c). In the sequences, the tutor's self-directed talk engages the student in different ways. Excerpt 2a begins with the tutor's clarification question and the student's response (Lines 1–7).

Excerpt 2a

```
1   TUT:        tsk what do you mean by, ((reads writing aloud)) we can
2               suffice to our personal experiences,
3   STU:        like our personal experiences would be enough
4               in order to have an illuminating answer,
5               we don't need to go into complicated
6               psychological topics.
7   TUT:        ((nods)) o:h okay, ((nods)) okay,
8         ->    i think it's just using {u::m °suffice
9         ->                             {((points with pen))
10        ->    .hh >let me see< we can suffice. {suffice.°
11        ->                                     {((thinking face))
```

Figure 9.4 Excerpt 2a, Line 11

```
12  STU:        i kinda translated from persian, i mea:n i thought
13              the sentence in persian, i translated that,
14              and that came out [in english,
15  TUT:                          [right, [right,
16  STU:                                  [i'm not sure if it makes
17              sense [like in english,
18  TUT:              [it- it- ((nods))
19  STU:        it doe:s, [but if it's awkward or not.
20  TUT:                  [it does.
21              yeah, i think it's cause, suffice, we don't really
22              use it as a verb for people,
23  STU:        okay,
24  TUT:        u:m it's usually i think inanimate objects,
25              or something u:m abstract that suffices.
26              but people don't suffice.
```

In Line 8 the tutor points to the word 'suffice' and problematizes its use. He then makes his thinking process visible in multiple ways. The embodied self-directed talk in Lines 8–11 consists of the repetition of the target word, *suffice*, and a meta-commentary, >*let me see*<. The turn is delivered at a lower volume than the surrounding talk and is accompanied by a thinking face and posture (Figure 9.4). As the turn trails off, the student explains how he came up with the sentence (Lines 12–14) and follows up with a question, asking for the tutor's help (Lines 16–17, 19). In response, the tutor explains that, while he understands the intended meaning, the use of the verb 'suffice' with the animate subject 'people' would be inappropriate (Lines 20–26).

In Excerpt 2b, upon the tutor's explanation, the student produces an upshot and seeks confirmation of his understanding, *So it's like passive, it's not active* (Line 27).

Excerpt 2b

```
27 STU:      so it's like passive, it's not active.
28 TUT:      s- it sounds like that, yeah.
29     ->    {°it suffices to: .hh it suffices°
30     ->    {((thinking face))
```

Figure 9.5 Excerpt 2b, Line 30

```
31           like it fill- something fulfills requirements.
32           like u::m (0.5) tsk i would say like >i don't know<
33           a certain course suffices to fi:ll u:m [a requirement.
34 STU:                                            [so it is active,
35 TUT:      i think, yeah, it would be used actively,
36           but i think just not for human objects.
37           <not for human subjects, i'm sorry.
38 STU:      okay.
```

After providing a tentative answer to the student's question in Line 28, the tutor produces self-directed talk, verbalizing the target verb with an inanimate subject, *it suffices to* (Lines 29–30, Figure 9.5). Subsequently, he provides a concrete example that illustrates the correct use of the verb (Lines 31–33). The student then revises his candidate understanding, asking another confirmation question, *so it is active*. In response, the tutor confirms the student's revised understanding and provides an additional explanation (Lines 35–37).

In Excerpt 2c the tutor again displays embodied self-directed talk as he attempts to revise the target sentence. After framing his turn as a candidate revision, he gazes down at the paper and lowers his volume. His self-directed talk involves repeating the target sentence as well as rehearsing the alternative form, *sufficient*, while visibly displaying a thinking posture (Lines 40–42).

Excerpt 2c

```
39 TUT:        So I think it'd be better to sa::y
40       ->    ((looks down)) °for an illuminating answe:r (1.0) tsk we
41       ->    can suffice to ((raises arm while making thinking face))
42       ->    our personal experiences. .hh sufficient° (0.5)
```

Figure 9.6 Excerpt 2c, Lines 41–42

```
43             it is sufficient, or it would be sufficient to
44             [look to our personal experiences.
45 STU:        [°sufficient°
46 TUT: ->     ((thinking face)) °for an illuminating answer,
47       ->    [it is sufficient-°
```

Figure 9.7 Excerpt 2c, Lines 46–47

```
48 STU:        [can we find another word to just-
49             to replace suffice with? {find another word fo:r
50 TUT:                                  {((nods)) sure, we ca:n
51       ->    ((looks down)) .hh °what should we say°
52       ->    °we can° {(3.0)
53       ->            {((moves lips))
54             for an illumin- illuminating answer,
55             we can simply look to our personal experiences,
56             [perhaps, we ca:n simply (0.5) consider
57 STU:        [°okay°
58 TUT:        our personal experiences,
59 STU:        ((nods)) okay, so how about simply ((takes notes))
60             like express that limit, and then another word
61             [like consider
```

```
62 TUT:    [look to, consider, reference,
63 STU:    °okay°
64 TUT:    cause by using simply, you're implying that
65         it's- it's enough.
66 STU:    it's enough.
67 TUT:    yeah, you don't need to go too- too far into it.
68 STU:    °mm-hmm°
```

In Lines 43–44 the tutor proposes a candidate revision, *it is sufficient,
or it would be sufficient to look to our personal experiences*. As the
student whispers the proposed word, *sufficient*, the tutor resorts back to
self-directed talk and repeats the candidate revision (Lines 46–47).
Instead of accepting the candidate revision, the student proposes to find
a different word (Lines 48–49). Accepting the student's proposal, the
tutor briefly engages in self-directed talk with a meta-commentary,
°what should we say° (Lines 51–53). He then produces the target sentence with another candidate revision, adding an adverb 'simply', and
using different verbs such as 'look to' and 'consider'. As the student
accepts the revision and produces its upshot (Lines 59–61), the tutor
repeats the alternative verbs (Line 62) and explains how the use of the
adverb 'simply' helps preserve the original meaning (Lines 64–65). The
sequence comes to a close with the student's acceptance of the tutor's
suggestion.

Overall, Excerpt 2 illustrates how the tutor's embodied self-directed
talk engages the student in the revision process in multiple ways. As the
tutor problematizes the use of the word 'suffice' (Lines 8–10), considers its
correct usage (Lines 29, 40–42) and rehearses the candidate revision
(Lines 46–47), the student explains how he came up with the word and
asks for help (Lines 12–19), displays and seeks the tutor's confirmation of
his understanding (Lines 27, 34), verbalizes the proposed revision (Line
45), and suggests a different revision (Lines 48–49).

In Excerpt 3 the participants search for a word to revise the written
sentence (emphasis added by the author): 'They do not have a direct benefit to *the one who does them*.' At first glance, the tutor's word search fails
without much uptake from the student. Nonetheless, the detailed examination of the embodiment reveals different moments of student engagement and alignment.

Excerpt 3

```
1 TUT:        ((reads writing aloud)) to the one who does them.
2             they do not have a direct benefit to:: (0.5)
3             trying to see if there's ((hand gestures)) single words.
4 STU:        yeah, [i couldn't find a noun.
5 TUT:              [yeah, the one who does them. ((looks away))
6             to thee:: tsk {(3.0)
7      ->                     {(((looks down while tapping desk with pen))
```

Figure 9.8 Excerpt 3, Line 7

```
8       ->   °to the one who does them, to::° {(5.0)
9       ->                                    {((taps desk with pen))
```

Figure 9.9 Excerpt 3, Line 9

```
10           tsk ((shakes head)) i don't think so.
11           {not one that i can think of.
12 STU:      {((smiles))
```

Figure 9.10 Excerpt 3, Lines 11–12

```
13 TUT:      i was gonna say actor, but ((shakes upper body))
14           {it's kinda not the right word.
15 STU:      {((shakes head))
16 TUT:      so i think it's fine. to the one who does them.
17           ((shrugs shoulders)) that's fine.
```

In Lines 1–2 the tutor reads the target sentence aloud; he first reads the
target phrase aloud (Line 1) and reads the rest of the sentence without the
target phrase (Line 2). He then explains what he is looking to do (Line 3).
Subsequently, the student aligns with the tutor by acknowledging the

search and accounts for his failed attempt, *Yeah, I couldn't find a noun.* In Line 5 the tutor begins the word search. He first looks away and repeats the incomplete phrase. He then looks down at the paper and starts tapping the desk with his pen. In Line 8 he repeats the problematized phrase at a distinctively lower volume, °*to the one who does them, to::*°. The student directs his gaze to the tutor (Figure 9.8) before looking down at the paper as the search continues (Figure 9.9).

In Line 10 the tutor conveys the end of the word search with a tongue click and a head shake. He then announces the result of the search, *I don't think so. Not one that I can think of.* The tutor shifts his posture by raising his upper body and the student looks at the tutor with a smile, displaying his alignment (Figure 9.10). Subsequently, as the tutor states the word that he thought of but thinks is inappropriate, *actor* (Lines 13–14), the student again displays his alignment by shaking his head with the tutor (Line 15). The sequence comes to an end with the tutor's assessment and the repeat of the target phrase (Lines 16–17). Along with his verbal turn, his visible body gestures such as shoulder shrugs indicate the end of the search sequence.

In summary, the excerpts above show how the tutor displays embodied self-directed talk as he problematizes student writing and makes suggestions for revision. The delivery of the self-directed talk is distinct as it is produced at a lower volume than the surrounding talk. The turn not only consists of verbal repeats, candidate revisions and meta-commentaries, but also nonverbal practices of looking down or away, holding thinking faces and postures, and tapping the desk. Such embodied practices elicit a wide range of student participation, from displaying alignment with smiles, head nods and head shakes to explaining his writing choice and asking for a different revision.

Explaining why

In this section the tutor's embodied self-directed talk reveals that he is not only concerned with what and how to revise student writing, but also with why the revision is necessary. In Excerpts 4 and 5 the tutor asks the why-question as a meta-commentary that constitutes his self-directed talk. That is, he asks himself a rhetorical question and reveals the process of responding to the question as an embodied practice. In Excerpt 6 the student asks the why-question and engenders a sequence that reveals the tutor's thought process in real time. The thought process includes considering a hypothetical scenario, making an assessment, and referring to a grammatical category and its rule to justify his suggestion for revision.

In Excerpt 4 the participants are discussing the following sentence (emphasis added by the author): 'In another example, why should our failure to graduate from college matter so much, *but* we don't care about the others' failures.' The tutor suggests the student revise the transition word from 'but' to 'yet' (Lines 1–4). Instead of accepting the suggestion,

the student responds with a question concerning parallelism, asking
whether the different subjects of the two clauses are the issue (Lines 5–7).

Excerpt 4

```
 1  TUT:      i think if you're going to use ((reads writing aloud))
 2            why should our failure to graduate from college
 3            matter so much, ((stops reading))
 4            instead of but, i think yet, yet we don't.
 5  STU:      but the: i don't need to make them parallel?
 6            i mean, these, they don't seem to be parallel,
 7            these two: parts of the comparison.
 8  TUT:      {(1.0) no, i think it's okay.
 9            {((moves lips))
10  STU:      it's okay?
11  TUT:      i think it was just but that was throwing me off.
12            i guess um they kind of have the same function,
13      ->    yet and but. {°how do i explain that?°
14      ->                 {(((looks away while making thinking face))
```

Figure 9.11 Excerpt 4, Line 14

```
15      ->    {(5.0)
16      ->    {(((looks down while maintaining thinking face))}
```

Figure 9.12 Excerpt 4: Line 15–16

```
17            i think yet makes it see:m i think yet has a stronger
18            connotation of it being an opposition between two ideas.
19            [cause there's the one part that we care about,
20  STU:      [mmm ((nods))
21  TUT:      we care about s:::: about so much if we fail.
22            yet, the other one, {there's the other part we don't
23  STU:                          {((nods))
24  TUT:      care at all, if other people fail.
25  STU:      i think i see that.
26  TUT:      yeah, ((nods))
```

In Lines 8–9 the tutor responds to the student's question, disconfirming his understanding that the two clauses need to be parallel. Subsequently, the student seeks another confirmation (Line 10), eliciting the tutor's further explanation. Starting in Line 11, the tutor begins his explanation by stating that the use of the transition 'but' is problematic. In Line 13 the tutor asks himself why, producing a meta-commentary, °*how do I explain that?*°, as self-directed talk (Figure 9.11). As he proceeds to look down while holding the thinking posture of resting his index finger on his chin, the student directs his gaze toward him (Figure 9.12). In Lines 17–24 the tutor provides a rationale for his suggestion to revise the transition word. Upon this further explanation, the student indicates his acceptance of the advice by nodding and providing an aligning response, *I think I see that* (Lines 20, 23, 25). The tutor's embodied self-directed talk reveals that he not only considers what and how to revise, but also attempts to explain why.

Excerpt 5 unfolds similarly as the sequence also concerns the transition word 'but' and the tutor asks a rhetorical why-question. Prior to the interaction shown below, the participants discussed the topic of formality in writing, and the tutor stated that 'it isn't typical in academic writing to start a sentence with "but"'. In Excerpt 5 the tutor points to a sentence that begins with 'but'. After the student marks the paper with a news receipt, °*oh*° (Lines 5–6), the tutor produces self-directed talk (Lines 7–11).

Excerpt 5

```
 1  TUT:        ((reads)) okay, and then here again with but.
 2              u::m (0.5) [yea:h
 3  STU:                  [u:h where is this?
 4  TUT:        ((points with pen)) right here, but.
 5  STU:        {°oh°
 6              {((marks paper))
 7  TUT:  ->    ((looks down)) °why is that?°
 8        ->    i would sa::y (0.5) if you take it out, it would just be:
 9        ->    °why has the myth of the individual's success been
10        ->    influential° {(1.0)
11        ->                 {((looks up while making thinking face))
```

Figure 9.13 Excerpt 5, Line 11

```
11 TUT:      [tsk it's a bit strange.
12 STU:       [would it be like hanging without-
13 TUT:      yeah, it seems like it's just out there.
14           i would sa:y, why comma, then comma,
15           why, then, has the myth of the individual's success
16           {been influential?
17 STU:      {((nods)) that sounds good. ((takes notes))
18 TUT:      yeah, cause by putting in then then,
19           it's referencing what you just said.
20           so it's like saying, in light of what i just said,
22           why is this true?
23 STU:      mm-hmm,
24 TUT:      ((nods))
```

As the tutor begins his turn by asking himself why, °*why is that?*° (Line 7), he shifts back and forth between addressing his turn to the student and engaging in self-directed talk. He first attempts to explain his rationale but leaves it as an incomplete sentence, *i would sa::y*. He then produces a hypothetical sentence, of which a part is delivered as self-directed talk, *if you take it out, it would just be: °why has the myth of the individual's success been influential°*. Here, he verbalizes the candidate revision by repeating the target sentence without the transition word 'but'. After displaying a characteristic thinking face (Figure 9.13), the tutor assesses his own candidate revision, *tsk it's a bit strange*. In an overlap, the student also conveys his reluctance to delete the transition word (Line 12). The tutor provides an aligning response to the student's question (Line 13) and proposes another candidate revision (Lines 14–16). After the student displays his acceptance of the proposal with nods, note-taking and a positive assessment, *that sounds good* (Line 17), the tutor adds an additional explanation to justify the revision (Lines 18–22). The sequence comes to an end with the student's acknowledgement (Line 23).

In Excerpt 6 the student explicitly asks the tutor to explain the rationale behind his suggestion for revision. The tutor then engages in a thinking process through which he attempts to justify his suggestion. The participants are discussing the use of 'much' versus 'very' in the following sentence (emphasis added by the author): 'So one may ask why the egocentric aspect of the myth should be so *much* appealing to the people.' After reading the target sentence aloud (Lines 1–3), the tutor suggests the student delete the word 'much' (Lines 4–9).

Excerpt 6

```
1  TUT:      ((reads writing aloud)) so one may ask why the
2            egocentric aspect of the myth should be so mu-
3            much appealing to the people.
4            (0.5)
5  TUT:      okay, so for he:re, i think so much appealing-
6            i think much is u::m extraneous,
7  STU:      °mmm°
8  TUT:      it'd be fine to say egocentric aspect of the myth
9            be so appealing. {or if- instead of much,
10 STU:                        {((marks paper))
```

```
11 TUT:       if you want to make it, if you want to emphasize
12            that it's very appealing, why should it
13            be so very appealing to the people.
14 TUT: ->    {((looks up while making thinking face))
15      ->    {°so much appealing°
16 STU:       {okay, ((looks at tutor))
```

Figure 9.14 Excerpt 6, Lines 14–16

```
17            so how come very would work there,
18            but much wouldn't work there,
19 TUT: ->    °so very (2.0) much (3.0) so very much
20      ->    [appealing, so much appealing°
21 STU:       [is it informal, or is it incorrect,
22 TUT:       i have a fee- i'm trying to think of what the rule would
23            be. i'm thinking cause very is a:n {(0.5) i don't wanna
24                                               {((smiles))
25            like call it the wrong grammatical thing. ((looks down))
26      ->    but u::m °it is much appealing°
27      ->    {(3.0)/((moves lips))}
28            cause i think, cause appealing is describing the myth.
29            (0.5) so appealing is being used as an adjective,
30            [right,
31 STU:       [((nods)) uh-huh,
32 TUT:       so when you're modifying- it's kind of modifying
33            the adjective, >i'm not sure what that word would be<
34            {but when you: when you modify the adjective to a degree,
35 STU:       {((looks at tutor and maintains his gaze))
36 TUT:       i don't think you put much. cause it's, u:::m tsk yeah,
37            i think that might be it. cause if you're saying
38            something's pretty, you wouldn't say much pretty,
39            [it's very pretty.
40 STU:       [°very pretty, i'd say°
41 TUT:       ((nods)) i think that's why.
42 STU:       okay.
43 TUT:       okay, that makes sense to me.
```

As the student marks the paper according to the tutor's suggestion (Line 10), the tutor continues with his turn, this time suggesting 'very' as a replacement for 'much' (Lines 9, 11–13). He then looks up and repeats the target phrase, °*so much appealing*° (Lines 14–15, Figure 9.14). In an overlap, the student first acknowledges the suggestion, *okay* (Line 16), and follows up with a question, asking for the rationale behind this replacement (Lines 17–18). Before answering the why-question, the tutor again engages in self-directed talk, verbalizing different alternatives (Lines 19–20). In another overlap, the student asks whether the revision concerns formality or accuracy (Line 21). In Line 22 the tutor begins to explain why 'very' instead of 'much' is appropriate in the target sentence.

His explanation reveals his thought process in real time. The tutor first considers the grammatical category for the target word 'very' (Lines 22–25) but changes his line of thinking to consider the grammatical function and category for the word 'appealing' (Lines 26–30). He then considers what should be modifying this adjective with an example (Lines 32–39). Throughout the tutor's turn, the student conveys his alignment with a continuer (Line 31), sustained eye gaze (Line 35), a partial repeat, °*very pretty, i'd say*° (Line 40) and an acknowledgement, *okay* (Line 42). The sequence moves to a close with the tutor's upshot, *okay, that makes sense to me* (Line 43). It is interesting to note that, with this upshot, the tutor assesses his own reasoning that has been revealed in real time throughout the sequence.

As shown above, the tutor's self-directed talk not only involves his suggestion for a specific revision, but also his justification for the revision. Whether initiated by the tutor's rhetorical question or the student's request, the tutor engages in various practices such as considering a hypothetical revision, verbalizing a revision, making an assessment and applying grammatical knowledge. These practices are made visible through embodiment, engaging the student at different moments to display alignment, convey his understanding and ask follow-up questions.

Attending to the big picture

The last two excerpts illustrate how the tutor engages in tasks that go beyond making and justifying specific revisions. Throughout the tutoring session he displays his orientation to the writing prompt and time management. The tutor's orientation is made visible with embodied self-directed talk. Meanwhile, the student shows that he is closely monitoring the tutor's thought process regarding these larger tasks.

In Excerpt 7 the tutor checks the prompt to make sure that their discussion is in line with the prompt. While the participants discussed the prompt at the very beginning of the tutoring session, here the tutor comes back to the prompt after discussing different aspects of student writing. The entire process of checking the prompt is made visible to the student via the tutor's embodied self-directed talk. Just prior to the interaction shown below, the participants discussed adding a paragraph. In Line 1 the tutor comes back to checking the prompt.

Excerpt 7

```
1  TUT: ->  tsk okay u::m (1.0) >°let's take a look at this again°<
2       ->  ((both look down at prompt))
```

Figure 9.15 Excerpt 7, Line 2

```
3  TUT:  ->   {°got that°, {°got that°, {°got that°, {°got that°,
4        ->   {((nods))    {((nods))    {((nods))     {((nods))
5        ->   {°did this°, °.hh oka::y talked about that°,
6  STU:       {((looks at the tutor))
```

Figure 9.16 Excerpt 7, Lines 5–6

```
7  TUT:       (2.0) tsk ((reads prompt aloud)) all in-text
8             works cited must be mla edition form.
9             okay, so you said you haven't specifically made this
10            ((looks up at student)) 1- mla yet?
11 STU:       no i should go over it to make it,
12 TUT:       okay,
```

As the tutor reaches for the prompt and produces self-directed talk, which consists of a meta-commentary, >°*let's take a look at this again*°< (Line 1), the student coordinates his gaze, looking down at the prompt along with the tutor (Figure 9.15). The tutor then proceeds to check the prompt against what the student has already written and what they have discussed during the session (Lines 3–5). He whispers his entire turn at a low volume, looking down and off to the side. Nonetheless, the process of checking off the prompt is made audible and visible to the student, and the student directs his gaze from the prompt to the tutor (Figure 9.16). In Lines 7–10 the tutor reads the last part of the prompt aloud and asks the student a question regarding citation.

In the last excerpt, the tutor displays his awareness of the time constraint and plans the tutoring session accordingly. In Line 1 the tutor stops reading the student's writing and asks for clarification. The student explains that he is using a secondary source (Lines 2–3) but is unsure of its citation (Lines 5–6). Upon the student's question regarding the citation, the tutor produces a meta-commentary, °*okay, let's see*°, as self-directed talk, while gazing away (Figure 9.17).

Excerpt 8

```
 1  TUT:        ((reads)) wait, so who's writing this,
 2  STU:        we:ll ((points)) t-these editors, i mea:n these writers
 3             are quoting this stuff, [so::
 4  TUT:                              [gotcha: [gotcha::
 5  STU:                                       [i probably need to
 6             have a different citation maybe?
 7  TUT: ->    u:::m for that, {((thinking face)) °okay, let's see°
 8  STU:                       {((takes notes)) i'll check it again.
```

Figure 9.17 Excerpt 8, Lines 7–8

```
 9  TUT:        yeah, we can take a look on the computer fo:r (.) that.
10             so it's ((points)) these editors quo:ting this man,
11  STU:        yeah.
12  TUT:        okay. yeah i'm not exactly sure, in mla,
13             how you would cite that, {but we can take a look.
14  STU:                                {((nods))
15             okay.
16  TUT: ->    {°so let me make sure we leave some time for that°
17       ->    {((looks at clock))
18  STU:        {((looks at tutor))
```

Figure 9.18 Excerpt 8, Lines 16–18

```
19 TUT: ->    {°the clock's moving, right°
20 STU:        {((looks at clock then at tutor)) i can do it
21             on my own if we don't have time.
22 TUT:        okay. have you:: do you know the resource?
23             [like-
24 STU:        [i have the mla book, so:
```

```
25 TUT:    oh you have the book. (okay, well th(h)en,
26 STU:                          (((smiles))
27 TUT:    you should have all the details then.
```

As the student states that he will check the citation information (Line 8), the tutor aligns with the student and suggests looking up the information on the computer together (Lines 9–15). Then, with a series of meta-commentaries that constitute his self-directed talk, the tutor reveals his planning process of checking the current time, allocating time for this task, °*so let me make sure we leave some time for that*°, and ensuring that the time is correct, °*the clock's moving, right*° (Lines 16–19). As the tutor turns his body and gaze to check the time, the student directs his gaze first at the tutor (Figure 9.18), then at the clock, and back at the tutor. Not only does the student monitor the tutor's planning process, he intervenes and proposes an alternative, *i can do it on my own if we don't have time* (Lines 20–21). Upon the student's proposal, the tutor checks that the student has an adequate resource and moves to closing the sequence.

In the excerpts above, the participants orient to the larger tasks that go beyond making specific revisions by checking and following the prompt and managing the time. The tutor's embodied self-directed talk reveals how he engages with these tasks and makes his thought process available to the student to closely monitor and intervene, if necessary.

Discussion

This paper has examined the embodied practices of self-directed talk in the context of college-level writing tutorial. The tutor's self-directed talk is audibly distinct as it is marked with quieter speech that consists of multiple repetitions and rhetorical questions. Moreover, the talk is visibly distinct as it accompanies averted eye gaze, thinking face/posture and hand gestures. Such an embodied practice reveals the tutor's ongoing thought process while he makes suggestions for revision, justifies the suggestions and attends to the larger issues of writing tutoring. Importantly, the analyses have also shown that the student attends to and engages with the tutor's thought process as they arrive at various writing decisions together. The student's engagement ranges from displaying alignment with smiles and nods to asking questions and suggesting an alternative candidate revision.

At the most basic level, this study describes a wide range of activities that the tutor attends to during the tutoring session. The tutor encounters various writing issues in student writing, including but not limited to grammar, word form, word choice, transition and citation. Not only does the tutor provide corrective feedback along with the rationale behind different alternatives, but he also ensures that the discussed revisions are in line with the prompt and allocates time for different tasks. More importantly, the detailed analyses of the tutor's self-directed talk – examining where it occurs, what it is composed of and how it is responded to – reveal the inter-actional dimensions of language use and embodied action (cf. Ford, 2004; Goodwin & Goodwin, 2005; Mondada, 2007; Schegloff, 1982). It has been shown that both participants carefully produce and monitor their unfold-ing turns to coordinate their actions; in particular, the student displays concurrent verbal and visible actions as the tutor's embodied thought pro-cess unfolds. As Smith (2007) maintains, when speech is uttered, whether it is addressed to oneself or to other interlocutors, it becomes a publicly available resource to all parties in interaction. This study highlights the role of embodiment in this public display of thought process.

The findings have useful implications for writing instruction, particu-larly in the tutoring context. Writing tutors require training that builds foundational linguistic knowledge and addresses various writing con-cerns, such as adhering to the prompt, stylistic requirements and time management. Furthermore, writing tutor training should allow tutors to consider and compare different alternatives. The analyses presented in this study reveal how a wide range of choices involved in writing are ques-tioned and revised on a moment-by-moment basis. As shown in the data excerpts, many grammatical and word choice issues may not have defini-tive answers and there exist different ways to make revisions. Throughout the revision process, writers need to problematize certain choices that they make, consider different alternatives, apply grammatical knowledge and assess their revisions. Therefore, training tutors to consider a wide range of linguistic alternatives and justifications for them would contribute to their instructional practice. Lastly, tutors can also adopt embodied self-directed talk as a tool for teaching by example and eliciting student par-ticipation. Monitoring and participating in the process of arriving at revision decisions upon considering different choices and rationales would benefit students as they learn how to write and revise independently.

References

Baumann, J., Jones, L. and Seifert-Kessell, N. (1993) Using think-alouds to enhance chil-dren's comprehension monitoring abilities. *The Reading Teacher* 47 (3), 184–193.

Bavelas, J., Gerwing, J. and Healing, S. (2014) Hand and facial gestures in conversational interaction. In T.M. Holtgraves (ed.) *The Oxford Handbook of Language and Social Psychology* (pp. 111–130). Oxford: Oxford University Press.

Bereiter, C. and Bird, M. (1985) Use of thinking aloud in identification and teaching of reading comprehension strategies. *Cognition and Instruction* 2 (2), 131–156.

Berk, L.E. and Garvin, R.A. (1984) Development of private speech among low-income Appalachian children. *Developmental Psychology* 20, 271–286.

Collins, A. and Smith, E.E. (1982) Teaching the process of reading comprehension. In D.K. Detterman and R.J. Sternberg (eds) *How and How Much Can Intelligence be Increased* (pp. 173–185). Norwood, NJ: Ablex.

Davey, B. (1983) Think-aloud: Modeling the cognitive processes of reading comprehen-sion. *Journal of Reading* 27 (1), 44–47.

Flavell, J.H., Beach, D.R. and Chinsky, J.M. (1966) Spontaneous verbal rehearsal in a memory task as a function of age. *Child Development* 37, 283–299.

Ford, C. (2004) Contingency and units in interaction. *Discourse Studies* 6 (1), 27–52.

Goffman, E. (1978) Response cries. *Language* 54 (4), 787–815.

Goodwin, C. (2000) Action and embodiment within situated human interaction. *Journal of Pragmatics* 32, 1489–1522.

Goodwin, C. (2013) The co-operative, transformative organization of human action and knowledge. *Journal of Pragmatics* 46, 8–23.

Goodwin, M.H. and Goodwin, C. (1986) Gesture and coparticipation in the activity of searching for a word. *Semiotica* 62 (1/2), 51–75.

Goodwin, M.H. and Goodwin, C. (2005) Participation. In A. Duranti (ed.) *A Companion to Linguistic Anthropology* (pp. 222–244). Oxford: Blackwell.

Hall, J.K. and Smotrova, T. (2013) Teacher self-talk: Interactional resource for managing instruction and eliciting empathy. *Journal of Pragmatics* 47, 75–92.

Kendon, A. (2004) *Gesture: Visible Action as Utterance*. Cambridge: Cambridge University Press.

Kristiansen, E.D. (2017) Doing formulating: 'Writing aloud voice' sequences as an interactional method. *Journal of Pragmatics* 114, 49–65.

Looney, S.D., Jia, D. and Kimura, D. (2017) Self-directed okay in mathematics lectures. *Journal of Pragmatics* 107, 46–59.

Markee, N. (2006) A conversation analytic perspective on the role of quantification and generalizability in second language acquisition. In. M. Chalhoub-Deville, C. Chapelle and P. Duff (eds) *Inference and Generalizability in Applied Linguistics* (pp. 135–164). Amsterdam and Philadelphia, PA: John Benjamins.

Mondada, L. (2007) Multimodal resources for turn-taking: Pointing and the emergence of possible next speakers. *Discourse Studies* 9, 194–225.

Olshavsky, J.E. (1977) Reading as problem-solving: An investigation of strategies. *Reading Research Quarterly* 12 (4), 654–674.

Palincsar, A.S. and Brown, A.L. (1988) Teaching and practicing thinking skills to promote comprehension in the context of group problem solving. *Remedial and Special Education* 9 (1), 53–59.

Schegloff, E.A. (1982) Discourse as an interactional achievement: Some uses of 'uh huh' and other things that come between sentences. In D. Tannen (ed.) *Analyzing Discourse: Text and Talk* (pp. 71–93). Washington, DC: Georgetown University Press.

Smith, H. (2007) The social and private worlds of speech: Speech for inter- and intramental activity. *The Modern Language Journal* 91, 341–356.

Smolucha, F. (1992) Social origins of private speech in pretend play. In L.E. Berk and R.M. Diaz (eds) *Private Speech: From Social Interaction to Self-regulation* (pp. 123–141). Hillsdale, NJ: Lawrence Erlbaum.

Steinbach Kohler, F. and Thorne, S.L. (2011) The social life of self-directed talk: A sequential phenomenon? In J.K. Hall, J. Hellermann and S.P. Doehler (eds) *L2 Interactional Competence and Development* (pp. 66–92). Bristol: Multilingual Matters.

10 Embodied Actions and Gestures as Interactional Resources for Teaching in a Second Language Writing Classroom

Yumi Matsumoto

This study investigates moments when embodied actions and gestures become prominent interactional resources for teaching in the context of a second language (L2) writing classroom. The data consist of video-recorded interactions from a freshman English as a second language (ESL) writing classroom at a US university. The sequences of talk-in-interaction selected for multimodal analysis involve an instructor employing another student's embodied actions as an interactional resource for explaining sentences that express requests. The data analysis reveals that when orienting to a student's state of nonunderstanding, the teacher quoted another student's (re)actions (see Keevallik, 2010) to explain the structure of requests. In other words, the teacher referred to and built on her student's embodied actions in the same manner in which teachers usually refer to and build on students' verbal comments. The analysis also demonstrates the emerging process of the teacher's decision, in which she employed both verbal and embodied interactional resources such as cut-offs, silences and gaze shifts. Such use of interactional resources enabled the teacher to think about appropriate teaching actions in response to her students' emerging needs. These findings offer an in-depth look at how an L2 teacher employed 'complex multimodal Gestalts' (Mondada, 2014: 139), including embodied actions and gestures, to orient to moment-to-moment interactional needs to achieve courses of action and larger instructional goals.

Introduction

Teaching is a complex activity. Teachers facilitate student learning by offering a range of meaningful instructional activities while responding to and managing their students' needs. By closely investigating the dynamics of classroom interactions, conversation analytic (CA) studies in L2 classrooms have revealed teachers' complex practices for managing various tasks (e.g. Hall & Smotrova, 2013; Sert, 2015; Walsh, 2006; Waring, 2008). In addition to their complex nature, L2 classroom interactions are not stable; rather, they are dynamic and variable practices that are constantly negotiated based on participants' orientations to co-constructed pedagogical phenomena (e.g. Seedhouse, 2004; Walsh, 2006). Accumulating detailed descriptions of actual classroom practices is necessary for demonstrating and understanding what sequences of teaching and learning look like. As Koshik (2002: 304–305) argued, 'we cannot investigate pedagogical effectiveness if we do not know in some detail what the practices of teachers are and what functions they perform'. Such descriptions can be transformative (Richards, 2005), because they provide new pedagogical insights and identify new interactional competencies that may inform teacher actions and practices in L2 classrooms.

In order to contribute to this important endeavor of describing and understanding L2 teachers' complex teaching practices, this study examines moments when embodied actions (bodily actions that contribute to meaning-making) and gestures (movements specifically associated with hands and arms) become prominent interactional resources for teaching. It is often the case that both embodied actions and gestures are considered to be embodied practices in CA studies. However, this study treats embodied actions and gestures separately because they might have distinctive functions as part of interactional resources for teaching. The data consist of video-recorded interactions from a freshman ESL writing classroom at a US university. The sequences of talk-in-interaction selected for multimodal analysis involve an instructor employing another student's bodily actions as an interactional resource for explaining the structure and meaning of a sentence that expresses a request. The data analysis reveals that while orienting to a student's state of nonunderstanding, the teacher quoted her student's bodily actions in order to explain a sentence expressing a request. The analysis also demonstrates that the students in the classroom paid more attention to the teacher when she used embodied actions to elaborate her verbal explanations, suggesting that embodied actions can be an interactional resource for L2 teachers.

These findings suggest that coordinating embodied actions with various semiotic modes – 'a web of resources formatting an action' or what Mondada named 'complex multimodal Gestalts' (Mondada, 2014: 139, emphasis in original) – is an important resource for teaching in L2 classrooms. Teachers should assemble multimodal resources by orienting to moment-to-moment interactional needs in order to achieve courses of action and larger instructional goals. The present study illustrates a single case in which an L2 teacher incorporates a student's embodied actions as part of complex multimodal Gestalts in order to explain a sentence expressing a request to her students. Following my detailed analysis, I offer a few pedagogical implications for L2 teaching.

Theoretical Framework

After briefly discussing the notions of multimodality, embodiment and nonverbality, I review CA studies that have investigated teachers' gestures and embodied actions in relation to teaching various linguistic aspects and turn-taking/allocating practices in the context of L2 classrooms.

Multimodality, embodiment and nonverbality

Recently, many researchers inside and outside of CA have paid close attention to multimodal, embodied and nonverbal aspects of social interactions. These three concepts entail slightly different epistemological orientations. While the term *nonverbal behavior* has been used to refer to various interactional resources including gestures, gaze and laughter, this concept has long been criticized. For instance, earlier gesture research (e.g. McNeill, 1985) noted that the term itself creates an opposition, and even a hierarchy, between verbal and nonverbal. Furthermore, it implies that language is the default and that nonverbal behaviors are secondary to language. Against this background, this study employs *embodiment* and, in particular, *multimodality*.

According to Mondada (2014), *multimodality* refers to various interactional resources mobilized by interactants for organizing their actions, which include gestures, gaze, body postures, body movements, prosody, lexis and grammar. Multimodality entails plural interactional resources (regardless of whether they are verbal or nonverbal) without considering, a priori, a hierarchy among them. Furthermore, these modalities are often intertwined, and interlocutors may use all the resources together or at times select one of them based on the activity in which they are engaging. *Embodiment* (or embodied actions) within CA, on the other hand, focuses particularly on the body and embodied practice as a whole, which includes gestures, facial expressions (e.g. smile), gaze shift, head movements, body movements and body postures. For instance, researchers who work on embodiment (e.g. Streeck, 2009) have examined the roles of embodied actions, which usually go beyond the study of gesture that typically focuses on hand- and arm-related actions.

In short, while these terms overlap, *multimodality* and *embodiment* highlight the importance of examining diverse semiotic resources *holistically* without separating language, body and nonverbality. Although Mondada (2014) prefers the term *multimodality* to *embodiment* due to the fact that the former entails the latter, I use both terms in this study because embodiment can highlight aspects of embodied actions and gestures within multimodal interactional resources. It is crucial to examine closely how these multimodal and embodied resources are assembled or coordinated by participants, responding to the contingencies of the progressivity of the action.

Embodied, gestural elements of L2 teaching

In recent decades, multimodal investigation of L2 classroom discourse, especially focusing on gestures and embodied actions for L2 teaching and learning, has gained popularity in the field of CA (e.g. Eskildsen & Wagner, 2015; Majlesi, 2018; Matsumoto & Dobs, 2017; Seo & Koshik, 2010; Sert, 2015, 2017; Waring *et al.*, 2013). Many studies have focused on the roles of teacher gestures in various L2 classroom contexts. For example, several studies (e.g. Belhiah, 2013; Käänta *et al.*, 2018; Waring *et al.*, 2013) examined interactional moments in which teachers engage with vocabulary explanations and definition-related work by employing speech and gestures/embodied actions and material resources.

Gestural interactions between teachers and students in L2 classrooms have also been the focus of more recent studies (e.g. Matsumoto & Dobs, 2017; Sert, 2015, 2017; Smotrova, 2017). For instance, Smotrova (2017) illustrated that gestures and embodied actions are interactional resources for teaching and learning L2 pronunciations. Eskildsen and Wagner (2013: 158) found that 'vocabulary is learned and taught and accomplished by recurring gestures that have emerged from shared interactional spaces'. Similarly, Matsumoto and Dobs (2017) found that teachers and students in ESL grammar classrooms repeatedly used abstract deictic and metaphoric gestures and that students used gestural catchments (i.e. recurrent gestures that replicate similar forms and meanings) to demonstrate their understanding of temporal concepts.

As for the roles of embodied actions, earlier CA studies (e.g. Mori & Hayashi, 2006; Olsher, 2004) have noted the embodied nature of L2 interactions in general and L2 classroom interactions in particular. Olsher illustrated the interactional practice of embodied completion (i.e. completing the sequential action with a gesture or other embodied display rather than with speech) of turns as sequential actions during group work in English as a foreign language (EFL) classroom contexts. Mori and Hayashi also analyzed cases of embodied completions during casual interactions between L1 and L2 speakers of Japanese, highlighting the coordination of both vocal and nonvocal resources for achieving intersubjectivity and language learning.

Furthermore, several studies (e.g. Käänta, 2012; Mortensen, 2008) have examined the interrelationship between turn-taking/allocation and teachers' use of embodied resources (e.g. gaze, body orientations, pointing gestures and nodding) in the context of content and language integrated learning (CLIL) and additional language classrooms. For instance, Käänta examined teachers' allocation of response turns to students in whole-class interactions, focusing on embodied allocation (i.e. turn allo-cations by teachers' embodied actions). Kääntä argued that these ephem-eral embodied resources become interactionally relevant for participants in managing speaker change and negotiating participation in multiparty classroom interactions. Mortensen closely investigated the role of teach-ers' gaze, especially achieving mutual gaze with students, in the process of teachers' turn allocation and selecting next speakers in Danish L2 classrooms.

In short, research through CA has revealed that embodied actions and gestures are interactional resources for L2 teaching/learning, specifically for explaining vocabulary and grammar, teaching pronunciation and managing and allocating turns. The present study analyzes moments in which a teacher employs both embodied actions and gestures while explaining the structure and meaning of a sentence expressing a request in ESL writing classroom interactions. Specifically, I take up the following questions: First, how does an L2 teacher coordinate embodied actions and gestures in ESL writing classroom interactions when a student displays lack of understanding? Secondly, how do the student and other classmates orient to the teacher's embodied actions? This chapter attempts to illumi-nate the complexities of L2 teaching practices and, in doing so, reveal possible distinctions between 'idealized' views of the work of L2 teaching and its *actual* L2 teaching practices.

Data and Methods

Participants and data collection

The participants for the present study were 19 international students (mostly freshman) and an experienced non-native instructor at a large public university in the United States. The students' nationalities were diverse, including Korean, Chinese, Indian, Malaysian, Kazakh and Mexican. All of the students' names that appear in this chapter are pseud-onyms. At the time of data collection, Teacher L, a female from Ukraine, was working as a postdoctoral teaching fellow, had resided in the United States for about six years and had taught an academic writing course for international undergraduates for about two years. I observed and video-recorded the classes regularly throughout the Fall 2013 semester. The source of the data for the single-case analysis is a corpus of video-recorded classroom interactions of the ESL academic writing course (29 hours in total).

A single-case analysis with a multimodal approach

This study employs sequential analysis (e.g. Sacks *et al.*, 1974; Schegloff, 2007) to closely examine moments in which embodied actions and gestures become prominent interactional resources for teaching. Sequential analysis is effective in explicating the detailed process by which interlocutors employ and orient to gestures and embodied actions as part of interactional resources. With the goal of a single-case analysis in mind, namely explicating a single phenomenon and developing a richer, deeper understanding of the phenomenon of interest (Hutchby & Wooffitt, 1998; Schegloff, 1987), I selected and examined one unique episode in which the instructor coordinated various interactional resources, in particular gestures and embodied actions, for achieving understanding in response to a student's lack of understanding.

Furthermore, this study employs a multimodal analytical approach (e.g. Mondada, 2014, 2016; Streeck *et al.*, 2011) in order to transcribe and analyze in detail interactional sequences in which a teacher integrates and coordinates multimodal, embodied interactional resources for teaching. In the context of classroom interactions, teachers and students constitute an embodied multiparty participation framework, namely an 'interactively sustained configuration of multiple participants' (Goodwin, 2000: 1518) accomplished through mutual orientation to the 'temporally unfolding juxtaposition of multiple semiotic fields', including prosodic resources, gestures, gazes, body positionings, the use of material artifacts and even spatial organization (Goodwin, 2000: 1517).

Data Analysis

Incorporation of a student's embodied action as resource for teaching

The excerpt for analysis (which is divided into three parts) involves the moment when, in response to a student's lack of understanding, Teacher L (TEA) elaborates on her question concerning differences between syntactic structures by switching among various actions. In particular, she employs embodied actions by another student, Shan (SHA) to explain the structure and meaning of a sentence expressing a request. In this sequence, the whole class is learning how to paraphrase by using examples in the textbook. In the following sequence, Teacher L nominates Ji-Min (JMI) to compare two example sentences: '*Explore* most prejudices and you will find a cruel stereotype at the core of each one.' and '*If you were to* dissect most human prejudices, you would likely discover an ugly stereotype lurking somewhere inside them.' Teacher L wanted Ji-Min to recognize the difference between requests ('Explore most prejudices') and conditional statements ('If you were to dissect most human prejudices,'). Because Ji-Min did not seem to understand the sentence expressing a request, Teacher L attempted to explain its meaning verbally, as seen in Part 1.

Part 1 *Shan, could you stand up?*

```
1  TEA:  and, what
2        {about, the:, sentence in the original uh, source paragraph,}
3        {gazes at textbook holding in both hands}
4        {explore(.) most prejudices.}=
5        {shifts gazes in JMI's direction}
6  JMI:  ={just like, general}
7        {gazes at textbook on desk}
8        {opinion?}
9        {looks at TEA while resting left elbow on desk}
10 TEA:  no, >it's not.<=
11 JMI:  =((looks at SJ who sits next to her right))
12 TEA:  does it tell you,
13       [{what to do?}
14        {brings left hand forward at chest level}
15 JMI:  [((smiles at SJ and then looks back to TEA's direction))
16       (1.8)
17 JMI:  yeah! hah [((keeps smiling))
18 TEA:            [if I tell you,
19       [{please stand up,}
20        {raises left hand from waist to lower chest level, with palm
21         facing upward and slightly cupped}
22 JMI:  [((gazes downward while smiling and covering mouth with left hand))
23 TEA:  {and uh:,}
24       {further raises left hand to neck level, with palm
25        facing upward, and then lowers it to waist level}
26       {go to the board?}
27       {quickly moves left hand to her right space, which seems to point
28        at blackboard, while gazing at JMI}
29       {(0.8)}
30 JMI:  {((looks down at textbook on desk))
31 TEA:  [{what would you do,}
32        {brings left hand forward at chest level, and holds it till line 37}
33 JMI:  [{(            )}
34        {body leans forward close to textbook while gazing it}
35       {(4.0)}
36 JMI:  {maintains same posture of leaning to textbook}
37       yeah,
38       {it is.}
39       {gazes up to TEA}
40       (0.6)
41 TEA:  {will you?}
42       {brings left hand forward at neck level with all fingers curled,
43        while gazing at JMI}
44       {(1.2)}
45 SSS:  {((several gaze downward and seem disengaged))}
46 TEA:  it-
47       (0.5)
48 TEA:  {okay,}
49       {holds left hand at chest level and shifts gaze to SHA's direction}
50       {let's,}=
51       {looks down at textbook in right hand, and shifts gaze to SHA}
52 JMI:  ={hah}
53        {gazes at SJ}
```

Figure 10.1 Lines 26–28 'go to the board?'

Figure 10.2 Lines 31–32 'what would you do,'

Figure 10.3 Lines 35–36   **Figure 10.4** Lines 48–49 'okay,'

In the sequence, Ji-Min displays a lack of understanding of Teacher L's question (Lines 1–4) in various ways, including hesitation signaled by rising intonation. More specifically, Ji-Min's response, 'just like, general opinion?' uttered with a rising inflection in turn-final position (Lines 6–8), seems to seek confirmation as to whether her response is correct and to solicit assistance from her teacher. Responding to Ji-Min, in Line 10 Teacher L says, 'no, >it's not.<', which is a rejection of her answer. Orienting to Ji-Min's state of understanding, from Line 12 onward Teacher L reformulates her question while using gestures. In Lines 12–14 Teacher L says, 'does it tell you, what to do?' while bringing her left hand forward at chest level. After a long pause (1.8 seconds), Ji-Min provides a minimal response, 'yeah!,' which displays understanding (Line 17). From Lines 18 to 31, Teacher L further reformulates her question. She states, 'if I tell you, please stand up, and uh:, go to the board? what would you do,'. In particular, when Teacher L says, 'go to the board?', she coordinates gestures (moving her left hand to her right, pointing at the blackboard) with speech (Lines 26–28, see Figure 10.1). Furthermore, in Lines 31–32, when she utters, 'what would you do,', she brings her left hand forward at chest level and holds this gesture (see Figure 10.2) until Ji-Min provides a response ('yeah,') in Line 37.

After Teacher L's reformulated question, a long period of silence (4.0 seconds in Line 35) ensues, in which Ji-Min is leaning forward and closely looking at the textbook on the desk (see Figure 10.3). This silence may signal her need to think. After this long pause, Ji-Min provides a response, 'yeah, it is.' while gazing back to Teacher L (Lines 37–39). In fact, her response is not directly answering Teacher L's reformulated question ('if I tell you, please stand up, and uh:, go to the board? what would you do,'), which signals lack of understanding.

After another short pause (0.6 seconds), Teacher L says, 'will you?' with a rising intonation (Line 41) to seek further response from Ji-Min. At the same time, Teacher L bodily displays her orientation to Ji-Min by bringing her left hand forward and gazing in her direction. After another long pause, Teacher L utters, 'it- (0.5) okay, let's,' in Lines

46–51. Note that 'okay,' marks a topic closing or *shift* (Beach, 1993; West & Garcia, 1988) along with a cut-off ('it-'). Teacher L's turn (Lines 46–51) seems to display the emerging process of her teaching actions, closely associated with what Smotrova (2017) and van Compernolle and Smotrova (2017) called *thinking for teaching*. Thinking for teaching is defined as 'teachers' moment-to-moment instructional decisions in the classroom' (van Compernolle & Smotrova, 2017: 2), which are often enacted through the gesture–speech interface. For example, Teacher L employs a discourse marker, 'okay,' while shifting her gaze to Shan and pointing in his direction at the same time (Lines 48–49, see Figure 10.4). Here, Teacher L employs both verbal and embodied resources (including a cut-off, silence and gaze shifts) for thinking for teaching. The following part (Part 2) demonstrates Teacher L's emergent teaching actions after her thinking-for-teaching moment.

Part 2 Shan, could you stand up?

```
50 TEA:   {let's,}=
51        {looks down at textbook in right hand, and shifts gaze to SHA}
52 JMI:   ={hah}
53        {gazes at SJ}
54 TEA:   ah:n,
55        {(2.2)}
56 TEA:   {looks down at list of students' names on desk}
57        [{Shan?}
58        {looks in SHA's direction}
59 JMI:   [(((looks at two classmates on her left while smiling))
60 TEA:   >could you stand up?<
61        (0.8)
62 TEA:   stand up!
63        {(2.0)}
64 JMI:   {(((looks in SHA's direction)))}
65 SSS:   {(((turns heads toward SHA)))}
66 SHA:   ((slowly stands up from chair))
67 TEA:   {thank you very}
68        {smiles at SHA}
69        {much.}
70        {beckons with left hand}
71        [˚have a seat.˚=
72 SHA:   [((sits down while glimpsing at JMI's direction))
73 TEA:   ={what does he do,}
74        {points at SHA's direction with left hand while gazing at JMI,
75         and drops left hand to desk}
76        (2.2)
77 TEA:   {what does he do,}
78        {does similar pointing in lines 74-75 while gazing at JMI}
79        (1.8)
80 TEA:   did he {stand,}
81               {raises left hand at chest level with all fingers stretched}
82        (0.5)
83 TEA:   {stand up?}=
84        {holds same gesture in line 81}
85 JMI:   ={yeah.}
86        {gazes at TEA while resting right elbow on desk}
87 TEA:   why?
88        (0.5)
89 JMI:   <you (.) told ˚him˚>
90 TEA:   {I asked}
91        {touches chest with left hand}
92        {him to do,(.) right?}
93        {points at SHA's direction with left hand, and holds it}
94        so I use,
95        {stand up!}
96        {raises left hand to chest level, with palm flat, facing upward}
97        (0.6)
```

```
 98  TEA:    {first I was polite to say, could you,}
 99           {looks in SHA's direction}
100           but then, I changed it,
101           {stand up, right?}
102           {gazes at JMI}
103  S??:     uh-huh,
104  TEA:     so
105           {it's a request,(0.8) right?}
106           {brings left hand forward, with palm facing upward at chest and holds it}
```

Figure 10.5 Line 65

Figure 10.6 Line 45

Figure 10.7 Line 66   **Figure 10.8** Lines 73–75   **Figure 10.9** Lines 77–78
'what does he do,'   'what does he do,'

Teacher L starts with a discourse marker, 'let's,', looks at the list of students' names on the desk, calls out 'Shan?' while looking in his direction, and then asks, 'could you stand up?' (Line 60) followed by 'stand up!' (Line 62). During the subsequent two-second gap (Line 63), Ji-Min shifts her gaze to Shan's direction, and then many other students in the classroom also turn their heads and shift their gaze toward Shan, which demonstrates their close attention (see Figure 10.5; arrows indicate gaze directions). In fact, in the earlier sequence (Line 45), those same students looked disengaged in the whole-class interaction, exhibited by their downward gaze (see Figure 10.6; arrows indicate gaze directions). There is a vivid contrast between the interactional condition in Line 65 and the one in Line 45, suggesting that Teacher L's action to employ Shan's embodied actions prompted several students to attend to and re-engage in the classroom interaction. In Line 66, responding to Teacher L's request, Shan slowly stands up from his chair (see Figure 10.7).

Teacher L employs two types of utterances when speaking to Shan – first 'could you stand up?' (polite; Line 60) and then 'stand up!' (more direct; Line 62) – in order to demonstrate the request (i.e. asking for some type of action) and its consequence (i.e. Shan stood up). She initiates this dialogue with Shan and makes the meaning of a statement of request visible based on Shan's embodied (re)action to her request. To resolve Ji-Min's lack of understanding, such an animated demonstration of the meaning of a statement of request can be more effective than verbal explanations, as observed in the previous sequence (Part 1). Furthermore, this embodied interactional resource can be shared and attended to by multiple people in the classroom, as exhibited by the students' gaze shifts (from downward to Shan's direction).

Right after Shan sits down in Line 72, Teacher L attempts to connect Shan's embodied action back to the grammatical structure and meaning of the request that Ji-Min does not seem to understand. Specifically, in Lines 73–75 Teacher L asks Ji-Min, 'what does he do,', while pointing at Shan with her left hand and gazing at Ji-Min (see Figure 10.8). After a long gap (2.2 seconds), which indicates a lack of uptake, Teacher L repeats the question while again pointing at Shan and gazing at Ji-Min (see Figure 10.9). The series of gestures here can be interpreted as *recurring gestures* (Eskildsen & Wagner, 2013, 2015) that construct cohesive discourse and facilitate the understanding and learning of the L2. Furthermore, building on the concept of *bodily quotes* (Keevallik, 2010) – meaning that bodily movements can be quoted similarly to words – it seems that Teacher L's employment of recurring gestures can be interpreted as a type of reported embodied actions or a 'quote' of previous action. Namely, Teacher L referred to and built on Shan's embodied actions in the same manner that teachers refer to and build on students' verbal comments. In this case, she pointed to, or 'quoted', the immediately prior visible bodily conduct of another student, Shan.

This reported embodied action gives Ji-Min and other students the opportunity to experience the meaning of a request and its intended effect as it was collaboratively enacted by Shan and Teacher L. In fact, it is clear that Ji-Min and other classmates attended to Shan's embodied action with their gaze and body orientation when Teacher L asked him to stand up (see Figure 10.5). Teacher L's use of various semiotic modes – including pointing and using reported embodied actions with recurring gestures – along with her verbal elicitation of another student's embodied action, makes her explanation more *contextualized* than when she relied on a single, semiotic (verbal) mode.

Probably because Ji-Min does not respond to Teacher L's question, as evidenced by another long silence (Line 79), Teacher L reformulates her question to make it more direct ('did he stand, stand up?') in

Lines 80 and 83. In response, Ji-Min provides a minimal token, 'yeah.'. And then in Line 87, Teacher L requests an account by asking, '<u>why</u>?'. Responding to this question, Ji-Min answers, 'you (.) told °him°' (Line 89). Subsequent to that, Teacher L makes a confirmation with Ji-Min by saying, 'I <u>asked</u> him to do, right?',[1] signaled by a rising intonation, and pointing in Shan's direction. Note that Teacher L refers back to Shan's embodied action by pointing in his direction (Line 93). Also from Line 104, Teacher L further double-checks with Ji-Min whether she understands that 'could you stand up?' is a request by saying, 'so it's a request, right?'. The final part (Part 3) exhibits Teacher L's shift in using her student's embodied action to using the textbook.

Part 3 *Shan, could you stand up?*

```
107   TEA:   {do we have a request here?}
108          {looks down at textbook while pointing at page with left hand}
109          explore?
110          (0.5)
111   JMI:   yeah.((looks up to TEA))
112   TEA:   {kind of,}        right?
113          {nods several times}
114          {and we don't have}
115          {shakes head several times while looking at JMI}
116          {the request, right?}
117          {turns to next page of textbook with left hand}
118   JMI:   {°yeah.°}
119          {nods while looking down at textbook}
```

Figure 10.10 Lines 107–108
'do we have a request <u>here</u>?'

From Line 107, Teacher L shifts her orientation back to the content of the textbook and connects with the example sentences by saying, 'do we have a request <u>here</u>?' while looking at the textbook and pointing to the page (see Figure 10.10). This turn clearly illustrates Teacher L's shift from the teaching mode of 'quoting' other students' bodily actions to the teaching mode of using the textbook. Responding to Teacher L's question, in Line 111 Ji-Min gives a minimal agreement token, 'yeah.', and then looks up to Teacher L. Then, in Lines 114–117, Teacher L makes a confirmation with Ji-Min by saying, 'and we don't have the request, right?' while shaking her head several times and looking at Ji-Min. Also note that Teacher L flips the page of the textbook to the next page while gazing at it (Line 117), which nonverbally displays that the two example sentences are located on different pages. Ji-Min responds to Teacher L with a minimal token, "°yeah.°" and nodding (Lines 118–119), which displays her understanding.[2]

As a whole, the excerpt demonstrates how Teacher L incorporates a student's embodied action into the classroom interaction and selects and coordinates multiple semiotic modes as relevant interactional resources to help Ji-Min understand the grammatical structure of requests. In particular, this study reveals that using and referring to students' physical actions to clarify a syntactic meaning can be effective. As several studies (e.g. Majlesi, 2018; Matsumoto & Dobs, 2017; Sert, 2017; Smotrova, 2017) have illustrated, gestures and embodied actions are means of making abstract concepts visible, concrete and memorable and thus facilitate students' understanding and learning.

It also suggests that students may pay more attention to such embodied actions than to their teacher's verbal explanations, as observed in several previously inattentive students paying attention to Shan's action (Part 2). Furthermore, Teacher L employs Shan's action for instructional purposes by coordinating pointing gestures so that the students can connect Shan's previous action with the reaction to Teacher L's request. It is worth noting that such pedagogical decisions are usually done in-flight through thinking for teaching. In this case, Teacher L employed and adapted both verbal and embodied interactional resources, such as cut-off, silence and gaze shift, to create space for thinking.

Lastly, Teacher L appeared to select various interactional resources available in the classroom that she considered appropriate for instructional purposes at specific moments and to adjust how she connected meaning by orienting to her students' needs and states of understanding. She improvised, shuttling between various embodied and material resources (textbook, quoting another student's bodily actions, and textbook in this case) in the classroom in order to construct understanding and create learning opportunities for the students.

Discussion and Conclusion

This sequential, multimodal analysis demonstrates an L2 teacher's use of multimodal resources, which appears to be effective for gaining the students' attention and possibly facilitating their understanding and learning. During classroom interactions, it appears that L2 teachers assemble and coordinate multimodal semiotic resources, including embodied actions, gestures, gaze and materials, by orienting to moment-to-moment interactional needs in order to achieve instructional goals.

With regard to the first question – How does an L2 teacher employ and coordinate embodied actions and gestures in ESL writing classroom interactions when a student displays lack of understanding? – the excerpt demonstrates that Teacher L quoted and connected another student's (Shan's) embodied action back to her request by asking, 'what does he do?', while pointing at him. In response to the second question – How do the student and other classmates orient to the teacher's embodied actions? – the excerpt demonstrates that both the student in question (Ji-Min) and other students attended to the teacher's embodied teaching practices. Right after Teacher L uttered her request to Shan, Ji-Min shifted her gaze in Shan's direction, and many other students in the classroom who had appeared disengaged prior to Teacher L's utterance also turned their heads and shifted their gaze toward Shan. This suggests that Teacher L's employment of another student's embodied actions was effective in getting her students' attention and re-engaging them in the classroom interactions.

Given the qualitative nature of this study with a single-case analysis approach, the findings cannot be generalized to other L2 classrooms and teaching practices. Nevertheless, these findings do suggest potential pedagogical implications, which I discuss below.

Implications for Pedagogy: Attention to Embodied, Interactional Achievement of Teaching

The first implication is that L2 teachers should be aware that coordinating embodied actions and/or gestures with various semiotic modes – 'complex multimodal Gestalts' (Mondada, 2014: 139) – is an important interactional resource for teaching in L2 classrooms. As Mondada argued, multimodal resources tend to be integrated in a holistic, complex way. Even further, multimodal resources are combined by interlocutors in various configurations, depending on the activity, its ecology, and its material and cultural constraints. Developing a multimodal orientation to L2 teaching might be treated as an important element of *learning to teach* for L2 teachers (e.g. Freeman & Johnson, 1998). Thus, this study suggests that L2 teacher education should inform L2 teachers about the importance of making use of multimodal resources coordinated with speech and underscore aspects of the embodied, interactional achievement of teaching along with teacher talk. In fact, such L2 teacher competencies and practices might indirectly influence how well students coordinate talk, gesture, gaze and other embodied actions in their classroom interactions because of its social, co-constructed nature.

Another important implication is that L2 teachers should recognize the roles of nonverbal resources (e.g. cut-off, silence, gesture and gaze) in *thinking for teaching* (Smotrova, 2017; van Compernolle & Smotrova, 2017) when they need to adjust teaching actions reacting to their students' state of understanding. Classroom interactions can be considered complex dynamic systems (Seedhouse, 2010), making it difficult for L2 teachers to anticipate and prepare what will happen; instead, teachers must constantly adjust their teaching based on the students' needs. The data analysis provides an in-depth view of how one teacher employed a variety of verbal and embodied resources to make instructional decisions on the fly. Such competencies in making timely decisions might be necessary for effective L2 teaching.

In conclusion, more empirical research is needed to illuminate how L2 teachers actually manage complex interactional activities in teaching through coordinating linguistic, sequential and embodied interactional resources and how they can jointly achieve such complex interactional practices with students in the context of L2 classrooms.

Notes

(1) This confirmation check might be a confusing explanation because Teacher L, in fact, instructed Shan to stand up and because her instruction did not come in the shape of a request. However, Teacher L's utterance, 'could you stand up?' (Line 60) at least is given in the form of polite request, unlike her utterance, 'stand up!' (Line 62).

(2) It is important to note that the multiple ways in which Ji-Min displays understanding, such as using the minimal token 'yeah.' and nodding, do not necessarily mean that she achieved understanding of the structure and meaning of requests. Ji-Min might simply have pretended to understand or 'let it pass', as illustrated in Firth's (1996) study. Yet, it is clear that Ji-Min displays understanding in the interactions.

References

Beach, W.A. (1993) Transitional regularities for 'casual' 'okay' usages. *Journal of Pragmatics* 19 (4), 325–352.

Belhiah, H. (2013) Using the hand to choreograph instruction: On the functional role of gesture in definition talk. *The Modern Language Journal* 97, 417–434.

Eskildsen, S.W. and Wagner, J. (2013) Recurring and shared gestures in the L2 classroom: Resources for teaching and learning. *European Journal of Applied Linguistics* 1 (1), 139–161.

Eskildsen, S.W. and Wagner, J. (2015) Embodied L2 construction learning. *Language Learning* 65, 419–448.

Firth, A. (1996) The discursive accomplishment of normality: On conversation analysis and 'lingua franca' English. *Journal of Pragmatics* 26, 237–259.

Freeman, D. and Johnson, K.E. (1998) Reconceptualizing the knowledge-base of language teacher education. *TESOL Quarterly* 32 (3), 397–417.

Goodwin, C. (2000) Action and embodiment within situated human interaction. *Journal of Pragmatics* 32 (10), 1489–1522.

Hall, J.K. and Smotrova, T. (2013) Teacher self-talk: Interactional resource for managing instruction and eliciting empathy. *Journal of Pragmatics* 47, 75–92.

Hutchby, I. and Wooffitt, R. (1998) *Conversation Analysis: Principles, Practices and Applications.* Malden, MA: Blackwell.

Kääntä, L. (2012) Teachers' embodied allocations in instructional interaction. *Classroom Discourse* 3 (2), 166–186.

Kääntä, L., Kasper, G. and Piirainen-Marsh, A. (2018) Explaining Hooke's law: Definitional practices in a CLIL physics classroom. *Applied Linguistics* 39 (5), 694–717.

Keevallik, L. (2010) Bodily quoting in dance correction. *Research on Language and Social Interaction* 43 (4), 401–426.

Koshik, I. (2002) Designedly incomplete utterances: A pedagogical practice for eliciting knowledge displays in error correction sequences. *Research on Language and Social Interaction* 35, 277–309.

Majlesi, A.R. (2018) Instructed vision: Navigating grammatical rules by using landmarks for linguistic structures in corrective feedback sequences. *The Modern Language Journal* 102, 11–29.

Matsumoto, Y. and Dobs, A. (2017) Pedagogical gestures as interactional resources for learning tense and aspect in the ESL grammar classroom. *Language Learning* 67 (1), 7–42.

McNeill, D. (1985) So you think gestures are nonverbal? *Psychological Review* 92, 350–371.

Mondada, L. (2014) The local constitution of multimodal resources for social interaction. *Journal of Pragmatics* 65, 137–156.

Mondada, L. (2016) Multimodal resources and the organization of social interaction. In A. Rocci and L. Saussure (eds) *Verbal Communication* (pp. 329–350). Berlin: De Gruyter Mouton.

Mori, J. and Hayashi, M. (2006) The achievement of intersubjectivity through embodied completions: A study of interactions between first and second language speakers. *Applied Linguistics* 27 (2), 195–219.

Mortensen, K. (2008) Selecting next-speaker in the second language classroom: How to find a willing next-speaker in planned activities. *Journal of Applied Linguistics* 5 (1), 55–79.

Olsher, D. (2004) Talk and gesture: The embodied completion of sequential actions in spoken interaction. In R. Gardner and J. Wagner (eds) *Second Language Conversations* (pp. 221–245). London: Continuum.

Richards, K. (2005) Introduction. In K. Richards and P. Seedhouse (eds) *Applying Conversational Analysis* (pp. 1–18). Basingstoke: Palgrave Macmillan.

Sacks, H., Schegloff, E.A. and Jefferson, G. (1974) A simplest systematics for the organization of turn-taking for conversation. *Language* 50 (4), 696–735.

Schegloff, E. (1987) Analyzing single episodes of interaction: An exercise in conversation analysis. *Social Psychology Quarterly* 50, 101–114.

Schegloff, E. (2007) *Sequence Organization in Interaction: A Primer in Conversation Analysis.* Cambridge: Cambridge University Press.

Seedhouse, P. (2004) *The Interactional Architecture of the Language Classroom: A Conversation Analysis Perspective.* Malden, MA: Blackwell.

Seedhouse, P. (2010) Locusts, snowflakes and recasts: Complexity theory and spoken interaction. *Classroom Discourse* 1, 4–24.

Seo, M. and Koshik, I. (2010) A conversation analytic study of gestures that engender repair in ESL conversational tutoring. *Journal of Pragmatics* 42 (8), 2219–2239.

Sert, O. (2015) *Social Interaction and L2 Classroom Discourse.* Edinburgh: Edinburgh University Press.

Sert, O. (2017) Creating opportunities for L2 learning in a prediction activity. *System* 70, 14–25.

Smotrova, T. (2017) Making pronunciation visible: Gesture in teaching pronunciation. *TESOL Quarterly* 51 (1), 59–89.

Streeck, J. (2009) *Gesturecraft: The Manufacture of Meaning.* Amsterdam: John Benjamins.

Streeck, J., Goodwin, C. and LeBaron, C. (2011) Embodied interaction in the material world: An introduction. In J. Streeck, C. Goodwin and C. LeBaron (eds) *Embodied Interaction: Language and Body in the Material World* (pp. 1–26). Cambridge, MA: Cambridge University Press.

van Compernolle, R.A. and Smotrova, T. (2017) Gesture, meaning, and thinking-for-teaching in unplanned vocabulary explanations. *Classroom Discourse* 8 (3), 194–213.

Walsh, S. (2006) *Investigating Classroom Discourse*. London: Routledge.

Waring, H.Z. (2008) Using explicit positive assessment in the language classroom: IRF, feedback, and learning opportunities. *The Modern Language Journal* 92 (4), 577–594.

Waring H.Z., Creider, S. and Box, C. (2013) Explaining vocabulary in the language classroom. *Learning, Culture and Social Interaction* 2, 249–264.

West, C. and Garcia, A. (1988) Conversational shift work: A study of topical transitions between women and men. *Social Problems* 35 (5), 551–575.

11 Collective Translations: Translating Together in a Chinese Foreign Language Class

Abby Mueller Dobs

Choral responding, through its collaborative achievement, is believed to foster a positive sense of social solidarity, provide students with a safe space to practice new language, and possibly serve to facilitate short-term memorization (e.g. van Lier, 1988). Yet, despite these suppositions and the relative frequency with which choral responses appear in transcripts of second language (L2) classroom interaction, choral responding, in its own right, remains under-researched. This chapter examines one distinct type of choral response identified as collective translation (CT), which involves the joint production of English to Mandarin translations. The data include video- and audio-recordings of one beginner-level Chinese foreign language class at a US university. The analysis reveals the multiple embodied cues the teacher uses to elicit and coordinate CTs (e.g. elongated speech, lip positioning and nodding). It illustrates how the majority of students orient to the teacher's cues to produce a unison response, but it also highlights how individual students orient to them differently, producing asynchronous talk and singular action. For instance, within one CT some students flaunted superior competence with speeded-up talk while others coped with language difficulties with slightly delayed automatic repetition. The findings are discussed in terms of their potential consequences for L2 teaching and learning.

Introduction

Conversation analytic (CA) classroom research on whole-class interaction has largely focused on teacher-fronted sequences, particularly initiation-response-feedback (IRF) sequences targeting a single student, or a group of students acting as one (e.g. Can Daşkın, 2015; Fagan, 2015; Hosada & Aline, 2013; Kääntä, 2015; Netz, 2016; Sert & Walsh, 2013).

Each of the three parts constituting the IRF has a specific instructional function. The initiation, delivered by the teacher, is commonly a question or directive that calls students' attention to the pedagogical focus at hand. This turn makes a student response relevant, in which students display their understanding of the ongoing instructional activity. Then the teacher offers feedback, often an evaluation of the student response (Mehan, 1979; Sinclair & Coulthard, 1975).

Even when classroom discourse is organized along the predictable lines of the IRF, teachers face the complex task of eliciting responses from and allocating response turns to their many students, and students alternatively face the complex task of securing turns. Students must recognize what knowledge or skill the teacher wants them to display and how they are to display it. CA researchers have detailed a variety of techniques that teachers employ to elicit student responses, including, for example, incomplete turn constructional units (Lerner, 1995), elsewhere referred to as elicitation completion devices (Margutti, 2006) or designedly incomplete utterances (Margutti, 2010; Netz, 2016; Sert & Walsh, 2013), a term coined by Koshik (2002). With this technique, teachers discontinue a turn before its completion, often with rising intonation and elongation, to solicit student self-correction or displays of knowledge through the completion of the turn. Hand gesture may also accompany a designedly incomplete utterance as a visual clue for the expected student response (Sert, 2015). Once teachers have generally made the content of an expected response clear, they must also indicate who is to supply the response. In contrast to the general assumption that it is the teacher who controls which students speak and when they speak, conversation analysts have documented how students and teachers *jointly* manage the turn-allocation of responses using a variety of verbal and nonverbal resources (e.g. eye gaze, hand raising, nodding and pointing). The teacher allocates turns to the students, but students also display their willingness to be next speaker and work to secure their recipiency (Kääntä, 2012, 2015; Margutti, 2006; Mortensen, 2009; Sahlström, 2002; Sert & Walsh, 2013), and non-selected students make way for selected students to respond (Hosoda & Aline, 2013).

Student responses to teacher elicitations are not always allocated to and provided by individual students, but relatively little attention has been paid to the coordination of responses involving multiple students, with the exception of the work of Ikeda and Ko (2011) and Ko (2009, 2013, 2014). Ko (2013, 2014) observes that a multiple response (MR) may occur when the teacher addresses an elicitation to the entire class and refrains from selecting an individual student as next speaker. In such cases, any student or several students have the opportunity to self-select. In the case that an individual student is nominated, MRs may still occur if the nominated student's response is in some way inadequate, providing opportunity for additional student actions, such as repair or elaboration.

One common type of MR is the choral response, which occurs when many students respond to a teacher elicitation in relative unison. In these responses, students match the tempo and loudness of their answers, which are treated 'as properly simultaneous' (Ikeda & Ko, 2011: 165). In reality, choral responses are not strictly simultaneous, but may be constructed by means of shadowing or echoing. Shadowing occurs when a student or multiple students begin to repeat a first speaker's turn, following a one- or two-syllable delay, but by the time they complete the response the student talk is often synchronized. Similarly, echoing occurs when a student or multiple students immediately repeat a first speaker's turn, partially or completely, and it often results in choral talk. Ikeda and Ko (2011) note that the two practices are often difficult to distinguish. In addition to detailing how choral responses are produced, Ikeda and Ko (2011) describe how choral responses are elicited. Choral responses typically result from teacher display questions with one correct, short and obvious answer (also see Abd-Kadir & Hardman, 2007; Lerner, 1993, 2002; Margutti, 2006). Teachers may also cue choral responses with gesture and codeswitching.

Choral responding is recognized as a highly collaborative activity (Jones & Thornborrow, 2004; Lerner, 1993, 1995, 2002), and L2 scholars have speculated that, through its joint achievement, choral responding may foster a positive sense of social solidarity, provide a safe space to practice new language as part of a supportive community, and possibly serve to facilitate short-term memorization (Chick, 1996; Toohey & Day, 1999; van Lier, 1988). Yet, despite these speculations and the relative frequency with which choral responses appear in transcripts of L2 classroom interaction (e.g. Anton, 1999; He, 2004; Lee, 2016; Walsh, 2002; Waring, 2008; Watanabe, 2016), choral responding in its own right remains largely under-researched. Additionally, when researchers have noted and analyzed choral responses, they typically represent the choral responses in a single line attributed to a generic group of students or to the class (for example, see Lerner, 2002). Single-line transcription fails to recognize any variation in the students' participation and potentially minimizes the interactional effort required for the students to coordinate so closely the co-production of their talk. This study contributes to the limited research on choral responding by describing one specific type of choral response – collective translation – in detail.

Collective translations (CTs) occur in a variation of the IRF sequence. A CT is elicited by a teacher initiation that includes the provision of a first language (L1) word, phrase or sentence; the student response, where the CT is located, includes the collaborative co-construction of an L2 translation. Excerpt 1 illustrates the basic structure of a collective translation. For the purposes of clarity, I have provided a simplified version of the transcript; a more detailed version is provided in Excerpt 4.

Excerpt 1¹

```
1    TEA:   na       zenme shuo >four and a< half hours.
            then     how   say
            Okay,   how do you say 'four and a half hours'?
2           (0.7)
3    S7:    uh,
4    SS:    si      g[e ban     zhongtou
            four    CL  half    hour
            Four and a half hours.
5    TEA:         [si ge BAn zhongtou
6    TEA:   hen   hao
            very  good
            Very good.
```

I made an analytic choice in calling this phenomenon collective translation rather than choral translation. First, collective translations are distinct from typical choral responses, as they are described in the literature on classroom interaction (e.g. Hardman, 2008; Heward, 1994; Lerner, 2002; Margutti, 2006). Unlike typical choral responses, the teacher may participate in the CT, producing the translation alongside the students, and the grammatical structure of CTs can also be more complex. A CT may consist of one or even multiple clauses, whereas a typical choral response consists of a single word or short phrase. In addition, choral responses occur across classroom contexts, whereas it is likely that CTs are unique to L2 classroom contexts, where language learning is the curricular objective and translation is a common exercise. Finally, as I observed the interactional development of CTs in the data, I noticed that student participation was not entirely uniform, so I use the term collective rather than choral to better account for any asynchronous talk and action occurring in the translations.

Data and Method

The data for this study come from a digitized corpus comprised of video- and audio-recordings of five class sessions from one beginner-level (second semester) Chinese foreign language (CFL) course at a US university. The class met every day for 50 minutes during the Spring 2013 semester. Figure 11.1 illustrates the classroom setup. Students are represented here as they are in the transcripts (S1, S2, etc.), and the researchers' positions are noted as R1 and R2. One camera captures student actions and the other captures teacher actions. Three audio-recorders, indicated by (a), were placed on student desks to better capture student voices.

Throughout most of each recorded lesson, the teacher stood behind or near the podium, and she made use of a PowerPoint presentation displayed on the projector screen to lead the class through series of form-based drills and question-answer exchanges.

Blackboard   Projector Screen   Camera

Podium

		S6		S5	S4	S3	S2	S1
S11			S10	S9	S8	(a)S7		
	S17(a)	S16	S15	X	S14	S13	S12	
						(a)S20	S19	S18
			R1	R2				

Camera

Figure 11.1 Classroom setup

I viewed the videos repeatedly and produced a basic CA transcript for each lesson. Through this process, I was struck by the teacher's and students' collaborative co-construction of English to Mandarin Chinese translations during whole-class interaction. I identified this joint action as collective translation, and the sequence of actions in which a CT occurs became the focus of my analysis. This paper concentrates on one class session containing 25 episodes of collective translation. I transcribed each of these episodes in greater detail, striving to capture the many subtleties and complexities of the students' co-produced talk. If I was able to discern an individual student's voice as asynchronous from the other students', even if only slightly so, I represented this student's voice separately in the transcript.[2] Despite the divergence of some students' voices, a unison response could be distinguished in each episode, and I represent this response as a single turn at talk in the transcripts (e.g. Line 4 in Excerpt 1).

Representing the many layers of slightly overlapping speech inevitably resulted in more complicated transcripts. While parsing through these layers may prove cumbersome for the analyst and the reader, they provide a more detailed picture of how teachers and students orchestrate a number of interactional practices to accomplish a collective translation. In particular, the analysis focuses on the multiple embodied cues the teacher uses to elicit CTs and to facilitate their choral co-production once begun. It illustrates how the majority of students orient to the teacher's cues and produce a unison response, but it also pays attention to how individual students produce asynchronous talk and singular action, often while orienting to the same cues.

Analysis

Five excerpts are presented in the analysis. The first three excerpts examine how the teacher and students coordinate the co-production of CTs consisting of a single word or phrase and the final two excerpts examine how the teacher and students coordinate the co-production of CTs consisting of entire sentences and elicited as part of a PowerPoint presentation.

Single word or phrase collective translations

The first three excerpts occur during the first 20 minutes of the class, which the teacher devotes to a long series of IRF sequences aimed at eliciting recently learned vocabulary and grammatical structures. Excerpt 2 illustrates how the teacher produces an elicitation typical of those prompting CTs that consist of a single word or phrase, and it illustrates how students orient to teacher cues to coordinate the synchronization of their response.

Excerpt 2[3]

Elicitation: zenme shuo: <u>traffic</u> <u>light</u>.
                          how   say
                          How do you say 'traffic light'?

Collective Translation: honglu deng
                          traffic light
                          Traffic light.

```
1    TEA:   zenme shuo traffic light.
2           ((0.7)
3    TEA:   (((rounds lips))
```

Figure 11.2 Preparatory lip positioning – hónglǜ

```
4    S12:   (((looks in notebook))
5     S7:   u:[h
6     SS:      [ho[:ng [lu deng
7     S8:          [hong[lus- (0.2) deng
8     S7:          [hong[lu honglu  [(°de°) deng
                                          PRT
9    S19:               [honglu deng
10   TEA:                      [honglu deng
```

In Line 1 the teacher begins her elicitation with the prompt `zenme shuo` (how do you say) and then verbally provides the English phrase <u>traffic</u> <u>light.</u> with added stress and falling intonation. In addition to this verbal prompt, which is characteristic of elicitations occasioning CTs, the teacher provides further cues to indicate her preference for a collective translation. In whole-class instructional interaction, teachers often coordinate the selection of individual students as next speakers verbally and through the embodied actions of pointing and head nodding (Kääntä, 2012) as is the case in this classroom. Thus, the gap that follows the teacher elicitation points to the absence of an individual student nomination and the preference for a CT. In addition, during this silence the teacher rounds her lips in exaggerated preparation for the articulation of the initial syllable in *hónglǜ dēng* (Figure 11.2). This cue strongly projects the content of the CT, and the majority of students simultaneously begin to chorally co-produce the translation – this is one of the only episodes in which individual turns do not precede the unison response (Line 6).

Three students begin their responses slightly behind the unison response, and differences in the ways in which they respond suggest they may be accomplishing different acts with their delayed speech. Without elongating the initial syllable of the translation, S7 and S8 catch up with the rest of the students' talk, but they promptly produce multiple disfluencies (Lines 7–8). On the other hand, S19 shadows the unison response, producing his entire translation a beat behind his classmates. S7's and S8's disfluencies suggest that they are not passively shadowing the unison response but actively assembling the translation. Lastly, in Line 10 the teacher concludes the sequence, repeating the students' response and confirming it as correct.

The next excerpt presents a similar translation, but one in which the teacher participates in the CT and one in which she does not coordinate the start of the translation with preparatory lip positioning that announces the initial syllable. Without this cue, a staggered start to the CT ensues. This particular CT occurs in a sub-series of IRF sequences devoted to eliciting the students' production of the ordinal prefix *dì*.

Excerpt 3

Elicitation: na   zenme   shuo the thir↑teenth
                                             then   how   say
                                             Okay, how do you say 'the thirteenth'?

Collective Translation: dishisan
                                             thirteenth
                                             Thirteenth.

```
1     TEA:   (na zenme shuo the thir↑teenth
2            (((looks from center to right side of class))
3            (0.8)
4     S7:    (uh
5     TEA:   (((gaze begins to shift from right to center))
6     S2:    di[sh[isan
7     S8:       [di[shisan ke
                       class
8     TEA:       [di[::,[{sh[isan
9                        {(((nods - See Figure 11.3))

10    SS:        [di[::,[sh[isan
11    S7:           [di:[si- sh- shi[san
12    S15:             [shisan
13    S1:                [looks down at phone, hidden in his hand
```

Figure 11.3 Emphatic head nod – shísān

In Line 1 the teacher again elicits the CT with the prompt na zenme shuo (okay, how do you say), and then draws attention to the English phrase for translation with additional stress and a marked rise in pitch. As in Excerpt 2, the subsequent gap and shift in gaze, i.e. the teacher's lack of individual nomination, serve as a cue for collective translation. Several students begin the translation (Lines 4, 6, 7) and then, in overlap, their classmates and teacher chorally produce the unison response, di[::,[sh[isan (Lines 8–10). The teacher and students producing this response match their prosody and tempo – a feature characteristic of choral talk – marking the initial syllable with significant elongation and slightly rising continuing intonation. Another cue the teacher employs to achieve synchrony is her emphatic head nod in Line 9 (Figure 11.3). Just prior to this nod, the teacher brings her head back (see the second image in Figure 11.3), an action Lerner (2002: 231) describes as 'a kind of "windup"' which projects her punctuation of the next syllable in sh[isan. This windup engenders a precisely timed turn completion from the students that coincides with hers. The teacher's cues also appear to assist S7's and S15's delayed participation (Lines 11, 12). As the teacher and students elongate the first syllable, S7 joins in the translation and, shortening the length of her own production of the syllable, she produces the remainder of the turn alongside the unison response. S15 does not produce the target form dì but, in timing with the teacher's nod, he produces the remainder of the translation in synchrony with the unison response.

It is important to note that dì is in fact a fourth-tone word, which is produced with a high pitch that falls across the articulation of the syllable. Thus, the pronunciation of the teacher and the students producing dì with slightly rising intonation more closely reflects a second-tone word, which is produced with a low pitch that rises across the articulation of the syllable. Interestingly, the students who begin producing the translation ahead of the unison response do not coordinate their unfolding talk to match the unison response. They do not elongate their production of the target form, and it is clear from the audio-recording that S8 pronounces dì as a fourth-tone word. S2's pronunciation is less clear. Finally, as is the case in all of these collective translations, some students refrain from participating, and they may coordinate this lack of participation with the teacher's cues as well; as the CT core begins and the teacher's gaze orients to other students, S1 hides the use of his cell phone and his lack of participation.

In Excerpt 4, the teacher elicits the collective translation in much the same way as she does in Excerpts 2 and 3. Like Excerpt 2, the teacher produces the CT with the students; however, in this excerpt she delays her involvement, and this delay is consequential to the students' participation. The target form in Excerpt 4 is *bàn* (half). Note that this is a more detailed transcript of the same episode presented in Excerpt 1.

Excerpt 4

Elicitation:
na   zenme shuo >four and a< half hours.
then how   say
Okay, how do you say 'four and a half hours'?

Collective Translation:
si   ge ban   zhongtou
four CL half hour (durational)
Four and a half hours.

```
1     TEA:  na zenme {shuo >four and a< half hours.
2                    {((presses palms together, slides RH away from body))
3           (0.7)
4     S7:   u[h:, si: [ge: [ba::[n:: ((0.2 s until line 14))
5     S2:     [>si ge< [ban [zhong
6     S9:              [si
7     S19:                  [si ge {(zhig thanghong) ((nonsense words))
8                                  {((tosses pen; watches it fall to desk))
9     SS:                  [si g[e ((0.4 s until line 13⁴))
10    TEA:                      [si ge [{BAn zh[ongtou.
11                                     {((nods head))
```

Figure 11.4 Emphatic head nod – bàn

```
12    S9:                    [si ge [ban
13    SS:                           [ban   zh[ongtou
14    S7:                                    [zhongtou
15    TEA:  hen hao
```

In Line 1 the teacher again elicits the CT with the prompt na   zenme shuo (okay, how do you say), and she increases the tempo of her talk through the first part of the English phrase, >four   and a< half hours. The faster speech draws attention to *half hours*, the part of the phrase that becomes translated into the target form of the elicitation, the *bàn* after the classifier and before *zhōngtóu*.

As in Excerpts 2 and 3, the gap in Line 3 serves as a cue for collective translation. Several students begin to produce the translation (Lines 4–6) ahead of the unison response (Line 9), and the different manner in which each of these students participates in the CT is of note. S7 begins the CT with an effort toward synchronization, evidenced by the excessive elongation and slowed-down speech. When the teacher and her classmates do not immediately join in, she adds additional elongation and a brief pause (Line 4). S2, on the other hand, produces > si ge < with increased tempo and marks the target form, ban, with emphasis (Line 5), perhaps as a means of highlighting his own competence and mastery of the form. Yet, in his failure to coordinate his speech, he also produces an inaccurate translation, failing to complete the entire word, *zhongtou*. S9 abandons his initial turn (Line 6) but begins again simultaneously with the teacher's translation (Line 12).

In Line 9 additional students overlap the early participators' talk and begin the unison response. Unlike the previous two excerpts, the teacher does not provide the lip positioning cue, and she does not begin her translation in synchrony with the students. Rather, the teacher joins the students' production a syllable behind them, and when she overlaps her translation with theirs (Line 10), the students interrupt the flow of their own speech with a brief pause. At this point the teacher nods her head (Figure 11.4). Again, the windup to this nod portends the teacher's production of the subsequent syllable, the target form of the CT, and students producing the CT in unison complete it in time with her. However, not all students organize their talk in accordance with the teacher's cue in this manner. S19, who begins his translation in coordination with the other students (Line 7), tosses his pen in the air and completes the translation with nonsense words, mimicking the Chinese language. S19's deviating talk and actions were clear to the analyst, who was able to discern them with the use of multiple recordings; however, because S19 sits in the back of the classroom, it is likely that his off-task behavior was concealed within the unison response and remained undetected by the teacher.

Sentence-length collective translations

The next two excerpts examine sentence-length translations that are also managed via a PowerPoint presentation. In Excerpt 5 the target structure is the quantifier *yīdiǎn* (a little). The English sentence to be translated is displayed on the projector screen. Above this English sentence, the title of the slide provides a grammatical formula, 'V+AdjV+一点' (verb+adjectival verb+yīdiǎn). The students' eye gaze in this episode reveals their orientation to the text on the PowerPoint throughout the co-production of the CT. However, despite the presence of this formula, the students and teacher persist in using a similar, but longer, grammatical structure that the students learned the day before: 'VO+V 得 AdjV' (verb object + verb *de* adjectival verb).

Excerpt 5

Elicitation: uh na   > zhe ge   zenme shuo< please drive a little <u>slower</u>.
                                          then   this CL how   say
                                    Uh, okay, this one, how do you say 'please drive a little slower'?

Collective Translation: qing   ni   kaiche   kai   de   man   yidian
                                    please you   drive-car drive PRT   slow a little
                                    Please, drive a little slower.

```
1    TEA:  uh na >zhe ge zenme shuo< please drive a little slower.
2    TEA:  so {the formula is on top
3             {((points to formula, 'verb+adjectival verb+ yīdiǎn'))
```

Figure 11.5 Points to
formula

```
4            (1.7)
5    S8:     kai che [kai de:,
6    S17:            [°kai che:,° ((4.6 s until line 14))
7    TEA:    qing ni[::,
8    S8:            [uh
9    S3:     kai che [kai (de) ((5.0 s until line 22))
10   TEA:            [<k[ai: che:: kai: de:,>
11   S8:               [>q[ing ni< ch- kai de
12   S19:                  [kai che: k- t- de:
13   SS:                   [<kai: che:: kai: de[::,> ((1.6 s until 22))
14   S17:                                      [kai de
15   S10:    man
16           [(0.4)
17   TEA:    [((purses lips))
```

Figure 11.6 Preparatory
lip positioning – màn

```
18    S8:   man [yi[↑dian
19    S19:       [yi[:,
20    TEA:         [{ma[n yidian
21                 {(((displays Chinese translation))
22    SS:             [man yidian
```

The teacher's elicitation in this episode is similar to those discussed above, but in this case the demonstrative zhe ge is added to the Chinese prompt and, following the English sentence to be translated, the teacher points to the grammatical formula that the translation will follow (Figure 11.5). It is at this point that the gap following the elicitation occurs. Two students begin the translation, each producing the final syllable of their turns with elongation and continuing intonation, a turn-design that provides space for others to join in the co-production of the CT.

However, as the students do not translate *please* in their responses, the teacher intervenes, producing the first component of the CT, qing ni[::,. The rest of the class does not immediately respond to the teacher's prompting, but S3 and S8 orient to it as a teacher-initiated correction, and they begin the translation anew. S3 immediately continues the translation where the teacher leaves off, kai che [kai (de) (Line 9), while S8 repeats the teacher's correction, including a translation of *please*, [>q[ing ni< ch- kai de (Line 11). Both students delay the completion of the translation.

In the meantime, the teacher overlaps the two early participators' talk and continues her production of the translation, slowing her speech and delivering it with significant elongation, [<k[ai: che:: kai: de:, > (Line 10). Nevertheless, rather than coordinating their speech to coincide with hers, students co-producing a unison response speak equally slowly, always a split-second behind the teacher. S10 immediately produces the next component of the translation, the adjectival verb *màn* (Line 15). No other students join her, and a brief gap ensues, during which the teacher purses her lips in exaggerated preparation for the articulation of the next syllable of the ongoing translation (Figure 11.6). Recall that this same cue facilitated a choral completion of the CT in Excerpt 2. Here, however, the students' eyes are directed toward the PowerPoint presentation rather than the teacher, and only S8 attends to the teacher's cue, producing the expected turn, man [yi[↑dian (Line 18). S19 begins to co-produce the remainder of the turn, but leaves it incomplete as the teacher continues with the translation and displays the answer in written form (Lines 20–21). At this point, the majority of the students shadow the teacher's talk and complete the translation in unison (Line 22).

The transcript reveals how CTs involving the translation of entire sentences are broken down into component parts and co-constructed across multiple turns, requiring much interactional effort to coordinate their co-construction. As there are no substantial pauses between one student's turn and the next student's turn, what might not be evident at first glance are the significant gaps between an individual student's turn and his or her next turn. For example, early in the CT and before the development of the unison response, S17 begins his construction of the translation °kai che:,° (Line 6), and 4.6 seconds elapse before he continues kai de (Line 14). In fact, he never even produces the target structure *yīdiǎn* or completes the entire translation. S3, who begins the translation quite fluently, kai che [kai (de) (Line 9), waits five seconds before completing it with the unison response. Even students chorally co-producing the translation entirely with the unison response wait 1.6 seconds between their turns. The teacher orients to the student gaps and shadowing as a display of confusion. She identifies the confusion as stemming from the mismatch between the underlying structure of the sentence the class is producing (verb object + verb *de* adjectival verb) and the grammatical formula displayed through the PowerPoint presentation (verb + adjectival verb + yīdiǎn), and she directly proceeds to explain the difference between the two constructions.

Excerpt 6 examines another CT that is coordinated in conjunction with the PowerPoint presentation. Like Excerpt 5, the CT is co-constructed across multiple turns, but in this case the sentence is longer, containing more grammatical constituents. The excerpt is rather lengthy, so the sequential analysis that follows will focus only on the teacher's cue use and the unison production of the translation.

Excerpt 6[5]

```
Collective Translation:      zai   diyi  ge   shizi lukou  wang  zuo  guai
                             LOC   first CL   intersection LOC  left turn
                             Make a left turn at the first intersection.

1    TEA:  kay there're two chunks of this sentence. which one would
2          you start first.
3          (0.4)
4    S9:   {zai:,
5          {((looking down, writing in lap))
6    TEA:  {At the f-irst intersection. or {make left turn.
7          {((LH points to second chunk))  {((LH points to first chunk))
8    S9:   [zai
9    TEA:  [what's the purpose of {these sentence.
10                                {((extends L arm, points to sentence))
11   S9:   make left [turn
12   TEA:            [make left turn. so anything description,
13         [(0.3)
14   TEA:  [brings forearm back toward body and start of sentence
15   TEA:  go[es to °(the front).°
16   S9:     [is the be- (0.5) begin[ing
17   S1:                            [zai:
18   TEA:  {would be:,
19         {((turns LH up and away from body))
```

Figure 11.7 Eliciting gesture

```
20              (0.2)
21      S1:     °zai°
22              (0.4)
23      S4:     [zai ((1.0 s until line 30))
24      S19:    [°di°
25 ──►  SS:     z[ai
26      S19:    [zai
27      TEA:    [zai
28              [(0.2)
29      TEA:    [points to second chunk of sentence
```

Figure 11.8 Focusing and
recalibrating gesture 1

```
30      S4:     di [yi ge
31 ──►  SS:        [di[: yi ge=
32      TEA:          [di yi ge
33      S?:     =kou
34      S19:    sh[:i:
35      S7:     sh[:
36      TEA:    [{sh[:izi (0.2) lu[kou
37              {((still pointing to the second chunk, four beats))
```

Figure 11.9 Focusing and
recalibrating gesture 2

```
38      S8:     [>shizi< ((1.0 s until line 41))
39 ──►  SS:     [sh[:izi
40      S7:       [shizi
41 ──►  SS:                        [°lukou:°=
42      S19:                        [>lukou<
43      TEA:    ={make a left turn
44              {((points to first chunk of sentence))
```

Figure 11.10 Focusing and
recalibrating gesture 3

```
45      S?:     [z-
46      S9:     [w[ang (.) zuo guai
47      S20:      [wang zuo (guai) ((first time participating))
48 ──►  SS:       [<wang zuo> [guai
49      S12:                  [wang zuo guai
```

First, unlike other elicitations, here the teacher explicitly divides the sentence into two 'chunks', embedding an IRF pre-sequence to identify which chunk the students should translate first (Lines 1–15), and she employs an English prompt, would be:,, while turning her left palm up and away from her body (Figure 11.7), instead of the usual *zěnme shuō*. Despite this division into two 'chunks', the unison response is actually constructed across five chorally co-produced turns (Lines 25, 31, 39, 41, 47), requiring the teacher and students to recalibrate their synchronization at each turn. The teacher uses a series of pointing gestures that facilitate this collaborative achievement.

In Line 25 the students begin the single-word first turn of the CT, z[ai, which the teacher quickly confirms, repeating them in overlap. At this point, the teacher points to the second chunk of the English sentence (Figure 11.8), which must be translated and produced first, and this gesture prompts the students to continue. The students elongate the first syllable of their next turn, [di[: yi ge= (Line 31), and this elongation creates space for the teacher to join in the translation in near unison (Line 32). From here, the teacher employs another gestural cue that coordinates the synchronization of the students' speech. With her finger still pointed to the second chunk of the sentence, she produces four beats corresponding to her production of the four syllables [sh[:izi (0.2) lu[kou (Figure 11.9), and the students produce their sh[:izi in unison (Line 39). Their °lukou:° is produced with some hesitation, slightly delayed and softened (Line 41). At this point, the teacher moves her pointing gesture back to the first part of the sentence (Figure 11.10) and states it aloud, make a left turn, and the students complete the CT with the choral co-production of [<wang zuo> [guai (Line 48).

Summary and Implications

This chapter has detailed the complex interactional work involved in accomplishing collective translations in one Chinese foreign language class. The analysis illustrates how the teacher elicits collective translations from students with the turn-design of her questions. Elicitations typically begin with a Chinese prompt, most commonly zěnme shuō, and end with the English word, phrase or sentence to be translated. The teacher draws attention to the specific language that will be translated into the target form with added stress, marked rises in pitch and/or faster speech. Then she refrains from nominating an individual student so a gap follows the elicitation. In Excerpt 5 she also employs an eliciting gesture, flipping the palm of her hand up and away from her body. Together, these features signal the teacher's expectation of a collective translation and, in response, the students co-produce the translation in relative unison. While individual student participation in a CT varies, at least to some extent, a single unison response still emerges through a chorus of student voices, which are hearably synchronous and indistinguishable.

The teacher and students use a variety of nonverbal cues, both prosodic and gestural, to coordinate the synchronization of their speech. For example, the teacher's preparatory lip positioning can project the first syllable of a CT, resulting in a synchronous start to the students' production of it (Excerpt 2), and the teacher's emphatic head nod can work to maintain or regain synchronicity midway through the production of a CT (Excerpts 3 and 4). These cues, however, may be overlooked when CTs are concurrently managed through a PowerPoint presentation and the students' visual attention is oriented to the text projected on the screen rather than the teacher's face (Excerpts 4 and 5). In such cases, gestural cues coordinated with the displayed text are more likely to be noticed (Excerpt 5). In all of the excerpts, the teacher and/or students use elongation and continuing, slightly rising intonation to synchronize their speech, but the analysis also reveals that while these cues facilitate the choral co-production of the CT, they may simultaneously disrupt fluency and accurate tone production. Interruption to the students' flow of speech is compounded in sentence-length CTs, which are co-constructed across multiple turns and require the synchronization of speech to be recalibrated at each turn; significant gaps between individual student turns, as well as turns constituting the unison response, are frequent (Excerpts 4 and 5).

Producing meticulous transcripts that detailed individual students' voices participating in choral responses proved important. While the teacher's cues generally appear to work toward achieving a uniform group response, not all students coordinated their speech to directly align with their classmates', and individual students performed a variety of actions within the CT. For example, several students produced the translations ahead of the unison response, or simultaneously with it, without efforts toward synchronicity and, in doing so, they produced the translations more fluently and with accurate tone production, possibly as a means of displaying that they had already mastered the target form (Excerpts 3 and 4). Others coordinated their talk so they produced translations a syllable or two behind the unison response. Some of these students produced certain disfluencies in their speech, for example self-correction, which suggests that they were actively assembling the translation without relying on hearing their classmates' production first, while others may have drawn on the support of their classmates' talk to produce the target language and participate in the translation. With their slightly delayed repetition, students coped with, and signaled to the teacher, language difficulties (Excerpts 2, 3 and 5). Still other students refrained from participating in the CT altogether, and some carefully coordinated off-task behavior in accordance with the unfolding CT. For example, one student timed his phone use with the teacher's shift in gaze (Excerpt 3) and another timed his nonsense words so they blended in with the accurate translation (Excerpt 4), perhaps as a means of coping with a lack of competence or quite simply out of boredom.

The findings from this study have implications for L2 teachers and teacher educators. First, they support previous assumptions that choral responses provide safe spaces for L2 students to practice new vocabulary and grammatical constructions. In the case of CTs, students may be bolstered by the joint effort of translating and protected by the anonymity arising from simultaneous talk. However, the analysis also provided a more complex picture of choral responding by means of collective translation, revealing that students do not simply parrot back the expected response in a single, strictly unified fashion; instead, individual students make of a CT what they will, perhaps shadowing their classmates' talk in order to confront unfamiliar language, or leading their classmates' talk in order to flaunt superior competence, or playfully diverging from their classmates' talk in order to alleviate mental strain. Previous research has not recognized choral responses as potential sites for the display of student agency. This surprising discovery is significant as language learning may be dependent on learner agency (van Lier, 2008).

The findings from this study certainly demonstrate the need for language teachers to be reflective practitioners with heightened awareness of how their participation and use of verbal and nonverbal cues in particular actions for teaching and learning shape student talk and how these actions may impede or enhance pedagogical goals. L2 teacher education programs must recognize the important roles that embodiment and nonverbal action play in the interactional organization of teaching and learning. As a researcher drawing on the theory and methods of CA, it is not in my purview to recommend or discourage the use of collective translation in other L2 classrooms, but I will conclude with a discussion of how the specific findings of this study may provide certain points of reflection for L2 teachers to consider when deciding for themselves whether and how to apply the action sequence in their own classrooms.

First, teachers should consider CTs and the cues employed in their coproduction in light of their pedagogical goals. Do they want to promote fluency? Do they want students to practice new language forms? Do they want to quickly review previously learned vocabulary before introducing new content? Do they want to increase students' opportunity to respond? Answers to questions like these will help teachers decide whether collective translation will be an effective means of student participation and what cues they would use to elicit and organize that participation. For example, if a teacher would like to practice new vocabulary and increase students' opportunity to respond, she might decide to elicit CTs from her students in order to accomplish these goals. All students have the opportunity to participate in each CT, and they need not fear being singled out if they have not yet mastered the vocabulary. If, like Chinese, the L2 is a tonal language, the teacher will need to decide whether the benefit of using slightly rising, continuing intonation to facilitate the synchronization of speech outweighs the risk of effecting inaccurate tone production. She may, instead, choose to use preparatory lip positioning and head nods. If the language to be translated will also be displayed in written form, the teacher may rather use gestural cues that are closely coordinated with the text. It may even be productive for the teacher to consider consistency in her cue use and to explicitly discuss this use with her students. Making student participation more predictable could ease the interactional effort required for them to participate in a CT and allow for greater attention to the language itself.

It would be impossible, perhaps even counterproductive (Käänta, 2015), for teachers to constantly monitor all of the many subtle, embodied and multimodal interactional practices they employ when orchestrating collective translations, or other sequences of action, but given the time and space for reflection, they might focus their attention on one or two. Slight changes in teachers' cue use could significantly shape the organization of classroom interaction, potentially enhancing students' opportunity for learning.

Notes

(1) Conventions for the grammatical gloss include CL (Classifier) and PRT (Particle).
(2) Of course, it would be impossible to represent 21 different voices linearly in a transcript, and the positioning of the recording devices influence which student voices may be heard more clearly and therefore transcribed with more precision. Thus, while this paper attempts to push current representations of the choral co-production of student talk, it is still limited in this regard.

(3) Another note about the transcripts is warranted here. Participants seldom produced any Chinese language outside the teacher elicitation and the CT, so to make the transcripts more readable I provide the Chinese-to-English translations of the teacher elicitation and the CT apart from the transcript of each excerpt. When a participant does produce additional Chinese language in a turn at talk, a translation is provided below it.

(4) Here, students complete the unison response across two turns, and I note the time that elapses between those turns. In subsequent transcripts, when individual students complete the translation across multiple turns, I also note the time that elapses between them.

(5) As the teacher elicitation in this episode is produced solely in English, I only provide a translation of the CT.

References

Abd-Kadir, J. and Hardman, F. (2007) The discourse of whole class teaching: A comparative study of Kenyan and Nigerian primary English lessons. *Language and Education* 21 (1), 1–15.

Anton, M. (1999) The discourse of a learner-centered classroom: Sociocultural perspectives on teacher–learner interaction in the second-language classroom. *The Modern Language Journal* 83 (3), 303–318.

Can Daşkın, N. (2015) Shaping learner contributions in an EFL classroom: Implications for L2 classroom interactional competence. *Classroom Discourse* 6 (1), 33–56.

Chick, K. (1996) Safe-talk: Collusion in apartheid education. In H. Coleman (ed.) *Society and the Language Classroom*. Cambridge: Cambridge University Press.

Fagan, D.S. (2015) Managing language errors in real-time: A microanalysis of teacher practices. *System* 55, 74–85.

Hardman, F. (2008) Teachers' use of feedback in whole-class and group-based talk. In N. Mercer and S. Hodgkinson (eds) *Exploring Talk in Schools*. London: Sage.

He, A. (2004) CA for SLA: Arguments from the Chinese language classroom. *The Modern Language Journal* 88 (4), 568–582.

Heward, W.L. (1994) Three *low-tech* strategies for increasing the frequency of active student response during group instruction. In R. Gardner III, D. Sainato, J.O. Cooper, T. Heron, W.L. Heward, J. Eshleman and T.A. Grossi (eds) *Behavior Analysis in Education: Focus on Measurable Superior Instruction*. Pacific Grove, CA: Brooks/Cole.

Hosada, Y. and Aline, D. (2013) Two preferences in question-answer sequences in language classroom context. *Classroom Discourse* 4 (1) 63–88.

Ikeda, K. and Ko, S. (2011) Choral practice patterns in the language classrooms. In G. Palloti and J. Wagner (eds) *L2 Learning as Social Practice: Conversation-analytic Perspectives*. Honolulu, HI: University of Hawai'i, National Foreign Language Resource Center.

Jones, R. and Thornborrow, J. (2004) Floors, talk and the organization of classroom activities. *Language in Society* 33 (3), 399–423.

Kääntä, L. (2012) Teachers' embodied allocations in instructional interaction. *Classroom Discourse* 3 (2), 166–186.

Kääntä, L. (2015) The multimodal organisation of teacher-led classroom interaction. In C.J. Jenks and P. Seedhouse (eds) *International Perspectives on ELT Classroom Interaction* (pp. 64–83). Basingstoke: Palgrave Macmillan.

Ko, S. (2009) Multiple-response sequences in classroom talk. *Australian Review of Applied Linguistics* 32 (1), 1–18.

Ko, S. (2013) *Understanding the Dynamics of Classroom Communication*. Cambridge: Cambridge Scholars.

Ko, S. (2014) The nature of multiple responses to teachers' questions. *Applied Linguistics* 35 (1), 48–62.

Koshik, I. (2002) Designedly incomplete utterances: A pedagogical practice for eliciting knowledge displays in error correction sequences. *Research on Language and Social Interaction* 35 (3), 277–309.

Lee, J. (2016) Teacher entries into second turn positions: IRFs in collaborative teaching. *Journal of Pragmatics* 95, 1–15.

Lerner, G.H. (1993) Collectivities in action: Establishing the relevance of conjoined participation in conversation. *Text* 13 (2), 213–245.

Lerner, G.H. (1995) Turn design and the organization of participation in instructional activities. *Discourse Processes* 19 (1), 111–131.

Lerner, G.H. (2002) Turn-sharing: The choral co-production of talk-in-interaction. In C. Ford, B. Fox and S.A. Thompson (eds) *The Language of Turn and Sequence*. Oxford: Oxford University Press.

Margutti, P. (2006) 'Are you human beings?' Order and knowledge construction through questioning in primary classroom interaction. *Linguistics and Education* 17 (4), 313–346.

Margutti, P. (2010) On designedly incomplete utterances: What counts as learning for teachers and students in primary classroom interaction. *Research on Language and Social Interaction* 43 (4), 315–345.

Mehan, H. (1979) *Learning Lessons*. Cambridge, MA: Harvard University Press.

Mortensen, K. (2009) Establishing recipiency in pre-beginning position in the second language classroom. *Discourse Processes* 46 (5), 491–515.

Netz, H. (2016) Designedly incomplete utterances and student participation. *Linguistics and Education* 33, 56–73.

Sahlström, J.F. (2002) The interactional organization of hand raising in classroom interaction. *Journal of Classroom Interaction* 37 (2), 47–57.

Sert, O. (2015) *Social Interaction and L2 Classroom Discourse*. Edinburgh: Edinburgh University Press.

Sert, O. and Walsh, S. (2013) The interactional management of claims of insufficient knowledge in English language classrooms. *Language and Education* 27 (6), 542–565.

Sinclair, J.M. and Coulthard, M. (1975) *Towards an Analysis of Discourse: The English Used by Teachers and Pupils*. Oxford: Oxford University Press.

Toohey, K. and Day, E. (1999) Language-learning: The importance of access to community. *TESL Canada Journal* 17 (1), 40–53.

van Lier, L. (1988) *The Classroom and the Language Learner*. New York: Longman.

van Lier, L. (2008) Agency in the classroom. In J. Lantolf and M. Poehner (eds) *Sociocultural Theory and the Teaching of Second Languages*. London: Equinox.

Walsh, S. (2002) Construction or obstruction: Teacher talk and learner involvement in the EFL classroom. *Language Teaching Research* 6 (1), 3–23.

Waring, H.Z. (2008) Using explicit positive assessment in the language classroom: IRF, feedback, and learning opportunities. *The Modern Language Journal* 92 (4), 577–594.

Watanabe, A. (2016) Engaging in an interactional routine in an EFL classroom: The development of L2 interactional competence over time. *Novitas-ROYAL* 10 (1), 48–70.

12 The Embodied Accomplishment of Teaching: Challenges for Research and Practice

Stephen Daniel Looney

The contributions to this volume document in fine-grained detail some of the embodied interactional contingencies of teaching. The contributions show that teaching is a complex task that involves the management of alignment, affiliation and multiple participant frameworks. In this conclusion, I will outline and discuss four central findings of the research presented here and how these findings are fundamental to an ethnomethodological conversation analysis (EMCA) conceptualization of teaching. Next, I will lay out four challenges that the studies present for future research in classroom EMCA. Finally, I will conclude with remarks about what the work in this volume means for those involved in teaching and teacher preparation and how findings from EMCA can be applied.

Summarizing the Contributions

The four central findings in the chapters are that teaching is embodied, teaching is contingent, teaching involves the management of alignment and affiliation, and teaching involves the management of various participation frameworks. First and foremost, teaching is embodied action. As outlined in the introduction to the volume, our conceptualization of embodied action (Goodwin, 2000, 2013, 2018) recognizes that all interaction is embodied and that multiple modalities and resources are involved. In this volume, particular attention is paid to gaze (Dobs; Park; Sert; Tadic & Box; Waring & Carpenter), gesture (Hall *et al.*; Matsumoto), facial expression (Looney & Kim), body positioning (Fagan) and objects in the environment (Reddington *et al.*). Embodied resources do not act in isolation. They are parts of constellations of resources that make up actions and practices. For example, when a writing tutor uses self-directed talk while suggesting revisions, his turns are designed with averted gaze, lower volume and language (Park). It is not one resource but a collection used just so *in situ* that make stretches of self-directed talk recognizable as pedagogical action. Additionally, teaching as embodied action recognizes the distributed nature of teaching and learning. For instance, Matsumoto's chapter shows how a teacher incorporates the embodied actions of students into her instruction. Likewise, the establishment of mutual gaze begets teacher-embodied go-aheads which in turn open up interactional space for student participation (Sert). We see in these studies that teaching is not just directing students to do this or that but acting with students to accomplish the instructional project.

The chapters in this volume repeatedly demonstrate that the work of teaching is contingent. It is not something that can always be planned out and involves recognizing and managing moments when students are struggling with course content (Fagan; Hall *et al.*; Looney & Kim; Reddington *et al.*). Teaching involves noticing and deciding when to contribute to ongoing interactions and when to withhold contributions (Fagan; Reddington *et al.*). Teaching also involves dealing with unsolicited contributions. Hall *et al.* demonstrates that actions for managing unsolicited turns could be as slight as raising one's index finger. On the other hand, Tadic and Box show that a teacher might actually take up the action projected by unsolicited student turns. By taking up unsolicited turns, the teacher validates students' experiences outside the class as relevant to the classroom. These are not moments that one can script in a lesson plan. They arise and must be dealt with in the moment. The choices that teachers make in the moment matter and influence the interactional trajectory, and thus opportunities for participation, of the instructional project.

Teaching involves the embodied management of alignment and affiliation (Stivers, 2008; Stivers *et al.*, 2011). As we have seen, the way in which students and teachers align (or disalign) with the action of the unfolding instructional project has interactional consequences. In Reddington *et al.*, a menu that a student uses during a storytelling triggers an affiliative interjection by the teacher. Despite the affiliative nature of the teacher's interjection, the student who was speaking and holding the menu does not align with the action it projects but instead works to maintain the floor and continue her storytelling. Looney and Kim show how a teacher manages disaligning student responses by teasing students. The teases not only affiliate with the humorous stances displayed by students around disaligning turns but realign the trajectory of the instructional project.

Finally, teaching involves the management of various participation frameworks (Dobs; Fagan; Tadic & Box; Waring & Carpenter). Fagan shows how a teacher moves from observer to participant during periods of group work. Reddington *et al.* unpack how a teacher influences the trajectory of a student's storytelling sequences by withholding participation or interjecting herself into the storytelling. Dobs analyzes how a teacher initiates a specific classroom activity – collective translations – and how students participate differently in the activity. Waring and Carpenter demonstrate how a teacher's gaze shifts at the end of turns shift the participant framework from dyadic to whole-class. Thus, we see that teaching is complex and rich and cannot be reduced to standing in front of a classroom presenting content knowledge to students. When we look at what teachers do in this volume's chapters, we see that they undertake a plethora of activities, including discussing students' life outside the classroom, monitoring small group work, teasing and suggesting revisions for a paper.

Four Challenges for Classroom EMCA

The chapters in this volume present four challenges for future EMCA research on classrooms. The first two challenges involve the further analysis of the embodied accomplishment of teaching. The second two challenges involve ethics and methods for data collection, storage and sharing. I am putting these challenges forward in the form of imperatives.

(1) Document the embodied interactional work of teaching

For decades now, EMCA scholars as well as others in related fields have worked to document the interactional work of teaching (Hellermann, 2003, 2005; Koschmann, 2011; Lee, 2006, 2007; Macbeth, 2004; Sert, 2015; Waring, 2008). Much of this work has focused on verbal and prosodic turn design in teaching. It is only recently that studies have considered nonverbal resources in teaching. This volume is the most recent contribution to this endeavor. The challenge for EMCA moving forward is to continue unpacking the embodied nature of the instructional project in adequate depth, accounting for both the multiplicity of resources that make up any one embodied action and how the use of those resources shifts and is shaped by the unfolding interaction. As Mondada (2014: 154) points out, analyzing video data 'notably complexifie[s] the insight into how human action and interaction is organized'. When we move from audio-recordings and transcription to video, our awareness of how interaction unfolds is broadened and sharpened. We see that we must account not only for the sequentiality of language use but also for the local arrangement of resources and the situated shaping of resources within the local ecology of the ongoing activity (Mondada, 2014).

In terms of the local arrangement of resources, we see when analyzing video that every embodied action teachers and students build involves the coordination of numerous resources, including body positions, facial expressions, gaze, gesture, linguistic material (spoken and written) and objects in the environment. Participants' coordination of resources creates '*complex multimodal Gestalts* that are both specifically adjusted to the context and systematically organized' (Mondada, 2014: 140). This complexity and multimodality raises issues for transcription. Mondada (2014) herself notes the challenges for presenting video data and creating transcripts that capture an appropriate level of detail. While I cannot provide all the answers for how best to represent embodied action, there are recent examples of data presentation that I find appealing (Goodwin, 2013; Kunitz, 2018). Both are examples of how less can actually be more. They rely primarily on images, instead of transcription, to do the work of presenting embodied action. Goodwin's (2013, 2018) figures often involve multiple still frames overlaid with arrows and circles directing readers' attention. Kunitz (2018) uses an ingeniously simple plus sign (+) in lines of talk to note where an accompanying screenshot below the transcription aligns. Clearly, there are limits to the number of still frames that can be included in a transcript and even the most high-definition pictures cannot help us with the presentation of prosodic features or other aspects of complex multimodal Gestalts. But these examples can serve as a starting point for how to present the embodied and sequential nuance of teaching.

EMCA studies must also account for the situated shaping of resources within ongoing ecologies of action. Mondada (2014) shows how during a business meeting a pen shifts from a tool for writing to a tool for guiding the attention of others, based in part on how the pen's user holds it. Undoubtedly, in the classroom, verbal and nonverbal resources are used in a variety of ways to achieve different purposes. If there is any classroom research on the situated shaping of resources, I am unaware of it, but speaking anecdotally there is evidence of this in the collection of geosciences data that Looney and Kim draw on in this volume. During a lab, Nora, the teacher, asks for a piece of notebook paper from a student and folds the paper to demonstrate a concept to a student. Thus, she turns an object that we often assume is for writing into a pedagogical tool to explain a concept in geology. While she is folding the paper, she comments that using the paper as part of her explanation probably will not work. Then, in subsequent interactions, the teacher reuses the paper as a pedagogical tool in a similar fashion but instead of doubting its efficacy lauds her innovation. While this anecdote does not meet the adequacy requirements for EMCA, future studies should look at how teachers and students draw on objects and other embodied resources across contexts in the accomplishment of different tasks as well as how the use of the same embodied resources across interactions can vary.

(2) Expand beyond the L2 classroom

While early seminal EMCA work on classroom interaction focused on a variety of classroom contexts (Lemke, 1990; Mehan, 1979; Poole, 1990), the majority of recent classroom EMCA has analyzed second and foreign language classroom interaction, particularly English as a second or foreign language classrooms (ESL/EFL). For EMCA to realize its potential to inform pedagogical practice, it must expand its focus beyond ESL and EFL contexts. Four studies in this volume do so (Dobs; Hall *et al.*; Looney & Kim; Park): Dobs' chapter looks at choral translations in a Chinese as a foreign language classroom; Hall *et al.* analyze interaction in an elementary school classroom; Looney and Kim investigate a university STEM lab; and Park explores writing tutoring dyads.

When we look at teaching in these different contexts, we can compare and contrast settings to help us understand both the general and the specific projects of teaching. For example, one general interactional undertaking that is found to be ubiquitous is the three-turn sequence known as initiation-response-follow up (IRF) (Mehan, 1979; Sinclair & Coulthard, 1975). In IRF sequences, teachers initiate the sequence, perhaps with a question, in the first turn. Students respond in the second turn, and the teacher follows up, likely with evaluation, in the third turn. The IRF has been noted to exist across numerous contexts, including urban elementary school classrooms (Mehan, 1979), ESL/EFL classrooms (Hellermann, 2003; Lee, 2007; Waring, 2008), university physics and geosciences labs (Looney, 2019; Looney & Kim, 2018) and medical school tutoring sessions (Zemel & Koschmann, 2011). There may be additional interactional events that are common across teaching contexts, but we do not yet know that.

In contrast to the ubiquity of the IRF, there may be projects that are particular to certain kinds of classrooms contexts. For example, projects like choral translations (Dobs) or storytelling (Reddington *et al.*) might be unique to specific types of second/foreign language classrooms. Future research must continue to locate the various specialized projects (Lynch, 1985) of the classroom and describe how they are constitutively constructed by competent members *in situ*. It should be EMCA classroom researchers' objective to 'bring the "reader" *into* the common settings of practical content' (Lynch, 1985: 6, quotation marks and italics in the original). In other words, it is our task to show the various projects of the classroom for what they actually are from teachers' and students' perspectives as demonstrated in embodied actions.

(3) Collect high-quality audio and video

Collecting high-quality audio and video data is a requisite for EMCA research. In EMCA, audio-visual recordings are '*records*' that act as 'both analytic "materials" and exhibits of discoveries' (Lynch, 1985: 7, italics and quotation marks in original). The richer the quality of the analytic materials, the richer the potential discoveries and the more convincing the arguments that can be put forward. Kimura *et al.* (2018) point out two institutional specifications that posit challenges for CA researchers. The first is the various spatial arrangements that occur in classroom contexts. These can make it difficult if not impossible to capture everything that is occurring in a classroom at any one point in time. For instance, STEM labs and other classrooms in which students engage in group work can be particularly difficult contexts for recording both audio and video. In such contexts, students and teachers move in and out of ecological huddles (Goffman, 1964) in which they at times obstruct the view of one another's face and/or hands. This also makes collecting clear audio challenging without a sophisticated arrangement of microphones. Thus, researchers must be cognizant of the various spatial arrangements of the classroom he or she is recording and be strategic in how he or she goes about producing recordings.

The second specification of classrooms the authors warn readers about is the location of pedagogical projects in the overarching instructional project, that is, when and where certain projects can arise during the unfolding of the class. If we return to the example of the STEM lab, we could note that some recurrent sub-projects occur at regular sequential positions in the overarching instructional project. At the beginning of labs, teachers give a brief lecture in which they review key concepts and the process of the lab. Following the lecture, students work in groups to complete the lab and the teacher circulates the classroom assisting students when they request help or when the teacher notices they need help. Toward the end of lab classes, teachers return homework and often handle housekeeping issues as students ask administrative questions while they are completing the lab. Thus, Kimura *et al.* (2018) recommend that researchers must be very familiar with the different projects in the context in which they are recording so they can plan and adjust to the shifting participant frameworks and spatial organizations of the class.

I would like to add two more suggestions for EMCA researchers. First, researchers need to consider using moving cameras and/or experimenting with the use of new technologies like body-mounted cameras. There is never going to be a complete record of the event, but the compact, light-weight and non-intrusive nature of commercially available recording equipment makes the potential for fieldworkers to 'be nimble [and] able to respond quickly' (Kimura *et al.*, 2018: 14) a reality. Using a combination of fixed and moving cameras, fieldworkers can literally move as teachers and students shift configurations. As one example, the data in Looney and Kim's chapter were gathered using a moving camera that allowed the person operating the camera to move and collect shots of the teacher inter-acting with small groups of students in a manner that would have been impossible with a fixed camera.

In addition to thinking about how we collect video, high-quality audio should also be a priority for EMCA researchers. Even at a time when audio-recording equipment, like video-recording equipment, is compact, lightweight and non-intrusive, there is immense variation in the quality of audio collected in different studies. Often, recordings are such that any-thing beyond an impressionistic analysis is impossible. While there was no in-depth analysis of prosody in this volume, classroom CA researchers have manually measured intonation contours (Hellermann, 2003). If we are going to analyze prosody using software like PRATT, recordings need to be of a high quality and free (or as free as possible) of white noise. Making such recordings requires the use of pre-amplifiers with low-pass filters. Additionally, sound must be collected from multiple sources, e.g. lapel microphones, shotgun microphones and table microphones. If research is going to do analytic justice to the embodied work of teaching, creating the highest quality recordings possible must be a priority.

(4) Foster collaboration across institutions

A final challenge for EMCA classroom research is to foster collabora-tion across institutions. One way to foster collaboration is through the use of large, shared collections of data. Two chapters in this volume demon-strate the potential for using large publicly available video corpora in EMCA research. The data sources used are the Corpus of English for Academic and Professional Purposes (CEAPP) (Looney & Kim) and TalkBank (Hall et al.). Such collections have many advantages. The first is that researchers can share large amounts of data over space and time. We all have more data than we will ever use and no one analysis of any stretch of interaction is exhaustive. By building shared open-access collec-tions, we have tools to collaborate across institutions and to train our students.

One example of a resource that is already online and available for researchers who want to share their data is CEAPP (ceapp.la.psu.edu). CEAPP is a website that allows users to browse and search transcribed classroom videos. Its twofold purpose is to advance research on teaching and learning, and to serve as a resource for the training of L2 teachers and international teaching assistants. CEAPP's capabilities enable researchers and language teaching practitioners to conduct cross-case, cross-corpora comparisons of various interactional practices in the classroom environ-ment. For example, the interface allows easy searching for transcripts of classroom interactions of intensive English program (IEP) and STEM courses. Users can specify a single or a combination of search criteria, including course type, course level, teaching context, date of a class and interlocutor. The CEAPP website can be used for research and pedagogi-cal purposes, and users can contribute their own data to CEAPP.

Concluding Remarks

The chapters in this volume make a significant contribution to our understanding of the embodied accomplishment of teaching as observable work. By using the analytic lens of EMCA to make teaching observable, we are able to move beyond the broad abstractions that we find in the literature on best practices and are left with the distilled essences of real classroom interactions. We are not trying to abstract a theory of teaching but to develop an empirically informed understanding of members' methods for accomplishing teaching. 'These studies are distinguished by their attempts to situate themselves within the settings of work they describe' (Lynch, 1985: 6). By improving our understanding of how teaching happens and is oriented to by participants *in situ*, we have given teachers and teacher preparation real examples of how teaching happens. Such detailed descriptions of the routine grounds of teaching offer to scholars of teaching, teacher educators, teachers and other stakeholders the opportunity to develop a reflective capacity for understanding the specialized nature of teaching and making sensible decisions in their own contexts of teaching.

References

Goffman, E. (1964) The neglected situation. *American Anthropologist* 66 (6), 133–136.

Goodwin, C. (2000) Action and embodiment within situated human interaction. *Journal of Pragmatics* 32, 1489–1522.

Goodwin, C. (2013) The co-operative, transformative organization of human action and knowledge. *Journal of Pragmatics* 46, 8–23.

Goodwin, C. (2018) *Co-operative Action*. New York: Cambridge University Press.

Hellermann, J. (2003) The interactive work of prosody in the IRF exchange: Teacher repetition in feedback moves. *Language in Society* 32 (1), 79–104.

Hellermann, J. (2005) Syntactic and prosodic practices for cohesion in series of three-part sequences in classroom talk. *Research on Language & Social Interaction* 38 (1), 105–130.

Kimura, D., Malabarba, T. and Hall, J.K. (2018) Data collection considerations for classroom interaction research: A conversation analytic perspective. *Classroom Discourse* 9 (3), 185–204. doi:10.1080/19463014.2018.1485589

Koschmann, T. (2011) Understanding understanding in action. *Journal of Pragmatics* 43, 435–437.

Kunitz, S. (2018) Collaborative attention work on gender agreement in Italian as a foreign language. *The Modern Language Journal* 102, 64–81.

Lee, Y.A. (2006) Respecifying display questions: Interactional resources for language teaching. *TESOL Quarterly* 40, 691–713.

Lee, Y.-A. (2007) Third turn position and teacher talk: Contingency and the work of teaching. *Journal of Pragmatics* 39, 180–206.

Lemke, J.L. (1990) *Talking Science: Language, Learning, and Values*. Norwood, NJ: Ablex.

Looney, S.D. (2019) Co-operative action: Addressing misunderstanding and displaying uncertainty in a university physics lab. In S.D. Looney and S. Bhalla (eds) *A Transdisciplinary Approach to International Teaching Assistants* (pp. 41–62). Bristol: Multilingual Matters.

Looney, S.D. and Kim, J. (2018) Humor, uncertainty, and affiliation: Cooperative and co-operative action in the university science lab. *Linguistics and Education* 46, 56–69.

Lynch, M. (1985) *Art and Artifact in Laboratory Science*. Boston, MA: Routledge & Kegan Paul.

Macbeth, D. (2004) The relevance of repair for classroom correction. *Language in Society* 33, 703–736.

Mehan, H. (1979) *Learning Lessons: Social Organization in the Classroom.* Cambridge, MA: Harvard University Press.

Mondada, L. (2014) The local constitution of multimodal resources for social interaction. *Journal of Pragmatics* 65, 137–156.

Poole, D. (1990) Contextualizing IRE in an eighth-grade quiz review. *Linguistics and Education* 2, 185–211.

Sert, O. (2015) *Social Interaction and L2 Classroom Discourse.* Edinburgh: Edinburgh University Press.

Sinclair, J.M. and Coulthard, M. (1975) *Towards an Analysis of Discourse: The English Used by Teachers and Pupils.* London: Oxford University Press.

Stivers, T. (2008) Stance, alignment, and affiliation during storytelling: When nodding is a token of affiliation. *Research on Language and Social Interaction* 41 (1), 31–57.

Stivers, T., Mondada, L. and Steensig, J. (2011) Knowledge, morality and affiliation in social interaction. In T. Stivers, L. Mondada and J. Steensig (eds) *The Morality of Knowledge in Conversation* (pp. 3–26). Cambridge: Cambridge University Press.

Waring, H.Z. (2008) Using explicit positive assessment in the language classroom: Three turn sequence, feedback, and learning opportunities. *The Modern Language Journal* 92 (4), 577–594.

Zemel, A. and Koschmann, T. (2011) Pursuing a question: Reinitiating IRE sequences as a method of instruction. *Journal of Pragmatics* 43 (2), 475–488.

Index

action, embodied 8, 19, 20, 49, 51,
    57, 60, 62, 76, 77, 100, 101, 104,
    105–106, 110, 116, 179, 181–182,
    184–186, 191, 192–194, 220–221
adjacency pair 3, 112
alignment 4, 18, 24, 39–40, 42, 49, 51,
    52, 90–91, 96, 137, 168, 170, 175,
    178, 218
affiliation 4, 9, 39–40, 42, 48–49, 50, 73,
    75, 133, 135, 137, 218
  affiliative 4, 37, 40, 42, 43–44, 52, 57,
      60, 61, 78, 92
  disaffiliative 4, 61, 63, 73, 75, 78

choral response 198, 200–201, 214
classroom interactional competence 143,
    148, 156
collective translations 9, 198, 200–201,
    202, 204, 206, 207, 213–215

ethnomethodological conversation
    analysis 2, 4–7, 37, 38, 40–41, 218,
    220–224
embodiment 75, 142, 147, 157, 168, 175,
    179, 183, 214
epistemics 103, 156, 219
  displays 103
  search sequences 103
  stance 8, 102, 103, 104, 107, 109, 110,
      117, 118
  status checks 104

frame 17, 18–19, 23, 24, 25, 27, 28, 32,
    33, 34
framework, participation 124, 125, 129,
    131, 135, 137, 138, 186, 218
framing 7, 15

gaze 7, 8–9, 18, 19, 28, 39, 42, 43, 44,
    58, 91, 103, 113, 123–124, 133, 142,
    143–147, 148, 150–151, 155–157,
    175, 178, 183, 194, 218, 219

shifts 8, 24, 28, 31, 32, 33, 86, 117,
    122–123, 124, 125, 126, 128–129,
    131, 133, 136, 137–139, 145, 152,
    160, 181, 183, 189–191, 193–194,
    205, 214, 220
  mutual 123, 142, 143, 144, 145, 147,
      155–157, 185, 219
  window 143
  withdrawal 146
Gestalts, complex multimodal 181, 182,
    183–184
gesture 7, 9, 32, 37, 39, 58, 59, 96,
    123–124, 139, 160, 170, 178,
    181–182, 183–185, 186, 191, 193,
    194, 199–200, 218
  metaphoric 107
  iconic 89, 96, 109, 122
  deictic 96, 123, 184

interactional competence 3, 28, 34, 95,
    97, 148, 156
IRF 6, 8, 17, 38, 46, 57–58, 59, 60, 62, 63,
    64, 65–68, 71, 76–78, 82, 198–199,
    200, 203, 204, 212, 222

marking the path 8, 100, 105, 106–109,
    116, 117
mobilizing elaboration 100, 110–116, 117
multimodality 122, 138, 143, 183, 221

practices
  interactional 19, 33, 34, 82, 182, 202,
      215, 224
  embodied 39, 124, 155, 182, 194, 195
preference 3, 39, 40, 64, 65, 145
  dispreference 58
  dispreferred 3, 4, 58–59, 78
project
  instructional 1, 6, 7, 9, 38, 42, 46, 48,
      51, 52, 57, 60, 64–65, 67, 69, 77,
      219–220
  pedagogical 5, 8, 137, 223

read-alouds 38–39, 42, 52
repair 3, 23, 27, 49, 91, 147, 199
resources, embodied 6–7, 8–9, 15, 18,
    19, 33, 39, 57, 59, 61, 63, 73, 81, 83,
    89, 95, 96, 123, 124, 138, 142–144,
    182, 183–186, 189, 193, 194–195,
    220–221

self-directed talk 8, 160–162, 163–164,
    165, 168, 170, 172, 178, 218–219
sequence organization 3, 5–6
storytelling 4, 8, 9, 38–40, 42, 84, 96, 219

teases 57, 60–62, 63, 66–67, 68–70, 71,
    73, 75, 76–77, 78, 219
thinking face 160, 163, 164, 166, 170,
    173, 178
thinking for teaching 189, 193, 194
turn allocation 6, 7, 123, 138, 143, 145,
    146, 185
turn taking system 3, 6, 143–145

unwillingness to participate 146

willingness to participate 146